"When all is said and done," Fred
Lockley once wrote, "people are just folks,
and if you feel a real and sincere interest
in them, and if you are a good asker and a
good listener, you will be rewarded by
getting good human interest stories." Lockley
(left), is shown here with Oregon pioneer
Ezra Meeker, in a photograph taken June 12,
1914. The flag was made in June, 1861, by
Mrs. W. F. Eastham, at or near Molalla.
(Photo courtesy of Oregon Historical Society)

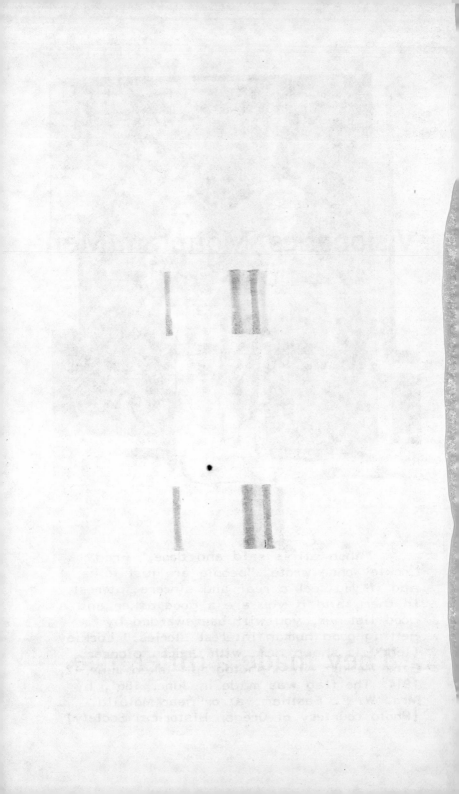

For...

Wayne Morse
United States Senator from Oregon
1945-1969

and

Tom McCall
Governor of Oregon
1967-1975

They, too, made a difference.

Acknowledgments

I would like to thank the following people for their part in the publication of **Visionaries, Mountain Men & Empire Builders**:

Malindi, Polly, and **Luke Helm,** for understanding what Simon Benson called "sticktoitiveness", addressing and stamping mailers, typing page numbers, and foregoing those several weekends at the beach while this book took shape;

and, **Chris Helm,** proofreader, lover, confidant, critic, companion, and best friend, who, after living with the **Lockley Files** for two years, understands my mania for these things and loves me anyway.

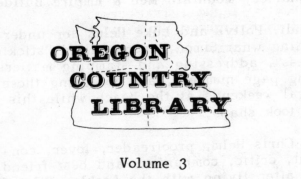

OREGON
COUNTRY
LIBRARY

Volume 3

Table of Contents

FOREWORD

Just over two years ago, I blew the dust off the first of those black three-ring binders and settled back in the Oregon Collection at the University of Oregon Library for what I thought would be a quick examination of some old newspaper articles. I was, of course, wrong. Those brittle yellow pages drew me through Fred Lockley's looking glass into a time in Oregon that I've always been sorry I missed. I sat there that day until my eyes refused to focus any more on the tiny graying print, and then came back, again and again through the next few weeks, until I had read all 58 volumes.

I felt envious of Fred Lockley. Imagine riding all over Oregon on a "lineback buckskin pony", or a "chainless Columbia bicycle", stopping here and there with a pioneer family, selling an advertisement or a subscription now and then, but, all the time, watching, asking, remembering, and writing about the fascinating folks you met. Imagine riding across Oregon and not having to cross a freeway or worry about being blasted off the road by a log truck. Imagine an Oregon with no disposable diapers splattered on its roads, an Oregon where deer and elk and bear are common sights, an Oregon where you can see Mount Hood from Portland almost every day, an Oregon where every deep breath, even in Eugene, fills your lungs with fresh air. This was Lockley's Oregon, seen, felt, smelled, pen and pad in hand, on the back of his lineback buckskin pony. He left it all for us, a treasury of vicarious experience, but it was filed away, locked up, forgotten by nearly everyone, and turning slowly to dust.

I found my own name in those old black books. Stories dimly remembered even by my parents, their skeletons told to me when I was a child, were suddenly right before me, fleshed out in the words of the people lived them.

"We started across the plains for Oregon a few months before my seventh birthday. That was in the spring of 1844," said Elizabeth Sager Helm, speaking to Lockley in her home near the Portland library. I'd heard of this lady, a relative of some sort, and how she survived the Whitman Massacre by hiding under the floor while the Indians murdered the Whitmans and other members of the Mission community. Suddenly, here she was, an almost mythical character who hadn't hidden under the floor but had taken refuge with others in an upstairs room and was then captured by the Indians and finally ransomed by Peter Skene Ogden.

"Each warrior had a knife in his

2

hand, with which, as he danced, he would lunge savagely at a supposed enemy...The chief was sitting cross-legged like a tailor. He sprang up as though his legs were wire springs and, coming up to my father, said, 'What you doing here? You no 'fraid of the Indians?'" This is Richard Watson Helm telling Lockley of his family's arrival in The Dalles after their wagon train followed Steven Meek around in circles in central Oregon for several weeks in 1845. "My father put out his hand and said, 'How do you do?'" and with those words my great-great-great grandfather, calm and stoic as a wooden chair, came to life for me. So...that's how our family came to Oregon.

My grandfather, too, was there. Dead since I was six, he rose out of those brittle old binders to tell Lockley of a more recent time in the west. "I had left that country in 1888, when I was a kid," he said of Sunnyside, Washington. "I had gone back as a farmhand for Ben Snipes in 1896, and this time, in 1911, I was returning as principal of the high school. I got a lot of satisfaction out of that."

My fascination with Lockley's subjects, though, stretched beyond the novelty of reading about my own family. These are tough, versatile, tenacious people. Their lives challenged the bounds of my imagination. Their stories are, in the words of one reviewer, "riveting". Vittwia St. Clair Chapman Mickelson "spirited away" wounded Civil War soldiers marked for amputation by the "Iowa butchers", Mary Geisel Blake and her mother are held captive and must listen while Indians systematically murder her father and three brothers, Mrs. Carter T. Allingham's father is "thoroughly fed up eating yams and monkeys" while he waits for a ship in Panama, and Jane Straight Bingham remembers "the Indians who had murdered Dr. Whitman and his party hanging with black caps over their heads on the gallows at Oregon City". When J. B. Wright reached Fort Laramie, "many of the trees had dead Indians tied in their uppper branches". J. A. Wisdom, a freed slave, was half white and half black. "My father," he says, "...figured that if there was a war the North would win and the slaves would be freed, so...he sold me for $400."

When I was a child my father would take us to visit my great grandmother, who lived in Portland and who came to Oregon--rather late, compared to the rest of the family--in 1872, by covered wagon. In my mind she sits in the shadows of her musty and cluttered parlor, frail and brittle like very old parchment, wearing long black dresses and saying nothing. My mother and sister and I sit at her feet trying to be quiet. I didn't like visiting my great grandmother, and I hardly noticed when she died and we didn't go there any more. It's possible, of course, that, even if I had been old enough to ask the right questions, she would have had nothing profound to say, but what an exciting experience it might have been if I'd only known enough to try.

I often mentally kick myself for

developing an interest in pioneer life
in Oregon only after the pioneers I had
a chance to know were dead. Finding the
Lockley Files was like a reprieve, another chance to talk with the pioneers,
and I could imagine myself once again
sitting in my great grandmother's parlor, not on the floor, but in a chair,
pad and pencil in hand--like Fred
Lockley--and hearing stories of near
escapes from the Indians, of cholera on
the Oregon Trail, of bears and wolves
at the door of a rude cabin thrown
hastily up against the winter rains, of
marriage at thirteen, of hunting,
clearing land for farms, and of making
a life in the wilderness of the Pacific
Northwest.

It was obvious to me that there
was too much of value here to be con-
signed forever to the oblivion of that
vault-like area of the Oregon Collection, so the publishing project of
which this foreword is a part gradually
took form in my mind. At first I
thought I might publish it all at once,
but my budget couldn't stand the cost
of one huge book and I couldn't stand
the idea of editing out enough good
material to shrink the book to fit
within those financial constraints. A
three-volume set was the answer. (Last
summer, however, while reading through
the Lockley Files once again in preparation for this volume, I read, for
the first time, the poetry with which
Lockley ended many of his columns. My
three-volume plan then stretched to
four. The fourth volume of the Oregon
Country Library, "A Bit of Verse: Poems

from the Lockley Files", will be published soon.)

Where the first two volumes relied almost solely on Fred Lockley's conversations with people who came to Oregon between about 1844 and 1880, this volume contains much of Lockley's expository writing, and spans a much greater period of time. "Visionaries, Mountain Men & Empire Builders" opens with the story of John Ledyard, who first saw Oregon from the deck of Captain James Cook's ship, in 1778. His incredible quest to return to Oregon took him across Siberia on foot in the dead of winter and finally led to his death in Egypt at the age of 38 in 1788. From that time on, a regular parade of interesting and influential people made themselves known in the Oregon Country, including John Jacob Astor, Jim Bridger, Peter Skene Ogden, Jesse Applegate, Joaquin Miller, and a host of others, right up to the 1920s and 1930s, when Abigail Scott Duniway, Simon Benson, and Sam Jackson stepped onto the stage. And Fred Lockley, with whom this book ends, wrote about them all.

Mike Helm
Eugene, Oregon
November, 1982

6

Otter

"...for I have trampled the world under my feet, laughed at fear and derided danger. Through fierce savages, over parching deserts, the freezing North, the everlasting ice, stormy seas, have I passed without harm..."

JOHN LEDYARD

The Endless Quest

Just as, while traveling some old-time
mountain road, you may happen on one of the ghost
cities of the West—some old-time mining camp,
long deserted and almost forgotten, so, while
reading some old-time document, you often run
across some almost forgotten character stalking
like a dim wraith through the pages of history.

In 1843, William Overton came from Memphis,
Tennessee, and took up a claim on the west bank
of the Willamette River, about midway between
Vancouver and Oregon City. Meeting Amos L. Lovejoy of Oregon City at Vancouver, Overton told him
of the claim he had taken up and offered him half of
it if he would put up the money to file on the
claim. They started by canoe for Oregon City,
stopping at Overton's claim, which Lovejoy examined. He accepted Overton's offer and suggested
to Overton that he build a cabin on the place.
Shortly thereafter Overton met Francis W. Petty-
grove and sold him the other 320 acres of his
claim for $50. Then and there Overton disappears
from Oregon's history, his only monument being
that Overton Street perpetuates his name. Colonel
J. W. Nesmith dismisses him in three lines by
saying, "Overton was a desperate, rollicking
fellow, and sought his fortunes in the wilds of
Texas, where, as I have heard, his career was
brought to a sudden termination by a halter."

9

While in Honolulu last winter I found that, instead of going to Texas to be hanged, William Overton had gone to the Sandwich Islands in 1846. Whether he died there or went elsewhere, I was unable to discover.

John Ledyard is another historic character of Oregon, though his name is rarely associated with Oregon's history. Probably one of the first white men to see the Oregon coast was Ferrelo, Cabrillo's pilot, who in 1543 sailed up the coast as far as the southern border of the Oregon Country. In the summer of 1774 Juan Perez sailed along the Oregon coast, going as far north as Russian America and putting in at and naming Lorenzo Harbor, later renamed Nootka Sound. Heceta Head, on the Oregon Coast, was named for Captain Bruno Heceta, who in 1775, while sailing along the Oregon coast, reported seeing an inlet which Captain Robert Gray later discovered to be the Columbia River. In 1778 Captain James Cook saw and named Cape Foulweather and Cape Perpetua, on the Oregon coast. Two men, members of his crew, Midshipman George Vancouver and John Ledyard, a corporal of marines, were destined to have much to do with the exploration and discovery of the Oregon country.

Because of John Ledyard's interest in and subsequent efforts toward the development of the Oregon Country, I am going to trace in some detail his early life. He was born in Groton, Connecticut, near old Fort Griswold, in 1751, and, by the way, his brother, Colonel William Ledyard, was in command of Fort Griswold and was killed in service while still a young man.

John Ledyard's grandfather, whose name was also John Ledyard, hailed from Bristol, England, settled at first on Long Island and later moved to Groton. John Ledyard's father was also named John. Probably John Ledyard, who was a born adventurer, inherited his love of the sea and his

love of travel from his father, who was a sea
captain. His father was engaged in trade with the
West Indies and died at the age of 35, leaving a
widow and four children--three sons and one
daughter. Young John Ledyard, when his mother
married again, was adopted by his grandfather, of
Hartford, for whom he had been named. When young
Ledyard's grandfather, John Ledyard, died, Thomas
Seymour, an attorney, became his guardian.

When John Ledyard was 19 years old, Reverend
Eleazar Wheelock, whose great-grandfather, Reverend Ralph Wheelock, had come to New England in
1637, invited young Ledyard to come to Hanover,
New Hampshire, to study philosophy and literature
in the school he had just founded. Dr. Wheelock
was a graduate of Yale, having taken his degree
in 1733. Two years later he was ordained pastor
of the church at Lebanon, Connecticut.

Because his salary was small, Dr. Wheelock
started a school, boarding the students at his
house. He conducted this school from 1743 to
1762, when he started an Indian missionary
school. In 1766 he secured an endowment of 10,000
pounds in England for the purpose of founding an
Indian school. Reverend Wheelock, being offered a
considerable body of land by Governor John Went-
worth if he would locate his school at what was
then Dresden, now known as Hanover, moved his
school to that place and received a charter from
King George III. The school was named Dartmouth,
after Lord Dartmouth, president of the board of
trustees. The school was moved to Hanover in
1770. At that time there was no settlement there,
so Dartmouth College was conducted in some hastily erected log cabins.

John Ledyard went there in 1772 to attend
the seminary conducted in connection with the
Indian school. Discovering that John Ledyard was
quick to learn, was a good mixer, and was of an
adventurous disposition, Dr. Wheelock urged him

to become a missionary to the Indians. In the early spring of 1772, John Ledyard dropped from sight and returned to college that fall, saying he had put in the summer wandering from one tribe to another, from the Six Nations up to the Canadian border, to learn their language and to become familiar with their beliefs and customs.

Discipline at Dartmouth in those days was rather severe, and John Ledyard chafed under it. He employed his leisure time in cutting down a large tree on the banks of the Connecticut River, and, with the help of his fellow students, he hollowed out this tree to make a dugout canoe 50 feet long and three feet wide. With a Greek Testament and a copy of Ovid and very little else, Ledyard launched his dugout into the Connecticut River and paddled down to Hartford, Connecticut, a distance of 140 miles.

Having put in a year at Dartmouth College, Ledyard decided that he could make better progress in studying divinity by becoming an assistant to a clergyman. Finding that a ripened scholarship was necessary to qualify as a candidate for the ministry, he decided to see more of the world before settling down, so he went to New London and shipped on board a vessel bound to Gibraltar. Captain Deshon, in command of the vessel, had known Ledyard's father, who was also a sea captain. At Gibraltar, Ledyard enlisted in the British Army. Captain Deshon secured his release and he returned to his ship, which went on to the Barbary Coast and from there to the West Indies. Ledyard spent a year as a sailor before returning to New London. Within a few weeks he secured another berth as a sailor on a vessel bound for Plymouth, England. From Plymouth he went on foot to London to look up some wealthy relatives of his father. When he went to the home of these relatives he was not received with open arms, for he was dressed in sailor garb and bore plentiful evidence of his tramp from Plymouth to London.

Ledyard then enlisted with the British Marines, sought and gained an introduction to Captain James Cook, who was just about to sail on his third voyage around the world, and persuaded Captain Cook to allow him to be a member of the expedition.

The Resolution and the Discovery, the former commanded by Captain Cook and the latter by Captain Clerk, left on July 12, 1776, for the Cape of Good Hope, where they were to take on board horses, cows, sheep, goats, hogs, rabbits, ducks, geese, turkeys, peacocks, and other livestock, to be used in trading with the natives of other lands. They spent a month in New Zealand and then sailed for Otahelte, as Tahiti was then called. From Tahiti they went to Tonga Taboo, where they arrived early in June and spent a month. Wherever they went they found the natives friendly and hospitable.

Some of the natives picked up small articles, and, as theft in those days was punishable in England by death, Captain Cook resorted to severe measures to teach the natives morality according to English standards. In discussing the harsh measures used to punish the natives, John Ledyard in his journal says:

"It must be remembered that the ability to perform the important errand before us depends very much, if not entirely, upon the supplies we might procure from these and other such islands, and Captain Cook should, of consequence, be very anxious and solicitous in this concern. But perhaps no consideration will excuse the severity which he sometimes used toward the natives. He would probably have done better to consider that the full exertion of extreme power is an argument of extreme weakness. Nature seemed to inform the insulted natives of the truth of this maxim, for before we quitted Tonga Taboo we could not go

anywhere into the country upon business or pleasure without danger."

When the Resolution and the Discovery anchored at Tonga Taboo, one of the head chiefs,
named Feenou, a man tremendously popular with the
natives, welcomed Captain Cook and his party,
giving them freely whatever they wanted. He put
himself at the disposal of Captain Cook during
the entire time of their stay, serving as guide,
securing food and forage and water for their animals, and doing everything in his power to make
the strangers welcome. The attentions were taken
pretty much as a matter of course. When the ships
were about to leave, this chief could not resist
taking two of the peacocks. Captain Cook took
Poulaho, the king of the island, a prisoner. His
warriors quickly gathered to avenge the insult to
the king's dignity. Chief Feenou promised that
the peacocks would be returned and begged that
the king be allowed his liberty. Captain Cook
placed a guard of marines with fixed bayonets
around the king and held him prisoner till the
peacocks were returned.

On August 14 the Resolution and the Discovery
cast anchor at Otahelte, in the Society Islands.
Six weeks after sailing from the Society Islands
for the coast of America they saw in the distance
a mountainous island, rising from the sea. This
land was not marked on any charts then in existence. Captain Cook discovered it was one of a
number of islands, which group he named the
Sandwich Islands. The natives brought presents of
sweet potatoes, yams, pigs, bananas and other
products of the island.

After ten days the ships departed for the
Pacific Northwest coast. A few weeks later they
anchored in Nootka Sound. The sailors aboard the
Resolution and Discovery traded nails, spikes,
buttons, files, and other such articles for sea
otter skins. These otter skins, which the sailors
purchased from the Indians at a cost of from

sixpence to a shilling, they later sold in Canton at an average price of $100. Ledyard discovered that some of the Indians of the Oregon Country had copper bracelets and knives, and they also had wampum of the same kind that he had found among the natives in the Six Nations, on the Atlantic seaboard.

In writing of the Oregon coast, Ledyard said:

"The light in which this country will appear most to advantage is in the variety of its animals and the richness of their furs. They have here foxes, sables, hares, marmosets, ermines, weasels, bears, wolves, deer, moose, otters, beavers and gluttons. The skin of this latter animal was sold at Kamtschatka, a Russian factory, for 60 rubles, which is near 12 guineas. Had it been sold in China it would have been worth 30 guineas. We purchased while here 1500 beaver beside other skins, but took none but the best, having no thought at that time of using them to any other advantage than converting them to the purposes of clothing. It afterwards happened that skins which did not cost the purchaser sixpence sterling sold in China for upwards fo $100. Neither did we purchase a quarter part of the beaver and other fur skins we might have done and most certainly should have done had we known of meeting the opportunity of disposing of them to such an astonishing profit."

From Nootka Sound Captain Cook sailed northward to Bering Strait in search of a Northwest Passage. On his way from the polar seas he stopped at the island of Onalaska. To Captain Cook's great astonishment the natives presented him with a cake of freshly made rye meal. They also had tobacco and some of them were wearing blue linen shirts. Captain Cook was anxious to explore the island, but he feared that if he sent out an armed party they would be cut off by the

Indians, and he could ill afford the loss of his men.

Lieutenant John Gore, first lieutenant of marines on board the Resolution, and John Ledyard were the only native-born Americans on board either the Resolution or the Discovery. Lieutenant Gore was born in Virginia in 1730 and accompanied Captain Cook on his first voyage around the world. When Sir Joseph Banks, president of the Royal Society, sent a ship to Iceland and the Hebrides, Lieutenant Gore was in command. Lieutenant Gore, who, by the way, became captain of the Discovery upon the death of Captain Clerk and succeeded to the command of the expedition when Captain Cook was killed in the Sandwich Islands, greatly admired John Ledyard. He suggested to Captain Cook that if he would call for volunteers, John Ledyard woud be glad to undertake the work of exploring Onalaska Island.

In speaking of this trip of discovery, John Ledyard in his journal says:

"Captain Cook assured me he was happy I had undertaken the venture, as he was convinced I would persevere. After giving me some instructions how to proceed, he wished me well and desired I would not be longer absent than about a week. If I did not return by that time he would wait another week for me, but no longer. A young Indian chief and his two attendants served as my guides. I took with me some presents, brandy in bottles and bread, but no other provisions, and by the advice of Captain Cook, went entirely unarmed."

The Indians took him afoot and in their native skin canoes to where there was a settlement of Russians. He had gone rather expecting that he might be killed, but in place of this he found the Indians very devout. He says:

"The Indians said prayers after the manner of the Greek Church. I could not but observe with what particular satisfaction the Indians per-

formed their devoirs to God, through the medium
of their crucifixes, and with what pleasure they
went through the ceremonies attendant on their
worship."

At the Russian village he found a number of
fur hunters. He also found a sloop lying in a
cove behind the village, equipped with an old
iron three-pounder. He says:

"I was no sooner informed that this sloop
was the same in which Bering had performed his
discoveries, which did him so much honor and his
country such great service, than I determined to
go on board of it. This vessel was from Kamtschatka and came from thence with the Asiatics in
order to establish a pelt and fur factory. They
have been here five years and they go over in
this sloop once a year, deliver their furs and
get supplies from their factory there. The native
who accompanied me went back to the village and
brought a canoe, in which we went on board Bering's sloop, where I remained above an hour."

John Ledyard persuaded three of the principal Russians to accompany him for a visit on
board the Resolution and the Discovery.

From Onalaska the Resolution and Discovery
shaped their courses for the two months' trip to
Hawyhee, as Hawaii was then spelled. When they
arrived at Hawaii they entered a bay on the south
side of the islands, anchoring near the town of
Kearakekua. Ledyard, in his journal, remarks that
in this town and in the nearby town of Kiverua
there were above 1400 grass houses and that a
prodigious number of outrigger canoes came out to
greet the visitors. He says they counted over
3000 canoes, surrounding their ships, in which
were over 15,000 natives, to say nothing of the
large number of natives who swam out and floated
about the vessels. That the natives welcomed them
whole-heartedly is proven by Ledyard's statement
that in addition to those in canoes and in the
water--

"The beach, the rocks, the tops of houses, the trees and the adjacent hills were covered with natives. The shouts of joy and admiration proceeding from the sonorous voices of the men, with the exclamations of the women, dancing and clapping their hands, the overturning of their canoes with their goods afloat and the squealing of the hogs brought out to us, formed one of the most curious prospects that can be imagined. Amidst this vast concourse all was peace, harmony, hilarity, and good nature."

The chief showed Cook where to put up his tents on shore and to erect his astronomical instruments. The chiefs put their official rods around the camp, which placed the camp under the restriction of the "taboo", so that no native would dare to enter the camp. Captain Cook, on his part, agreed that his sailors should not leave camp after sunset, but as a matter of fact, most of them were A.W.O.L. after the first day. The charms of the soft-voiced, liquid-eyed sirens proved irresistible.

While the sailors were securing supplies, filling their casks with fresh water and exploring the island, John Ledyard secured permission of Captain Cook to climb Mauna Loa, whose elevation Captain Cook estimated to be about 18,000 feet. One of the gunners of the Resolution and the botanist accompanied Ledyard but they were unable to gain the summit of the snow-covered mountain.

Captain Cook punished severely any fancied transgressions of the natives, which caused their friendship for the visitors to cool. Ledyard says that one untoward event after another caused the natives to show the symptoms of uneasiness at the presence of the white visitors. The master's mate on board the Resolution asked the natives to assist his sailors, and when they did not move promptly he struck them. A chief interposed. The mate of the Resolution ordered the chief to have his people assist him, which the chief refused to do. This angered the mate, who had his crew fall upon the natives and beat them up with trunnels. The natives gathered in a threatening manner and Corporal Ledyard's guard of marines was ordered out "to make a show of resentment".

The one thing that probably caused more resentment than anything else done by the white man was the action of Captain Cook in offering Priest Kikinny two iron hatchets in exchange for the hardwood fence which surrounded the graves of their ancestors and their sacred Morai. In describing what took place John Ledyard says:

"Captain Cook was as much chagrined as the chiefs were surprised, and, not meeting with the easy acquiescence he expected to his requisitions, gave orders to the sailors to ascend the Morai, break down the fence and load the boats with it. He led the way himself to enforce his orders, the dismayed chiefs, dreading his displeasure, following him upon the Morai to behold the fence that enclosed their noble ancestors and the images of their gods torn to pieces by a handful of strangers, without the power of opposing their sacrilegious depredations."

To see the depository of their dead--the place where the images of their gods were kept and their solemn ceremonies performed--desecrated by the white men turned the attitude of the natives from friendship to hostility.

After 19 days on shore, the Resolution and the Discovery left, to the manifest satisfaction of the natives. Shortly after leaving they encountered a violent gale, which injured the foremast of the Resolution, so Captain Cook gave orders to return to the island for repairs. In his journal Ledyard gives a very minute and exhaustive recital of the incidents that led up to the killing of Captain Cook. To insure good treatment by the natives, Captain Cook sent a

guard to the home of Teralobu, the principal
chief, an after threatening the chief they made
him accompany them to the shore, with the intention of taking him on board. The other chiefs
and the natives protested, as they feared that
the white men were either going to carry their
principal chief away or kill him.

One of the natives acting in a threatening
manner, Captain Cook fired at him with a blank.
Seeing that he was unhurt the native continued to
go forward in defense of his chief and to prevent
him being taken on board the Discovery. Captain
Cook this time fired at him again, the ball entering the native's groin. In describing what
then happened, John Ledyard says:

"Captain Cook, perceiving the natives were
determined to oppose his designs, and that he
should not succeed without further bloodshed,
ordered Mr. Phillips, lieutenant of marines, to
get his men into the boats, which were lying
ready to receive them. This was effected by the
sergeant, but as they began to retreat, Captain
Cook was hit with a stone. Perceiving the man who
threw it, Captain Cook shot him dead. The officer
in the boats, observing the guard retreating and
hearing this third discharge, ordered his men to
fire. The guard on shore faced about and also
fired and the attack became general. Captain Cook
and Mr. Phillips, perceiving a general fire
without orders, quitted Chief Teralobu and ran to
the shore to put a stop to it. They joined the
guard, who fired as they retreated. Cook, having
reached the margin of the water, waved with his
hat to cease firing and come in. While doing this
a chief stabbed him with one of our iron daggers,
just under the shoulder blade, which passed quite
through his body. Cook fell with his face in the
water and immediately expired.

"Mr. Phillips, not being able to use his
fusee, drew his sword and, engaging the chief who
had killed Cook, dispatched him. His guards were

20

all killed but two. They plunged into the water and began swimming to the boats. Mr. Phillips stood for some time the butt of all their force, and, being as complete in the use of his sword as he was accomplished, his achievements struck the barbarians with awe. Being wounded and growing faint from loss of blood and excessive action, he plunged into the sea, sword in hand, and swam to the boats. He was scarcely taken on board before he saw one of the marines that had swum from the shore, lying flat upon the bottom. Phillips ran aft, threw himself in after him, brought him up with him to the surface of the water and both were taken in the boats. The boats, lying off without the reach of any weapons but stones, had received no damage. Being at leisure, they had kept up an unremitted fire and caused great havoc among the natives, particularly among the chiefs, who stood foremost in the crowd and were most exposed. Lieutenant Gore, who commanded as first lieutenant under Cook, on the Resolution, perceiving that the guard on shore was cut off and that Cook had fallen, fired two round shots into the middle of the crowd. The effect of the shots operated so powerfully that it produced a precipitate retreat from the shore. We lost beside Captain Cook, a corporal and three marines."

From the Sandwich Islands, the ships sailed northward, anchoring in the harbor of St. Peter and St. Paul. They passed through Bering Strait and upon their return went to China around the Cape of Good Hope and returned to England after an absence of four years and three months.

After the four-years' trip with Captain Cook, John Ledyard, native of Groton, Connecticut, found himself homesick to see his mother. He arrived on board of a British man-o'-war in December, 1782, in Long Island Sound. He received shore leave and went to Southold, New York, where his mother kept a boarding house, most of her boarders being British officers. Ledyard asked if he could be accommodated as a lodger. His mother replied that he could, and showed him a room. Presently he took a seat by the fireplace, in company with several officers. His mother passed through the room several times, eyeing him closely each time. Finally she put on her spectacles and said, "I beg your pardon for my rudeness, but I must have a better look at you. You resemble very much my son, who has been absent for eight years." He then told her that he was her son, and they had an affecting and affectionate reunion. From Southold Ledyard went to Hartford. He spent four months in Hartford, during which time he wrote his journal of Cook's voyage.

His imagination had been fired by the fact that furs purchased at a cost of sixpence on the North Pacific coast found ready sale in China at more than $100. He went to New York and visited many wealthy merchants, trying to interest them in sending a ship to what is now the coast of Oregon and Washington to trade for furs, but the merchants would have none of him. They tapped their heads significantly, for they regarded him as a fanatic and a visionary.

From New York he went to visit his cousin, Dr. Isaac Ledyard, in Philadelphia, to see if he could interest the merchants there in outfitting a ship to go to the North Pacific coast. In writing of his experience in Philadelphia, he says:

"I have been so often the sport of fortune that I durst hardly credit the present dawn of bright prospects. But it is a fact that the Honorable Robert Morris is disposed to give me a ship to go to the North Pacific Ocean. I have had two interviews with him at the finance office and tomorrow I expect a conclusive one. What a noble hold he instantly took of the enterprise. I have been two days, at his request, drawing up a minute detail of the plan and an estimate of the

outfits, which I will present him tomorrow. I am
to take the lead of the greatest commercial enterprise that has ever been embarked on in this
country--one of the first moment, as respects the
trade of America. If the affair is concluded, as
I expect it will be, it is probable I shall set
off for New England to procure seamen, or a ship,
or both, for Morris is wrapped up in the idea of
Yankee sailors."

In speaking of Ledyard's enthusiasm for this
venture, Jared Sparks, who had access to all of
his journals and correspondence, says:

"At this time no such mercantile adventure
had been attempted either in this country or in
Europe, nor is it known that anything of the kind
had ever been contemplated. Ledyard's knowledge
of the resources of the Northwest coast in furs,
derived from his observations while there, together with the enormous advances which he had
seen paid in Canton, on the original cost, had
convinced him that great profits might be realized by a voyage fitted out expressly for this
trade. The furs could be purchased extremely low
and paid for at such prices as the buyer might
choose to offer. So strong had grown Ledyard's
confidence in the accuracy of his opinions that
he applied the whole energy of his mind and
character to the task of creating interest in his
project among the merchants who had the means of
carrying it into effect and without whose pat-
ronage nothing could be done. No merchant was
found willing to hazard his money or his reputation in an adventure so novel in its kind and
so questionable in its promise--a scheme not only
untried, but never before thought of.

Poor Ledyard was destined to have one disappointment after another. He went to Boston,
where he secured a vessel, and after making it
ready for the voyage the owners decided to send
it elsewhere. From Boston he went to New London,
where he made arrangements to charter the con-

tinental frigate Trumbull. After engaging this
ship for a voyage to the Northwest coast it was
diverted elsewhere. He then made arrangements to
charter the Count d'Artois, a French ship, but
once more he was doomed to be disappointed. Finally he secured a ship in New York harbor of 300
tons, but the men who were investing the money in
the enterprise decided that it was too old for a
voyage of such hazard, so it was condemned.

Finally Lady Luck looked his way and Daniel
Parker was sent to New York to purchase a ship
and to have it in readiness by next spring. He
bought a ship, and when Ledyard was ready to
outfit it for its long voyage he was told that he
would have to postpone his trip to the Northwest
coast until the ship made one more trip to Canton. Finally Ledyard was able to interest Captain
Deshon, the owner of a new ship, in a trading
expedition to the Northwest coast. Ledyard, while
still a youth, had sailed with Captain Deshon's
uncle. Captain Deshon said he would be glad to
join with Ledyard in any mercantile adventure
which was safe, practicable, and afforded a rea-
sonable prospect of gain. Ledyard was such an
enthusiast over the possibilities of establishing
trade between Boston and the Pacific Northwest
coast, and he drew so rosy a picture of the profits to be derived from such a voyage, that Captain Deshon changed his mind and refused to go on
with the venture. Captain Deshon thought it was
possible that they might realize a profit of 100
percent, but when Ledyard told him that he could
trade files, knives, mirrors, beads, hawk bells
and other goods costing not to exceed a shilling
for furs that would sell in China for $100, Cap-
tain Deshon concluded that Ledyard was altogether
unreliable and refused to further consider the
matter. A few years later Captain Deshon said
that he had looked over Ledyard's prospectus and
plans, and that it had proved correct in its
minutest details.

Ledyard interested a few acquaintances in Boston, who promised to give the matter consideration, but they wanted to wait until some ship could go to China to confirm Ledyard's statements about the high price paid for furs there. Some members of this group later sent the Columbia and the Lady Washington the Pacific Northwest, and on his second voyage Captain Robert Gray discovered and named the Columbia River.

Being unable to interest anyone in America in his plans, Ledyard decided to go to France and seek Jefferson, who was known to be a man of broad vision. Robert Morris gave Ledyard letters to various merchants and others in France. Ledyard was thought to be a dreamer by the merchants of New York and Boston, because he told them that after procuring a consignment of furs on the Northwest coast he would send the ship to China, where the supercargo could dispose of the furs at an immense profit, while he himself would cross the American continent, afoot or by canoe, to the headwaters of the Mississippi, and thence make his way back to New York City by the time the ship returned from China, so that he would be there ready to make another voyage in the ship.

Landing in Spain, Ledyard made his way from Cadiz on board the French ship Bourbon to Brest. His letters from Robert Morris proved an open sesame to the merchants of France. A company of merchants chartered a ship for the intended voyage and mutual engagements were drawn up and signed. The merchants, however, made it a part of the agreement that he should not set sail until the following spring, as they feared the vessel would be wrecked in the stormy gales of winter. His plan was to leave France and pass around Cape Horn into the Pacific Ocean. He passed the time from October to the following February with as much patience as he could and then began equipping the vessel for sea. The French merchants decided to obtain from the king a commission that would clothe the vessel with public character and enable the owners to claim, in the name of the king of France, all islands or unknown regions that might be discovered. A memorial was sent to the king's ministers, applying for letters of recommendation to all European public agents residing in the ports of the world at which the vessel might touch. On February 23, 1875, Ledyard wrote:

"My affairs in France are likely to prove of the greatest honor and advantage. I have a fine ship of 400 tons and in August I expect to sail on another voyage around the world, at the end of which, if heaven is propitious, I hope to see you. In the meantime, may the God of nature spread his mantle over you all. If I never see you more, it shall be well. If I do, it shall be well--so be happy and of good cheer."

Poor Ledyard! Once more his hopes were dashed to the ground, for the king's ministers doubted the wisdom of a French ship making a trip of this kind, so the merchants withdrew their support from the plans. From L'Orient, Ledyard went to Paris to see Thomas Jefferson, who was minister from the United States at the court of France. Thomas Jefferson heartily approved of Ledyard's plans, and, moreover, thought them practical. He told Ledyard that he was interested not only from the profits to the American merchants to be made from such a trip but because of its bearing on the political interests of the United States. Not only had western America not been explored, but formal possession had not been taken of it. Jefferson believed there might be possibility that, though the western coast of America was separated from the United States by such an immense amount of territory, yet the time might come when the dominion of the United States would reach from sea to sea, or at least, if this did not occur, that a republic would be set up on the shores of the Pacific, colonized by Americans. Not only was Thomas Jefferson in hearty sympathy with Ledyard's plan, but he promised to do all he could toward its consummation. He introduced him to Paul Jones, who was in France to secure payment for the prizes he had taken during the Revolutionary war, particularly for the capture of the Serapis and the Countess of Scarborough, which had been sent into French ports.

John Paul Jones was carried away by Ledyard's plan. He agreed to go in with Ledyard and pledged all of the private fortune he expected to realize from the prize money due him. He promised to use his influence at the French port to furnish two vessels well armed. If the French king refused to furnish the vessels, John Paul Jones agreed to raise the money himself to purchase two vessels.

After much discussion, John Ledyard and John Paul Jones came to the following agreement: They would outfit two vessels and cruise up and down the Pacific Northwest coast, purchasing furs. Meanwhile, they would establish a trading post and build a stockade in which Ledyard, with a surgeon and 20 soldiers, would remain to purchase furs from the Indians, while one of the vessels, in command of John Paul Jones, would go to China with the cargo of furs. When sufficient furs had been collected to furnish another cargo, it would also go to China, where Jones would trade the furs for silk and tea and go around the Cape of Good Hope to Boston and New York, where he would dispose of his cargo and secure more trade goods and supplies, to return by way of Cape Horn to Nootka Sound, or wherever they had established their trading post.

John Paul Jones advanced considerable money to Ledyard for the purchase of cargo, for they were both determined that nothing should prevent them from carrying out their plans. Meanwhile, John Paul Jones was summoned to L'Orient, where he had to wait three months in negotiations to secure the prize money due him. He found the French king and his ministers would do nothing in the matter, and it was also found that, even with the prize money, John Paul Jones was unable to outfit two ships and carry the project through as planned. So the plan was abandoned.

Disappointed in this, Ledyard decided to outfit one vessel and he started to raise the money among the merchants in Paris. Once more his enthusiasm and sureness of large profits discouraged his backers.

Disappointed in this, Ledyard decided to outfit one vessel, and he started to raise the money among the merchants in Paris. His plan was to gather a cargo of furs along the coast of the Oregon Country and send it to China in charge of the supercargo while he would return afoot and alone across the continent to Boston to study the prospects for trade and to make friends with the various Indian tribes. When the Paris merchants learned that he was planning to go alone, on foot, thorugh unexplored country for near 4000 miles from the shores of the Pacific to the Atlantic seaboard, they shook their heads and refused to put in their money.

The Marquis de la Fayette and Thomas Jefferson did all they could to create a favorable impression for him with the authorities. In writing of Thomas Jefferson, Ledyard says:

"Mr. Jefferson is an able minister, and our country may repose confidence in him equal to their best wishes. Whether in public or private, he is, in every word and action, the representative of a young, vigorous, determined state. His only competitors here, even in political fame, are Vergennes and LaFayette. In other accomplishments he stands alone. The Marquis de la Fayette is one of the growing characters in this kingdom. The marquis is a warm friend of America.

"It will be difficult for any subsequent plenipotentiary to have as much personal influence in France as Dr. Franklin had. I had the pleasure of being at his house before his departure, and, although bent down with age and infirmities, the excellent old man exhibited all the good cheer of health, the gay philosopher and the kindness of a friendly countryman."

After discussing the matter with Thomas Jefferson, John Ledyard decided to investigate the fur industry in Russian America, hoping that the knowledge so gained might be helpful in persuading his fellow countrymen in Boston or New York to take up the fur trading industry. He also planned to carry out his original intention of walking from the Pacific Northwest coast across the continent to the Atlantic seaboard. Since he could find no one to put up the money for a ship, he decided to travel overland, mostly afoot, through Europe, across Asia and then cross Bering Strait by boat, walk the length of Russian America to Nootka Sound, on down the Pacific Northwest coast, and thence cross the interior of America to Boston.

Thomas Jefferson gave his hearty approval to Ledyard's plan and agreed to forward his desires in every way possible. He saw M. de Simoulin, the minister plenipotentiary from Russia to the court of France, and he also interviewed Baron de Grimm, the minister from Saxe-Gotha at the French court. Grimm was the private agent of the empress of Russia. Both of these men, in behalf of Thomas Jefferson, wrote a request to the empress asking permission for John Ledyard to travel through her dominion. While waiting for the letters to make their slow progress to St. Petersburg, John Ledyard moved into a little cottage at the edge of the royal forest and each day he ran for many miles to harden his muscles and keep him trim for his 10,000 mile walk.

For five months he waited for a letter from the empress, and finally, becoming impatient, decided to walk to St. Petersburg to present his petition to the empress in person. During the five months he had been waiting he had spent much time with Thomas Jefferson, talking over his plans to establish a fur factory on the Pacific Northwest coast and also his plans of exploring the country between the Pacific Ocean and the Mississippi River. He also frequently saw his friend the Marquis de la Fayette. In speaking of his relations with La Fayette at this period, he said:

"I walked to Paris this morning and saw the Marquis de la Fayette. I esteem him, and even love him, and so we all do, except those who worship him. I make these trips to Paris often--sometimes to dine with this amiable Frenchman, and sometimes with our minister, who is like a brother to me.

"I die with anxiety to be back in the American states after either having come from the Pacific to the Atlantic or penetrated to the Pacific Ocean. The American Revolution invites a thorough discovery of the continent. The honor of doing it would become a foreigner, but a native only can feel the genuine pleasure of such achievement. In the name of amor patriae, let a native explore its resources and its boundaries. It is my wish to be the man. What fate intends is always a secret, but fortitude is the word. Farewell for the present. I have just received intelligence which hurries me to London."

Ledyard went at once to London, in answer of the summons of Sir James Hall, who had met him in France. To Ledyard's unspeakable joy, he found an English ship about to sail for the Pacific Ocean. Sir James Hall had interceded in his behalf with the owners, who had agreed to give him a free passage and set him ashore at Nootka Sound or at any other place on the Pacific Northwest Coast that he might choose. Before going aboard he wrote to Thomas Jefferson:

"Sir James Hall has presented me with 20 guineas, pro bono publico. With this money I bought two great dogs, an Indian pipe and a hatchet. My want of time as well as of money will prevent my going otherwise than indifferently equipped for such an enterprise (to go afoot from the shores of the Pacific Ocean across the continent to Boston). You know how much I owe the amiable La Fayette. Will you do me the honor to present my most grateful thanks to him? If in my travels I find a mountain as much elevated above other mountains as he is above ordinary men, I will name it Mount La Fayette."

If ever a man had hard luck it was John Ledyard. Whenever things looked pretty bad for him, conditions changed, and they grew worse. Inasmuch as the interior of America was unknown, Ledyard decided to be put ashore at Nootka Sound, make his way down the coast, follow some large river inland, and, if there were mountains in the interior of America, to cross them and thus come to some other river that led eastward toward the Mississippi River, from which point he would make his way to Virginia. If adverse fate had not interfered, Ledyard might have been the discoverer of the Columbia River. He wrote to Jefferson that he believed he could walk across the continent in about three years, and he felt sure, from his knowledge of the Indians, that the peace pipe which he carried, and the fact that he was traveling alone, would guarantee his safety.

Sir Joseph Banks, president of the Royal Society, entered warmly into his designs, as he believed that Ledyard would be able to make, in his trip across the continent, many worthwhile discoveries that would add to the geographical knowledge of the world. Colonel Smith, who had been secretary of legation to Mr. Adams, the American minister at London, also was enthusiastic as to the value of the trip. He wrote to John Jay, secretary of foreign affairs in the United

States, in reference to Ledyard's proposed trip:

"In consequence of some allurements from English noblemen, Ledyard came here with the intention of exploring the Northwest coast and the country. A vessel being on the point of sailing for that coast, after supplying himself with a few necessary articles for his voyage and march he procured a passage on the ship, with a promise from the captain to land him on the Western coast, from which he would attempt to march through the Indian nations to the back parts of the Atlantic states, for the purpose of examining the country and its inhabitants. He expects to be able to make his way through and thus become possessed of information of the country and its people that will be of great advantage to our country. It is a daring and wild attempt. Determined to pursue this object, he embarked last week, free and independent of the world, pursuing his plan unembarrassed by contract of obligation. If he succeeds, and in the course of two or three years should arrive at our country by this amazing circuit, he may bring some interesting information. If he fails and is never heard of more, which I think most probable, there is no harm done. He dies in an unknown country, and if he composes himself in his last moments with the reflection that his progress was great and the undertaking what few men are capable of, it will soothes his mind. He is perfectly calculated for the attempt--robust and healthy and has an immense passion to make discoveries which will benefit society. It may not be improper for your excellency to be acquainted with these circumstances and you are the best judge of the propriety of extending them further."

Probably Ledyard spent the happiest hours of his life as the vessel went down the Thames and put out to sea. At last he was embarked on his great adventure--at last the obstacles were overcome. Soon a faster vessel overtook the one on which he was embarked, with orders from the government to return. The vessel put back to Deptford expecting only a temporary delay, but the officers of the government compelled the owners to abandon the voyage.

In writing to his relative, Dr. Ledyard, John Ledyard said:

"This will inform you I have disembarked from the ship which was bound to the Northwest coast of America, on account of her having been seized by the custom house and exchequered. My heart is too much troubled at this moment to write you more."

Ledyard wrote to his friend, Thomas Jefferson, "I am going across Siberia, as I before intended, on foot."

Sir Joseph Banks, Sir James Hall, Colonel Smith, Dr. Hunter, and other scientists headed a subscription to raise money for his trip. From London he went to Hamburg. By January, 1787, he was in Copenhagen. Here he met Major Langhorn, an American officer, whose baggage had been seized because he had been unable to pay his hotel bill. Ledyard had started on his journey across Russia and Siberia and thence down the coast of Alaska to Nootka Sound,, with ten guineas. His sympathy was so profoundly stirred to find another traveler who had been buffeted by fate that he immediately gave him all the money he had, to relieve his distress.

From Copenhagen Ledyard made his way, toward the end of January, to Stockholm. Had it been summer he could have readily crossed the Gulf of Bothnia to Finland, or, had the gulf been frozen over, as was usually the case, he could have walked across, but the floating ice prevented the passage of a boat, and the gulf was not entirely frozen over, so the only alternative was for Ledyard to walk completely around the gulf to St. Petersburg, a distance of 1200 miles, through a very thinly settled district. In other words, he would have to walk 1200 miles to make a distance of 50 miles across the gulf.

Ledyard set out in the heart of winter, without money or friends, afoot and alone, on what everyone considered a desperate undertaking. He traveled through storms and intense cold, averaging a little more than 30 miles a day, reaching St. Petersburg toward the last of March, seven weeks after leaving Stockholm. After traveling afoot through Denmark, Sweden, Swedish Lapland, Swedish Finland, and Russian Finland, he found that his clothes were worn to shreds and his shoes were almost non-existent, but he was on his way, and happy that he was at last started on his great adventure. Writing to Thomas Jefferson from St. Petersburg, he says:

"An equipment is now on foot here to go to the sea of Kamtschatka, the first to visit the Northwest coast of America. It is to consist of four ships. This and the expedition that went from here 12 months since, by land, are to cooperate in a design of some sort in the northern Pacific Ocean."

At St. Petersburg he formed the acquaintance of Professor Peter Simon Pallas, a German naturalist and traveler, who, in 1768, at the invitation of Empress Catherine II, had come to St. Petersburg to take the chair of natural history in the Imperial Academy of Science. Later he had served as naturalist on a six-year trip of exploration through Russia and Siberia. He befriended Ledyard and introduced him to an eminent physician, a member of the Royal Society of Physicians, who promised to procure for Ledyard a royal passport. Dr. Pallas took Ledyard to the French minister, who promised to dispatch the letter of application for the passport to the necessary officials. Unfortunately for Ledyard, the empress and Prince Potemkin, with many members of the Russian court, as well as the Austrian and French ambassadors, were in the Crimea.

From Smolensk they had gone to Kief. The empress apparently had no time or inclination to give a ragged American adventurer a royal passport. Fortunately, Ledyard became acquainted with an officer, a member of the family of the grand duke, who promised him that he would be able to arrange to secure a passport. Ledyard had already waited two months for his royal passport, but his new-found friend, the Russian officer, secured it for him in two weeks.

Dr. William Brown, a Scotchman employed by the empress as a physician, was leaving for the province of Kolyvan at about the time Ledyard secured his passport. Dr. Brown invited Ledyard to accompany him, as going with him, in a government conveyance, would save more than 3000 miles of walking. Ledyard eagerly accepted the invitation.

They left St. Petersburg early in June and drove to Moscow. From Moscow they drove in a kibitka drawn by three horses to Kazan, a distance of over 500 miles. After spending a week in Kazan they crossed the Ural Mountains to Tobolsk, where they arrived on July 11. They finally arrived at Barnaoul, capital of the province of Kolyvan, which was as far as Dr. Brown was going. Here Ledyard met the governor of the province, dined with him twice, and also met a number of former army officers, all of whom treated him with great kindness. He had already come on his journey, from St. Petersburg to Barnaoul, 4539 verstrs, or, to put it in miles, 3026 miles.

Writing from Barnaoul to Thomas Jefferson on July 29, 1787, Ledyard says:

"How I have come thus far, and how I am to go still further, I must disclose to you on some happier occasion. I shall send this letter to St. Petersburg in the care of Professor Pallas, who will transmit it to you, together with one for the marquis in the mail of Count Segur...Those who have heard of America flock around to see me.

Unfortunately the tattoo marks on my hands procure me and my coutrymen the appellation of wild
men. I am treated with the greatest hospitality
here. We have two stars that shine even here, and
the healths of Dr. Franklin and General Washington have been drunk in compliment to me at the
governor's table."

The governor of the province assigned a
corporal to go with Ledyard and arrange that he
should travel at government expense with the
courier who took the post. They traveled in a
three-horse kibitka, reaching Tomsk, 300 miles
distant, in two days and three nights. Usually
the peasants at whose houses the travelers stayed
served them barley soup, onions, quass, bread and
milk, and would accept no pay. Occasionally,
however, Ledyard paid one kopeck for a meal. Inasmuch as one English penny was worth ten ko-
pecks, it can be seen that Ledyard lived very
economically. From Tomsk he went on with a corporal and in the government post to Irkutsk,
which was 1155 miles from Barnaoul. In writing
from Irkutsk, Ledyard says:

"The rains have begun--they have set in severely. I have had a very fatiguing journey from
Barnaoul. Going with the courier, driving wild
Tartar horses at full speed over wild and rugged
country, breaking and upsetting our kibitkas,
beswarmed with mosquitoes, hard rains all the
way, so that when I arrived at Irkutsk I had been
for the last 48 hours wet through and through and
covered with a mass of mud."

At Irkutsk he made the acquaintance of a
brigadier general, a colonel and a major, also a
former adjutant in the French army who had served
at Quebec and was familiar with the Indians of
that country. Governor Jacobi, governor of the
province, granted Ledyard permission to go with
the government post and saw to it that he had
good accommodations. In his journal he records
his astonishment that among the Kalmuks the same

type of moccasin is used as with the Indians in America. He also found them living in wigwams, or tepees, similar to those of the American Indians.

From Irkutsk he went by post to the Lena River, a distance of 150 miles. Here he ran across Lieutenant Laxman, an officer in the Swedish Army, and together they embarked in a small boat for the 1400-mile trip to Yakutsk. On August 30, Ledyard records in his journal:

"We stopped at a village this morning to procure stores. They killed a sheep for us, gave us three quarts of milk, two loaves of bread, cakes made of carrots and radishes, one dozen fresh and two dozen salt fish, some onions and some straw and bark with which to thatch up the roof of our boat, for 14 pence, or about 28 cents. The mountains are full of bear and wolves. We see plenty of wild foul, which we shoot as we please. In the river are salmon trout. My soldier courier stole our brandy, got drunk, was impertinent and I was obliged to handle him roughly."

Ledyard arrived at Yakutsk on September 18, having been 22 days coming down the Lena in the small rowboat. His next traveling was done on a sledge drawn by an ox, the driver, a Yakuti Indian, mounted on the back of the ox, which he guided by a cord fastened through the cartilage of its nose.

At Yakutsk, Ledyard dined with the governor general and asked him to provide him transportation to Okotsk, a distance of 635 miles. The commandant, however, shook his head and told him that the winter had so far advanced that he had better stay as his guest till the following spring. It was now the middle of September and the commandant told him that by the middle of the following May he could resume his journey. In spite of every argument that Ledyard could advance the commandant assured him that the governor general had sent orders to render all possible service and kindness to the American traveler and, in his opinion, the greatest kindness he could render him was to prevent him from leaving until the following spring. The governor general told Ledyard that he would be happy to have him as his guest during the winter. It is quite probable that Governor Jacobi had sent secret instructions to the commander at Yakutsk to detain Ledyard.

In November, Captain Billings arrived at Yakutsk. Captain Billings and Ledyard had served together under Captain Cook on his voyage of discovery, Billings having been the assistant to Astronomer Bayley of the Cook expedition. Both Billings and Ledyard were surprised and delighted to meet in the heart of Siberia. Captain Billings had entered the Russian service and been placed in command of an exploring expedition. Ledyard became a guest of Captain Billings for the next five weeks at Yakutsk and accepted his invitation to return with him to Irkutsk, a distance of more than 1500 miles, to spend the rest of the winter. Captain Billings was going to Irkutsk to secure supplies, which were to be shipped to Okotsk, at which point there were some vessels on which Billings was going to make a voyage to the American coast as soon as spring opened up. Captain Billings invited Ledyard to be his guest until the vessel sailed, at which time he could take him as a passenger to Russian America, as Alaska was then termed. With Captain Billings, Ledyard left Yakutsk on December 29 and traveled by dog team and sledge, up the frozen reaches of the River Lena, negotiating the 1500 mile trip in 17 days.

Here fate dealt the crowning blow to Ledyard's hopes. On February 24 the governor general received orders from the empress to arrest Ledyard and send him under guard to the private inquisition at Moscow. Ledyard, with his two guards, went by sledge through the rigors of a Siberian winter, at full speed, to Moscow.

Shortly after being arrested, Ledyard wrote in his notebook:

"My hopes are once more blasted. What secret machinations have been at work? What motive? Her royal majesty of all the Russias has nothing but her own pleasure to consult--she has no nation's resentment to apprehend. I am the minister of no state or monarch--I travel under the common flag of humanity, which serves the world at large. If death--then my journeyings will be over sooner. Though born in the freest of civilized countries, yet in my present state of privation I have a more exquisite sense of the immortal nature of liberty than I ever had before."

The charge against Ledyard was absurd. He was arrested as a French spy in Siberia. Writing in his journal a little later, he says:

"I am in Neeshna, in a vile, dark, dirty, gloomy damp room. The soldiers who guard me are doubly watchful over me when in a town, though at no time properly so, through their consummate indolence and ignorance. Though treated like a felon, I will not appear like one by flight. I am emaciated. It is more than 20 days since I have eaten anything that might be termed food, and during that time I have been traveling in an open kibitka. I am treated in all respects like a convict, except that I have to support myself with my own money. Were I charged with any injury done either to this or to any other country, I would be more resigned. But to be arrested in my travels at the last state but one--to be seized, imprisoned and transported in this dark and silent manner, without even a guess as to my destination--treated, in short like a subject of Russia--under such circumstances resignation would be a crime against my dear native land."

It is supposed that the rest of Ledyard's journal was seized and destroyed. Writing from London to a friend, he said:

"I penetrated through Europe and Asia, almost to the Pacific Ocean, but in the midst of my career was arrested, a prisoner to the empress of Russia by an express sent after me for that purpose. I was a prisoner under guard during the winter and spring, was banished from the empire and taken to the frontiers of Poland, making the journey of 6000 versts in six weeks. The cruelties and hardships I shall leave untold."

When released at the Polish frontier he was told that instructions had been issued if he was ever found again in Russia or Siberia he would be hanged. He finally arrived in London, ragged and emaciated.

The headquarters of The Russian American Fur Company were at Irkutsk. The governor general of all the eastern parts of Siberia lived there. When the Russian fur traders at Irkutsk learned that Ledyard was going to travel down the Alaskan coast and on to Nootka Sound they were afraid that he would learn what immense profits were being made in the fur trade and also learn with what severity the Russian fur traders treated the Alaskan natives, whom they made virtual slaves. Undoubtedly, the governor general of Irkutsk sent a courier to the empress, which resulted in her having Ledyard arrested and deported from the country.

His deportation from Russia made John Ledyard more eager than ever to have his fellow Americans engage in the fur trade on the Pacific Northwest Coast, and he was also equally eager to explore the country lying between the Pacific and Atlantic Oceans. Sir Joseph Banks of London, who had befriended Ledyard on every occasion, recommended Ledyard to the African Association, as a man of indomitable courage. Ledyard visited Mr. Beaufoy, secretary of the African Association, who, in describing his interview with Ledyard, said:

"Before I learned from the note from Sir Joseph Banks the name and business of my visitor I was struck with the manliness of his person, the breadth of his chest and the openness of his countenance. I spread the map of Africa before him and, tracing a line from Cairo to Sennar and thence westward in the supposed direction of the Niger, I told him that was the route by which I was anxious that Africa might be explored. He said he would consider himself fortunate to be trusted with the venture. I asked him when he could set out. 'Tomorrow morning,' was his response. I told him I was afraid that we should not be able in so short a time to prepare his instructions and to procure for him the requisite letters, but that if the committee should approve of his proposal all expedition should be used."

Writing from London, Ledyard says:

"By my acquaintances in London my arrival was announced to a society of noblemen and gentlemen who had for some time been fruitlessly inquiring for some person to travel through the continent of Africa. I was asked and consented to undertake the tour. The society have appropriated a sum of money to defray the expenses. I dine with them this day week, and within the month shall be on the move. My route will be from here to Paris, thence to Marseilles, across the Mediterranean to Alexandria, then to Grand Cairo, beyond which is unknown, and my discoveries begin. Where they will terminate you shall know, if I survive. Do not think because I have seen much of the world, and will see more, that I have forgotten America. I could as soon forget you, myself, and God."

Ledyard was hopeful that the money he made in exploring parts of Africa might help finance him in establishing the fur trade on the Pacific Northwest Coast. His proposed trip to Africa was to occupy three years. Just before leaving London for his African trip he wrote to his mother:

"Truly is it written that the ways of God are past finding out and his decrees unsearchable. Is the Lord thus great? So also is he good, and I am an instance of it, for I have trampled the world under my feet, laughed at fear and derided danger. Through fierce savages, over parching deserts, the freezing North, the everlasting ice, stormy seas, have I passed without harm. How good is my God, and what rich subjects have I for praise, love and adoration. I have full and perfect health. I pray God to bless and comfort you all. Farewell."

When the secretary of the African Society told him of the dangers and hardships he would encounter, Ledyard said:

"I have known both hunger and nakedness to the utmost extremity of human suffering. My distresses have been greater than I have ever owned or ever will own to any man. Such evils are hard to bear, but they never yet had power to turn me from my purpose. If I live I will faithfully perform to the utmost extent my engagement to the society. If I perish in the attempt, my honor will be safe, for death cancels all bonds."

Ledyard spent a week in Paris visiting Thomas Jefferson, La Fayette, and other old-time friends. Once more he and Jefferson discussed the matter of exploring the western part of America.

Ledyard arrived at Cairo on the 19th of August and a few days later was introduced to Aga Mohommed, the confidential minister of Ismael, one of the four ruling beys. He was promised letters and protection while passing through Turkish Nubia and also was promised letters to the chiefs who lived far inland. Under date of October 14, he writes:

"I went today to the market place where they vend the black slaves who come from toward the interior parts of Africa. There were 200 of them together. I was told by one of them that came from west of Sennar, about 55 days journey, which may be 400 or 500 miles. One of the slaves--a Negro chief--told me the Nile had its source in his country. The name of the country these savages come from is Darfoor, well known on account of the slave trade as well as its trade in gum and elephants' teeth. Most of the slaves appear a harmless, wild people, and are mostly young women."

Ledyard spent most of his time in the slave market, talking to the slave traders and to the slaves themselves, securing information as to the country through which he was to travel. He investigated the type of trade goods, finding that he would have to carry with him for trade with the natives, soap, red linen cloth, antimony, razors, scissors, beads and mirrors. He records that he found in the loads brought in by the caravans elephants' teeth, Sennar gum, gold, ostrich feathers, but principally slaves."

The last letter Ledyard wrote was addressed to Thomas Jefferson, and after describing very minutely conditions in Africa, he said:

"From Cairo I travel southwest about 300 leagues to a black king. There my present conductors leave me. Beyond that I shall go alone. I expect to cut the continent across between the parallels of 12 and 20 degrees of north latitude. If possible I shall write you from the kingdom of this black king. If not, do not forget me. I shall not forget you--indeed, it will be a consolation to think of you in my last moments."

Either the heat or the food or some germ he contracted while visiting the slave market made Ledyard ill. The doctor prescribed what at that time was the common remedy, vitriolic acid. The dose given him was so large that it was thought the medicine would kill him if the disease did not, so he was given a large dose of tartar emetic. He died that night and was buried next day.

He died in November, 1788, and was 38 years of age. In writing of him, the secretary of the African Society said:

"Such instance of decision, energy, perseverance, fortitude and enterprise have rarely been witnessed in the same individual, and in the exercise of these high attributes of mind his example cannot be too much admired or imitated."

Shortly before his death he wrote to Jefferson relative to organizing an expedition to cross the American continent to the Pacific. In 1792, President Jefferson employed his secretary, Captain Meriwether Lewis on an expedition of this kind, but it reached no further than Kentucky.

While Ledyard was in Russia, his former associates built the ship Columbia in the North River and purchased the Lady Washington and employed Robert Gray of Boston as captain and John Kendrick of Wareham, as captain of the other ship. They sailed in September, 1787, visiting the Pacific Northwest forts to establish trade between the Atlantic seaboard and the Pacific Northwest. This trip resulted first in the organization of a company which sent the Columbia and the Lady Washington to the Oregon Country and later in the sending of an expedition to explore this country, which resulted in its settlement by Americans.

That the American flag in place of the British flag now floats over the Oregon Country is due, in no small part to John Ledyard, the Connecticut Yankee who, dying in his thirties while trying to discover the source of the Nile, was still working and writing and talking about the establishing of trade routes between Boston and the Oregon Country.

Oregon Journal
May 5, 1929
October 7-18, 1929

JOHN JACOB ASTOR
Fur Trader

John Jacob Astor, founder of Astoria, had a
hard childhood. While he was still a boy, his
mother died. His father and his stepmother quar-
reled bitterly, and because the stepmother could
not take it out on her husband, she usually
vented her anger on her stepson. Young John
Jacob, when things became too strenuous and
tropical, would go to the home of a boyhood
friend and sleep in their woodshed. He would have
to be on hand early in the morning, however, to
deliver the meat. (He worked for his father, a
butcher.) Because the village boys teased him on
account of his father being a drunkard, he did
not mix in village sports.

The village of Waldorf (Astor's birthplace,
in Germany) took its religion seriously. Most of
its residents were Catholics. Young Astor was a
Protestant. The line of cleavage was very distinct in those days and the more young Astor
thought the matter over the less prospect he saw
for himself in his native village. Professor
Valentine Jeune, a French Protestant, was his
teacher. Because young Astor had such an unhappy
home life, and also because he was so eager to
learn, the teacher took special pains with him.
He taught him to read, write, cipher to the Rule

of Three, to sing the church hymns and to learn the catechism by heart.

John Jacob Astor was confirmed on Palm Sunday, 1777. Immediately after confirmation German boys, at that time, were either apprenticed to a trade, or, if their fathers had no money to buy an apprenticeship, they tried to find a position as laborer or servant. To be apprenticed to a carpenter or blacksmith cost approximately $50. An apprenticeship to an instrument maker or a jeweler cost $200. John Jacob Astor's father had no money whatever, so an apprenticeship was out of the question. He wanted his son to continue to deliver meat and to help him in butchering stock, but this business was very distasteful to young Astor, so finally his father consented to allow him to join his brother in London, if he would work at home for a few years more.

When young Astor was 17 years old, he put all of his earthly possessions into a large handkerchief and with this suspended from a stick over his shoulder he started afoot for the Rhine. He had less than two dollars in cash to pay his way to London. He landed a job as an oarsman on a timber raft. In those days the timber from the

Black Forest was fastened into rafts and these rafts were rowed down the Rhine with huge sweep oars, from 60 to 80 men being employed with each raft. It usually took about two weeks to row a raft to the seaport. He was paid $10 for his work, which was more money than he had owned altogether up to this time.

He secured work where his brother was an apprentice, with the firm of Astor & Broadwood, manufacturers of flutes and pianos. He put in the next two years working hard and during this time he saved every cent he could, learned to speak and to read and write English and read all he could get hold of about the new land, America.

In November, 1783, he invested five guineas

in a steerage ticket, which included his meals of sea biscuit and salt beef. He invested five guineas in seven flutes and took with him five guineas to start in business in America. They arrived, after a very stormy, rough passage, in Chesapeake Bay in January, where the ship became frozen in the ice and where the steerage passengers were compelled to stay on board for the next two months.

"He told Astor that with a small pack of trinkets he could travel among the Indians and pick up furs at about a fifth of the value he could sell them for.'

Young Astor had struck up an acquaintance with a fellow voyager, a German, who also had emigrated to America a few years before, friendless and without money. He had bought furs from the Indians and had done so well that he was now returning to America with goods and was going to start a store. He told Astor that with a small pack of trinkets he could travel among the Indians and pick up furs at about a fifth of the value he could sell them for.

It was March before the ice broke up and the ship could go to Baltimore. Astor went to New York City to live with his brother Henry. Young Astor wanted to become an apprentice to a furrier but he knew he had no money to pay for an apprenticeship. To his great joy and astonishment, he found that in America, instead of paying to learn the business, a young man was paid for his services while learning.

The day after he reached New York he secured a job with Robert Bowne, a Quaker, who was engaged in the business of buying, curing, and exporting peltries. He paid young Astor two dollars a week and his board and lodging. His job was beating furs to keep the moths out of them. After a month, Mr. Bowne raised young Astor's wages. The Indians and trappers bought their furs to Bowne's place of business. Young Astor was a living question mark. He asked them all about the habits of various animals, where they were trapped or killed, and learned all he could about the Indian tribes and what goods they liked best.

Soon his employer, seeing his interest in the fur business, taught him all he could about the quality of various furs and sent him on a fur-buying trip. With a pack of trade goods on his back he struck out afoot and walked to Lake George, where he purchased a canoe and began trading with the Indians on the various lakes and streams in that district. He was very successful on this trip. For a few nails, some bells, or for a small dab of vermilion paint he was able to get excellent furs. There and then he established the principle that guided him in life, of giving as little as possible for as much as possible.

In 1786 Astor started in business for himself. He was 23 years old. In those days beaver skins were still abundant in New York and John Jacob Astor learned not only to drive a hard bargain, but to know furs. He worked 16 to 18 hours a day. He not only bought his own furs, but he cured them, beat them, packed them and sold them. When there were only wigwams on the site of Rochester, he picked that out as the site of a future city, as he did also at Buffalo. He traveled on foot and by canoe all over New York state, buying furs.

With a few bales of prime skins he bought a steerage ticket for London and there visited the great fur houses and established connections which became invaluable to him later. He also became the American agent for the firm of Astor and Broadwood and on his return from London he gave up his shed in Yard and Water Streets and moved to a small store on Gold Street between Fulton and Ann. His sign read, "Furs and Pianos".

The first time John Jacob Astor's name appeared in the New York City Directory was in 1790. One line was devoted to him, "Astor, J. J., fur trader, 40 Little Rock Street". He married Sarah Todd, a young woman of some social pretension and also having a very satisfactory dot (dowry), amounting to $300. She soon became as good a judge of furs as her husband and was an expert at sorting and buying furs. Within a few years he carried out a cherished plan of buying a ship of his own in which to take his furs to England.

He became an expert on the Chinese trade. He sent his first ship to Canton in 1800. From then on the money began rolling in. This money he loaned on business property in New York City at good interest. If the borrower failed to pay interest, Astor was perfectly willing to foreclose and take over the property. For the first 15 years of his residence in New York he and his wife lived in the shop in which he conducted business.

Astor had a genius for making money. Among his maxims to get ahead were give the least and get the most, and get all you can and keep what you get. Although hard and close, Astor was one of the boldest, ablest, and most fearless business men in the country.

In 1800 about 6,000,000 pelts were sold annually. Practically all hats were made of beaver skin. Astor was able to buy beaver skins for less than a dollar in trade goods. He sent these beaver skins to London where he was able to realize five dollars for them. This money, invested in cutlery, musical instruments, or cloth, would

bring a return for his original dollar investment
of at least eight dollars. He averaged $30,000 on
each shipload of furs sent to China, though at
times he made as high as $70,000. Astor would
ship his furs, as well as ginseng, iron, lead,
and other metals to Whampoa, near Canton. There
he would exchange his cargo for tea, chinaware,
and cassia. He could buy good tea for 35 to 40
cents a pound and in New York this tea sold
readily for a dollar a pound or more.

When Astor arrived in New York the population was about 25,000. Astor realized that New
York City was bound to grow, in spite of the
prediction of many there at that time that it
could never be a city of over 50,000 because
people wouldn't live so far out from a business
center. Astor, whenever he had money to invest,
bought farms in the suburbs of the city. He
bought Aaron Burr's estate on Richmond Hill,
consisting of 160 acres, at $1000 an acre. Many
shrewd business men thought he would never get
his money back. Ten years later he was selling
this land at $1500 a lot. Later, Mr. Astor pur-
chased 51,102 acres of land in Putnam County, New
York. On this deal he made a half a million dollars. His agents constantly searched the mortgage
records, and Astor bought every mortgaged farm or
mortgaged property he could find in and about New
York City. During the war of 1812 and during the
panic of 1837 he foreclosed on 60 different properties. As a result of his shrewdness he left an
estate of over $30,000,000. To his eldest son,
William Backhouse Astor, he left the bulk of his
fortune.

In spite of his hardness and in spite of the
fact that it seemed as if he worked first, last,
and all the time for himself, in the founding of
Astoria one can see that he had a vision of helping to build a greater America. John Jacob Astor
believed that in time to come there would be a
great city on the western coast of America, such

as New York City on the Atlantic seaboard. He planned to establish a trading post at the mouth of the Columbia. He also planned to secure lands there so that in time to come, when the city he founded, Astoria, should become the metropolis of the Pacific coast, he would be able to profit as he had in New York from the increased value of his real estate.

On June 23, 1810, he organized the Pacific Fur Company. His partners were Alexander McKay, who had gone with Sir Alexander MacKenzie on both of his exploring expeditions to the northwest

---

"There and then he established the principle that guided him in life, of giving as little as possible for as much as possible."

---

coast of America in 1789 and 1793. He also secured two other trusted employees of the Northwest Company--Duncan MacDougall and Donald McKenzie. Later he took in Wilson Price Hunt of New Jersey.

One hundred shares of stock were issued, 50 shares being owned by Mr. Astor, and the other 50 divided among his associates. Mr. Astor agreed to furnish the vessels, trading goods, provisions and arms and ammunition. Mr. Astor further agreed to stand any loss which should occur during the first five years. Wilson Price Hunt was appointed principal agent for the first term of five years and was to maintain his headquarters and the company post at the mouth of the Columbia River.

One expedition was to go by sea and one by land. Wilson Price Hunt was put in charge of the expedition by land. Mr. Astor hired Lieutenant Jonathan Thorn, who was on leave of absence from the United States Navy, to command the Tonquin, a ship of 290 tons burden, having a crew of 20 men and mounting ten guns. In addition to the crew, four of Astor's associates went on the Tonquin--McKay, McDougal, David Stuart and his nephew, Robert Stuart--and 12 clerks, most of whom had been engaged in the Indian trade in Canada. These clerks were paid $100 a year, the money to be paid at the end of the five year contract. In addition to this, there were 13 French-Canadian voyageurs, each of whom had enlisted for a five-year term. These men were to handle the canoes and bateaux used in trading on the Columbia River and its tributaries. In addition to the trading goods, which formed the cargo of the Tonquin, Mr. Astor sent seeds and other materials to make a permanent settlement. The United States authorities ordered Captain Hull, in command of the frigate Constitution, to serve as a convoy to the Tonquin until it ws safely off the coast. The Tonquin put to sea on September 8, 1810.

Captain Thorn fell afoul of the partners before the ship was 24 hours out of port. He ordered them to extinguish the lights in the cabin at eight o'clock. The partners refused to obey what they considered a needless infraction of their rights. Captain Thorn told them they were on the high seas, and if they did not obey him he would put them in irons. McDougal, drawing out his pistol, invited Captain Thorn to try it. From then on the whole trip was one of bitter contention and crossed purposes.

While in France during the World War (WW I), one of my fellow workers was Mrs. Vincent Astor--and, by the way, she was a most charming, capable, and hard-working young woman. Her husband, Vincent Astor, was an ensign in the Navy.

Oregon is indebted to the generosity of Vincent Astor and to the enterprise of Ralph Budd, president of the Great Northern Railroad, for the monument on Coxcomb Hill at Astoria, dedicated to the memory of Captain Robert Gray, the discoverer of the Columbia River, and to John Jacob Astor, founder of Astoria.

Someday someone will write a book which will show John Jacob Astor in his true light--a patriot and far-seeing American. He was willing to risk his fortune to establish a trading post at the mouth of the Columbia, from which point he could open up the trade of the Orient. It was not merely to make more money that he established this trading post, for he was working with President Jefferson to hold the western part of the United States as a part of our country.

In discussing the founding of Astoria, Agnes C. Laut, in her book, "The Conquest of Our Western Empire", says:

"Astor was a personal friend of President Jefferson and knew that Congress, in order to stop the frightful abuses of liquor traffic among the Indians, was about to pass a law excluding the foreign and unlicensed traders from setting up fur posts in the American territory. The law, it may be added, was more honored in its breach than in its observance, for beyond the Mississippi there was no law nor any means of enforcing law."

At a banquet held in the Beaver Club of the Northwest Company at Montreal, plans were being discussed to hamper the trappers and traders of the Hudson's Bay Company. At this banquet was John Jacob Astor.

"There is a little plain man," says Miss Laut, "hair cut very short, with the high forehead of an idealist, with brains behind his ideals, sharp eyes that bore into other men's designs like a corkscrew, tight lips that keep their own counsel--diplomatically suggesting that as the clash between Hudson's Bay and Nor'westers and Americans is costing so much in life and profits, it would be wise for Nor'westers and Americans to avoid further clashes with lawless free traders, by combining for the Pacific fur

53

trade.

"The agreement between Vancouver and Don Quadra has left the most valuable fur trade area between New Spain and Alaska a no-man's land. Why not combine, avoid the ruin of different prices, competition, liquor traffic, and divide th profits? They could find a strong military station at the mouth of Gray's Columbia River to defy Indian attack and open the sale of fur directly to China, bring back Chinese silk and teas and send their ships out again, with no empty hold on any leg of the trade around the world. They could string a chain of fur posts up Lewis and Clark's trail from the Missouri to the Columbia, and control the fur trade west of the Mississippi, without encroaching on the Hudson's Bay Charter to the north.

"John Jacob Astor's suggestion was received in frigid silence. The Montreal traders are a proud, stiff-necked lot of highlanders. Astor says he will put up $400,000 in cash as his part. If the Nor'westers feel that proportion unfair, he will put up two-thirds and they can put up one-third. With war threatening between the United States and Great Britain—with bloody civil war wasting the resources of the Nor'westers and the Hudson's Bay, $400,000 cash would have broken either of the British companies flat, and Astor, an individual American citizen, could propose that seriously, nonchalantly, as though $400,000 in coin were a casual possession.

"The Napoleonic wars had crippled British finances. Neither Hudson's Bay nor Nor'westers could look to home banks for any financing to tide them past the slump in fur values. They must make their profit from the fur trade itself and here is Astor proposing to divide those profits among three companies. They refused his offer. There were some partners present who did not sniff at Astor's plan, among whom was Alex McKay, who had gone with Mackenzie to the Pacific.

"There was Duncan McDougal, a great mixer with the Indians, and a good trader, but too self-important and fussy to obtain the place among partners to which he felt entitled. There was David Stuart, too easy-going for these ruthless Nor'westers. There was his nephew Robert—a fine fellow, but too loyal to David for swift promotion. There was Alexander Henry. Before Astor returned to New York, he engaged several partners for the Pacific Fur Company.

"Alexander McKay was to be chief trader on the coasting vessel going around the horn; McDougal, chief bourgeois at the fort to be built on the Columbia with full proxy power for Astor himself; the Stuarts, to be traders for the posts inland from the Pacific.

"Astor was to put up $400,000 and go 50-50 with the partners on all profits, but bear all loss if the venture failed. The papers were drawn up for twenty years, but if the venture proved a losing one, it was to be mutually dissolved in five years. In other words, with war impending, Astor risked half his fortune on a chance that would have bluffed out a gambler.

"McKay was empowered to gather up a dozen voyageurs for inland waters and a dozen clerks to come down to New York by canoe and board Astor's ship the Tonquin, to sail to the mouth of the Columbia River."

The Tonquin, after a stormy and turbulent voyage, in more ways than one, from New York to the mouth of the Columbia, anchored near Chinook Point on the north shore. In telling of the coming of the Astor party and their adventures after arriving at the mouth of the Columbia, Miss Laut says:

"Pens were at once built to herd in the hogs and goats left alive from the gales. Thorn was disgusted to see McDougall hob-nob familiarly with the one-eyed Chief Concomley, who had known Lewis and Clark. McDougall knew his job as trader. The Astorians must have the friendship of the Indians, and the Indians advised him, as they advised Lewis and Clark, to build on the south shore, where there was better hunting, better anchorage, and more shelter from gales. In crossing from the north to the south shore in their frail birchbark canoes, the inland voyageurs came to grief in an upset of a flood tide. The Canadians would have drowned but for Chinooks and Clatsops dashing to the rescue in dugouts and tossing the helpless men into the righted canoes-- every paddle had been lost in the upset--and towing the canoes ashore.

"The place chosen for their trading post was the site of modern Astoria. High enough to be out of the tide's reach, sheltered by Coxcomb Hill to the rear and about 15 miles inside the bar. While the builders were busy, McKay, who was the chief trader, set off up the Columbia in a canoe with young Robert Stuart and four voyageurs, as far as the Cascades to spy out the possibilities of trade."

Oregon Journal
January 8 & 9, 1930
May 19, 19??

THE MCKAY FAMILY

Fur Traders and Indian Fighters

"My grandfather, Thomas McKay, came with his father, Alexander McKay, from Mackinaw in the summer of 1810 to establish a post at the mouth of the Columbia River which was to serve as a depot for furs gathered from the Rocky Mountains and the coast country," said Miss Leila McKay of Portland. "From Astoria the furs were to be shipped to China, where they were to be exchanged for tea, silk and sandalwood, to be sold in Boston and New York City.

"John Jacob Astor organized the Pacific Fur Company 1810, and my great grandfather, Alexander McKay, was one of the partners. The trading goods were sent around the Horn aboard the Tonquin in charge of Captain Jonathan Thorn, a man who could not brook opposition. He was obstinate, set in his ways, arbitrary and intolerant. The Tonquin started from New York City in September, 1810, and arrived off the mouth of the Columbia in March, 1811. The bar was rough, but Captain Thorn insisted that one of the ship's yawls be manned and sent out to sound the bar and discover a channel. Four sailors were thus drowned. Captain Thorn, against protests, had the other yawl launched and sent six more more sailors on the quest. This yawl was overturned on the heavy seas and four of the sailors were drowned. A day or so later the Tonquin sailed in over the bar and anchored in a small harbor on Vancouver Island.

"You can't rush Indians, nor can you insult them. Captain Thorn decided that the Indians must do business with him in his way and not after their leisurely fashion. My great-grandfather went ashore to get in touch with the Indians farther inland and to get them to bring their furs out to the ship. While he was gone Chief Nookamis, with a large number of his tribesmen, went aboard the Tonquin with furs. Captain Thorn, a typical Yankee, wanted to get the furs for a tithe of their value. His offers in trade goods were so low that the Indians refused to exchange. Captain Thorn became furious, so he seized a sea otter skin that Chief Nookamis was offering him and rubbed it in the face of the chief and ordered him off the boat. Because they did not go as fast as he thought they should, he kicked them, and, becoming enraged at his lack of success in dealing with them, he used his fists most effectively to teach them a lesson of the superiority of the white man.

"My great-grandfather, on his return to the Tonquin, learned from the Indian interpreter what had happened, so he knew that unless they set sail at once the Indians would try to avenge their insults. Captain Thorn refused to listen to advice, and said he would settle the Indians and teach them a lesson with his cannon and small arms. When my great-grandfather went to him again, with a demand that, for the protection of the lives of those on board and on account of the value of their cargo, they should go to some other point to trade, Captain Thorn became furious and abusive and refused to move the Tonquin a foot.

"Next morning at daybreak a canoe with 20 unarmed Indians in charge of Chief Shewish came aboard to trade. John Jacob Astor had given orders to Captain Thorn to allow but a limited number of Indians aboard at one time, but Captain Thorn decided that, as he was master of the ship, he would let as many come aboard as wanted to. Canoe after canoe came alongside, and the Indians clambered aboard. The officer on watch did not like to disturb Captain Thorn, who was not yet up, and as he had no orders to keep the Indians off he let them come aboard to wait till Captain Thorn got up and was ready to trade. The officer

---

"Our family has been engaged in almost all the Indian wars of Oregon..."

---

on watch did not like the looks of the Indians, so he called my great-grandfather to come up on the deck and talk with the Indians. He also decided to wake Captain Thorn. My great-grandfather saw the Indians meant trouble. He told Captain Thorn the only thing to do was to set sail and clear the deck of the Indians. Captain Thorn refused to do so, for the Indians told him they would trade with him on his own terms. They traded their furs for long, keen-bladed knives. That was the only thing they seemed to want.

"Captain Thorn, seeing the Indians gather into knots on the deck in place of going back to their canoes, ordered the anchor hoisted and sails set. In a loud and angry voice he ordered the Indians to leave. In an instant the Indians drew their war clubs from beneath their fur mantles and attacked the white men. They stabbed Mr. Lewis. They felled my great-grandfather with a war club and threw him overboard so the squaws could kill him with their clubs and knives.

"Chief Shewish told his tribesmen he wanted to deal with Captain Thorn himself, so he attacked him with a long knife. Thorn drew a heavy clasp knife and with one blow ripped Chief Shewish open, killing him. Thorn was soon the center of a struggling mass of Indians who were trying to get in effective blows, but he killed or crippled several and made his way to the wheel, where an Indian felled him with a war club and he was hacked to pieces and thrown overboard for the squaws to finish.

"The crew defended themselves with hand-spikes, but were soon overpowered and killed. Seven of the crew were aloft setting the sails. The armorer, Stephen Weeks, and two more were killed as they came down to the deck, but the other four got to the captain's cabin, from which they opened fire on the Indians, who jumped overboard and took to their canoes. The four men turned a cannon on the canoes and killed a considerable number.

"Mr. Lewis, who was the first man stabbed and had been left for dead, was seen by the Indians next morning, leaning against the rail of the Tonquin. He motioned for the Indians to come aboard. The four sailors had escaped during the night. The Indians clambered aboard. The Indian interpreter, who had come from Astoria, had been spared by the Indians, as he was one of their own race. He came aboard with the Indians. Soon the decks were covered with Indians intent on plunder. Lewis had disappeared below. Suddenly there was a terrific explosion that tore the Tonquin to fragments. More than 100 Indians were killed by the explosion of the powder magazine.

"Next day the four sailors were captured and brought to the Indian camp and killed by slow torture. They told the interpreter before they died that Lewis, the ship's clerk, and planned the blowing up of the Tonquin in revenge for his mortal wounds. The interpreter escaped and made his way back to Astoria and gave full particulars of the tragic fate of the Tonquin and its crew.

"I was born at The Dalles, though I have made my home here in Portland for many years. My father, Dr. William C. McKay, was born at Astoria, March 18, 1824. His father, Thomas McKay, was born at Fort William, Canada, in 1797, and was the son of Alexander McKay, born in Scotland.

"My mother's maiden name was Margaret Campbell. She was born at Fort Donvegan, January 13, 1834. She was the fifth daughter of Colin Campbell, chief factor of the Northwest Fur Company. She spent her girlhood in the Peace River country up to the time she was sent to school at Fort Gary, now Winnipeg....On May 24, 1854, when she was 20, she accompanied her brother-in-law, James Sinclair, and her sister, from the Red River country to Wallula, on the Columbia River, where Sinclair was sent to take charge of the Hudson's Bay Post. My mother drove a two-wheeled Red River cart pulled by a black ox the entire distance. My father, who had taken up a place in 1851 on McKay Creek, near the present town of Pendleton, heard of the arrival of the Red River brigade at Fort Wallula and rode to Wallula to welcome the newcomers. There he met and fell in love with my mother, and thereafter was a frequent visitor at the fort.

The Indians were restless in the winter of 1854. Kamaiakun was sending runners to stir up the tribes east of the Cascades over the broken promises of the white men, telling them that unless they fought to retain them the white men would soon crowd them from their hunting grounds and the land where their fathers lay buried. Peu-peu-mox-mox, who had in times past proved a loyal friend of the white settlers, was now an open and avowed enemy, because the white men had murdered his son in cold blood.

"It was decided that it would be cheaper to pay some of the money promised the Indians when the treaty was signed in which they gave up their land, than to have an Indian war, so Nathan Olney was sent to Fort Wallula from The Dalles with $500 in silver and some presents for Peu-peu-mox-mox, as the first installment of payments due under the treaty. Peu-peu-mox-mox refused the presents or the money in payment for the murder of his son. Nathan Olney and James Sinclair, the Hudson's Bay factor at Wallula, saw that the chief's action meant war, so they notified the settlers to take refuge at The Dalles. Sinclair took the powder and lead stored at Fort Wallula and dropped it into the river so the Indians would not make use of it. Indian Agent Olney, with my uncle and aunt, Mr. and Mrs. Sinclair, and my mother, Margaret Campbell, as well as most of the settlers and miners, left by canoe or bateaux for The Dalles.

"On March 26, 1856, the Yakima Indians attacked,, at the Cascades, the white men who were building a warehouse and two portage bridges. My uncle, James Sinclair, was one of the first killed by the Indians.

"That fall, on October 6, 1856, my father and mother were married at The Dalles, and theirs was the first marriage license issued at The Dalles.

"My great-grandfather, Alexander McKay, married a woman of the Ojibway tribe. My grandfather, Thomas McKay, who was 14 when the Astor trading post was established at the mouth of the Columbia, came with his father to what is now Astoria in the spring of 1811. He was to have gone with his father aboard the Tonquin on its trading voyage for sea otter skins when it sailed in 1811, to Vancouver Island, but just before the Tonquin sailed he took sick, so his father left him with the men who were building the stockade and trading post. If he had gone I wouldn't be here, for, with the exception of the Indian interpreter, everyone aboard the Tonquin was killed by the Indians while the ship was anchored at Clayoquot Sound, Vancouver Island.

"Dr. John McLoughlin married Alexander McKay's Indian wife at Fort Williams, so my grandfather, Thomas McKay, became Dr. McLoughlin's stepson. Thomas McKay was half Scotch and half

Indian. He was tall, dark, and very powerful. He
was a man of great courage and daring. He married
the oldest daughter of the chief of the Chinook
tribe, and my father, Dr. William Cameron McKay,
was born at Astoria in 1824. After the death of
his first wife my grandfather married the
half-breed daughter of Mr. Monture, a clerk of
the Hudson's Bay Company. They were married at
Fort Vancouver by Bishop Blanchet. To them was
born a son, Donald McKay. My grandfather, being
the stepson of Dr. McLoughlin, was given large
authority and had great influence with the Indians all over the Pacific Northwest.. He had
charge of many important expeditions.

"In 1832 Nathaniel J. Wyeth of Cambridge,
Massachusetts, came overland to establish a
trading post, but his ship, with his trading
goods, was wrecked in the south seas. Dr. Mc-
Loughlin entertained him at Fort Vancouver that
winter. Wyeth came out again in 1834 and established Fort Hall as a trading post. His ship, the
May Dacre, with supplies, arrived safe, and he
established a trading post on Sauvies Island. He
sent supplies up the Columbia to Fort Hall. Unable to compete with the Hudson's Bay Company,
Wyeth sold out to Dr. McLoughlin. Dr. McLoughlin
had my grandfather, Thomas McKay, and John McLeod
go with Wyeth to Fort Hall to take over that
trading post. While they were there Jason Lee and
his party came to Fort Hall, and on July 17,
1834, preached a sermon to the mountain men,
trappers, and to the men with Wyeth. One of the
men with my grandfather was killed by a fall from
his horse that afternoon, so my grandfather asked
Jason Lee to preach his funeral sermon, which he
did the following day.

"My grandfather married the oldest daughter
of Chief Com-comly, head chief of the Chinook
tribe at the mouth of the Columbia. Archibald
McDonald married the second daughter, known by

the whites as Princess Sunday. She died shortly
after the birth of her first child, Ranald Mac-
Donald, who was taken to the lodge of his
mother's sister, Car-cumcum. When Ranald was bout
a year and a half old his father took him to what
is now Winnipeg, then known as Fort Garry. On
September 1, 1825, Ranald's father married Jane
Klyne, and shortly thereafter they returned to
Fort George, at the mouth of the Columbia. Ranald
and my father attended school at Fort Vancouver
in 1833. The teacher was John Ball, who came with
Wyeth and started his school in November, 1832.
Ranald's father was a graduate of the University
of Edinburgh. When Ranald was little his stepmother would make long trips from Fort Langley or
Fort Colville to Fort Vancouver, and on the return they would travel on a pack horse, Ranald in
a woven basket on one side of the saddle and his
step-brother, Angus, in a basket on the other, to
balance the load.

"In the days of the provisional government,
in 1846, the legislature granted my grandfather,
Thomas McKay, a charter to construct and operate
a toll road from the settlement on the Santiam
River, now Albany, across the Cascade and Blue
Mountains to his claim at what is now Boise.
Stephen A. D. Meek's petition to construct a toll
road at what now is the McKenzie Pass Road was
refused, but S. K. Barlow was given permission to
build a toll road around Mount Hood.

"Immediately after the killing of Dr. Whitman and the others at Waiilatpu my grandfather
raised a company of volunteers on French Prairie
for the Cayuse War. He was captain, Charles McKay
first lieutenant, Alexander McKay second lieutenant, and Edward Dupois orderly sergeant. A
flag with a lone star and several stripes was
presented to the company. In presenting it he
said: 'This flag we are expected to defend. We
must defend it.' And they did.

"Colonel Gilliam in February went with his

64

volunteers to The Dalles. From there they marched to Meek's crossing of the Deschutes, where they had a skirmish with the Deschutes Indians. From there they started for the Whitman Mission. They met the Indians at Sand Hollow, about eight miles from Wells Springs. My grandfather's company was on the extreme right. Five Crows, head chief of the Cayuses, had told his warriors that his med-

"The Indians, who have been converted to Christianity, find it hard to understand how men who profess to be Christians will defraud, deceive and betray them and refuse to keep promises solemnly made, and yet insist that the Indian must keep his part of the bargain."

icine was so strong that the white men's bullets could not harm him. War Eagle said he could swallow all the bullets the white men could fire at him. These chiefs told their people they would not let the volunteers cross the Umatilla River. To prove that the white men's bullets could not hurt them, these chiefs rode at full speed at my grandfather's company. My grandfather, who was a noted shot, shot War Eagle through the head, killing him instantly, while Lieutenant Charles McKay, with a double barreled shotgun loaded with buckshot, wounded Five Crows so badly he had to surrender command.

"The Indians fell back. They kept up an occasional fire, but there was no more charging of the volunteers, who reached Whitman Mission three days later. A day or so later, in a skirmish, an Indian killed William Taylor. Nathan Olney, an old-time friend of my grandfather, grappled with the Indian, seized his war club and struck him over the head, and, in the hand-to-hand struggle that ensued, killed the Indian with his knife.

"In September, 1848, a company was organized at Oregon City to go to the California gold diggings. There were 50 wagons in the train and over 150 men. Peter H. Burnett was elected captain, and my grandfather, Thomas McKay, was elected pilot. He took them by the old Applegate Trail to Klamath Lake, and there headed for the old trail across the Sierras, but they ran across a newly opened wagon road made by Peter Lassen. They reached the summit of the Sierras on October 20, and shortly after overtook Lassen, who had started out with ten wagons, but, finding it impossible to travel through the heavy timber with wagons, they had cut them down to carts, while some had abandoned the carts and used their oxen as packhorses. Lassen and his party had been without flour for a month and were about starved out. The Oregon train took them under their wing, and the Oregonians, who had 75 axemen ahead of their train, soon cleared a road and reached the newly discovered diggings.

"I wish you could have interviewed my mother. She and father had a most adventurous life. Mother lived at Wallula with her brother-in-law, Mr. Sinclair. She was left in charge of the post while the Sinclairs went to The Dalles. This was in 1855. Mother heard the Indian drums at night, so she asked Mr. McBean, the interpreter, to see what the Indians were doing. He went to the camp of Peu-peu-mox-mox and found the Indians war dancing. They had the scalp of Mr. Bolen, agent of the Yakimas, and another fresh scalp. My father came over from his place on McKay Creek the next day, and Mother told him of it. He didn't think the Indians would go on the warpath. A day or so later Peu-peu-mox-mox and his warriors came to the post and demanded the key to the building where the powder and lead were kept. Mother said, 'You cannot have it. You will have to kill me if you get the key from me.' They liked her courage, so they held a council and told her they would come back later to get it. My brother-in-law and Nathan Olney threw all the powder and lead in the Columbia, and they all went to The Dalles. In the war that ensued, my brother-in-law was killed in the attack on the Cascades.

"My grandfather was the chief factor at Fort Hall, which had been purchased from Nathaniel Wyeth. He decided to send my father to Scotland, where my grandfather's father was born, so that Father could be educated. The other two boys, Alexander and John, were to go to Wilberham to receive their education at the school Jason Lee attended.

"My grandfather on his way east stopped at Waiilatpu to visit Dr. Marcus Whitman. He was to go north by way of Fort Garry and thence to Montreal and on to Edinburgh. Dr. Whitman said to my grandfather, 'This country is going to belong to Americans, Mr. McKay. Why don't you send William to an American college in place of making an Englishman of him?'

"My grandfather said, 'I have not the money to send William as well as my other two sons to an American college.'

"Dr. Whitman said, 'If you will send him to Fairfield, New York, where I received my schooling, I will put up the money for his schooling and take it out in goods. As you ship the goods up the Columbia to Fort Hall you can put them off at Fort Walla Walla for me.'

"My grandfather agreed to this proposition, so Father went on across the plains with his two brothers to attend an American school. Father put in five years at the academy and medical college. He returned in 1843 with the yearly express for the Hudson's Bay Company. As Father was only 19 years old they could not give him a doctor's diploma, but his professor, Dr. F. H. Hamilton, gave him a license to practice medicine till he was 21, at which time he could secure a regular diploma.

"Father clerked for Mr. McKinaly in his store at Oregon City. In 1849 he went to the gold diggings on Trinity River. In 1851 he moved east of the mountains and started a store on the Boise-Salt Lake City road on Houtamia Creek, now called McKay Creek. Father's store was burned by the Indians in the war of 1855. Vic Trevitt of The Dalles, who is buried on Memaloose Island, used to be a frequent visitor. Father moved to The Dalles in 1856 and he and Mother were married there that same year. Father's best man was Ben Stark, for whom Stark Street is named. The bridesmaid was Ruth Buckingham, later Mrs. John G. Campbell, house mother of Bishop Scott Academy for years.

"We had a large flagpole in our yard (in The Dalles). Each morning when the flag was raised and each evening at sunset when Father lowered it, he had all of us children come out and stand at attention. He said it would be a good example to others and that it would impress loyalty to our country in our own hearts. Father served as interpreter to Governor I. I. Stevens of Washington Territory when he was making treaties with the Indians.

"Our family has been engaged in almost all the Indian wars of Oregon. My grandfather, Captain Thomas McKay, raised a company of volunteers on French Prairie and fought in the Cayuse Indian War in 1847-48. My father served as scout and interpreter in the war of 1855-56. My brother Tom was in the fight at Willow Springs and William Lamar, who was killed there, was engaged to my sister. My brother Jim, now a rancher in Grant County with Mr. Disosway, made a breakneck drive from Pendleton to Walla Walla to get guns and ammunition when Pendleton was forted up at the time of the Bannock-Piute War. Mr. Disosway took a heavy cold, which turned into pneumonia, from which he died.

"Father was assistant surgeon to Major Throckmorton when he was stationed at Pendleton at the time of the Indian wars. Major Edward S. Farrow, one of the officers, was a cousin of Sam Jackson, publisher of the East Oregonian. My father's half-brother, Donald McKay, saved the life of Major Granville O. Haller and the others in his command. A. J. Bolon, the agent of the Yakimas, had gone to see Kam-i-ah-kan to notify him that his tribesmen must not bother the miners who were passing through the Indian country. This was in 1855. Skloom, sub-chief, met Bolon. Bolon told him if the Indians did not behave the soldiers would be sent up there to kill them. While Bolon was on his way back to The Dalles he was killed by a young Indian, one of a party of three Yakimas. They built a fire, and after killing Bolon's horse they put the bodies of Bolon and his horse on the fire and burned them up.

"Major Haller, who was at The Dalles, started with 107 officers and men, with supplies for a month's campaign on pack horses. My father's brother Donald was to go as scout, but Major Haller changed his mind and told him he would have to serve as chief packer in place of scout. They left The Dalles on October 3, 1855. On the 6th they had a skirmish with the Indians, in which one soldier was killed and seven were wounded. The Indians, who numbered about 700, surrounded Haller's command. The soldiers took up their stand on a ridge and after nightfall retreated to a higher ridge nearby. Major Haller saw they would probably be wiped out. He said to my uncle, Donald McKay, 'McKay, you know this country as well as the palm of your hand. You will have to get us out of here.'

"My uncle said, 'I am not a scout. I am a packer.'

"Major Haller said, 'Now is your chance to prove you are a real scout. I want you to get a courier out to The Dalles and send word to Lieutenant Day to bring his company of the Third Artillery at once.'

"My uncle took one man and got him through the surrounding Indians, and returned. Next day the Indians kept up their fire, killing two more soldiers and wounding 13. That night my uncle discovered a trail over the steep bluff, and the soldiers started for The Dalles. They would have escaped without detection, but some of the soldiers halted and built a fire, and the Indians discovered they were escaping. They kept up a running fight from then on, and Haller finally, with a part of his force, reached The Dalles.

"General Canby and my father were warm friends. General Canby wanted my father to go with a band of Warm Springs scouts to the Lava Bed country at the time of the trouble with Captain Jack and his band. Father could not get away, so his half-brother Donald went in charge of the scouts. Donald served with Major Haller; also with General Canby and with General Crook and many other army officers. At the time the council was held by General Crook, A. B. Meacham and others with the Snake Indians in Antelope Valley, my uncle Donald McKay served as interpreter. Donald spoke Shoshone fluently. In fact, he spoke seven Indian languages and, of course, by means of the sign language, could make himself understood in any tribe. He took the contract in early days to take the mail by way of the Barlow Trail from Portland to eastern Oregon points. He traveled the route winter and summer, but it was tough going in winter.

"My father took A. B. Meacham from The Dalles to the Warm Springs Reservation for his first visit there. The Warm Springs Indians used to live at Tygh Valley, but in the treaty made in 1855 they were compelled to accept lands at the Warm Springs Reservation and give up their former home in Tygh Valley. My father was the interpreter, so he knew all about it.

70

"The Indians, who have been converted to Christianity find it hard to understand how men who profess to be Christians will defraud, deceive and betray them and refuse to keep promises solemnly made, and yet insist that the Indian must keep his part of the bargain. The Indians do not understand how a thing that is not right morally can be right legally. For example, when the treaty was made with the Tenino Indians the government took away the improvements made by John Mission and Billy Chinook, promising them that the government would reimburse them for what the white men wanted and took. What happened? The usual thing. The Indians got nothing for what they gave up, and, of course, had no redress. My father used to help the Indians whenever he could to secure their rights, and he tried to prevent advantage being taken of them.

"Winip-Snoot, the Umatilla chief, came to my father one day and said, 'We want a church like the Indians at Lapwai.' The Indians met at first at the home of Moses. Father wrote to Mr. Corbett in Portland, who sent an organ, some chairs and some hymn books. My brother Tom put up a church, and soon the work was gaining ground. This work resulted in the establishment of the Presbyterian Mission on the Umatilla Agency.

"Occasionally unscrupulous white men that attempt to defraud the Indians come out second best. You used to live in Pendleton, so you probably have heard how How-lish-wam-po, chief of the Cayuse Indians at the Umatilla Agency, cleaned up the white gamblers in 1867. When I was a girl in Pendleton I loved to ride, and the Indians taught me many a trick in riding.

"There is something about a horse race that stirs the blood. How-lish-wam-po had a pony sired by a thoroughbred out of a Cayuse mare that was one of the swiftest race horses for anywhere from five miles up that was ever bred east of the mountains. The Indian race course was on the bottom land along the Umatilla River was over two and a half miles long. There was a stake at the end of the course. The riders had to turn around this stake and return to the starting point.

"Joe Crabb, a white man, got hold of a horse that had beaten every horse it had raced with. Crabb timed the Indian's race horse. He measured the course. He timed his own horse and found that his horse could make it in less time than the pinto. He managed to get hold of the pinto and, with a good man on it, he raced it with his horse, and there was nothing to it. His horse came out ahead and didn't exert itself. He challenged How-lish-wam-po to a race. The challenge was accepted.

"When an Indian horse races against a horse owned by a white man the Indians, out of loyalty, will bet on their own horse. Joe Crabb knew this, so he taunted the Indians till they bet everything they had on the pinto. The Indians starve down a race horse before a race, feeding him but little and racing him each evening.

"On the day of the race nearly everyone living in Pendleton was on hand to watch the race. The Indians turned out en masse. Joe Crabb had passed the word to some of his friends to bet their limit on the race, as he had raced the two horses, and the Indian horse didn't have a look-in.

"The Indians, when they learned that Crabb had stolen the pinto one night and tried the two horses together, seemed to hesitate. How-lish-wam-po, the owner of the pinto, sent back for more horses to bet. In front of the stakeholders were blankets spread with great heaps of twenty dollar gold pieces. The Indians not only bet their horses, but their saddles and their treasured ornaments. They bet all they had, rather than seem to go back on their chief and his race horse. The white men, who knew they had a sure thing, did everything in their power to get the Indians to bet all they had, for they knew how susceptible an Indian is to the gambling fever.

"Joe Crabb's racer was a blooded horse, and shone in the sunlight, while the pinto looked unkempt. A young Indian boy, naked except for a breechclout, rode the pinto.

"Well, there isn't much more to tell. Joe Crabb's famous race horse made a noble race, but was no match for the pinto. The jockey, with his silver spurs and his jaunty cap and crimson silk uniform, gave up the race after running four miles, and the pinto swept in alone. The pinto ran the five miles and a quarter and 83 yards (for they measured the course afterwards to know its exact length) in 9 minutes 51 seconds. This was the fastest time ever made up to that time, and for all I know it may never have been beaten.

"After the race How-lish-wam-po gave Joe Crabb the saddle horse he had won from him, and also gave him a handful of double eagles. He said to him, 'Next time you steal my racing horse to try him out, be sure you get the right horse. The horse you stole that night and tried out was the half-brother of my racer.'

"How-lish-wam-po won about $20,000 on the race, and the Indians were flush for a long time after the race. How-lish-wam-po, to show that he was a good sport, issued a challenge to all comers. He offered to pay the expenses of any horse from wherever it came that would beat his pinto over the five and a quarter mile course. He could have done it, for he owned several thousand Indian cayuses and had lots of money. His pinto was never beaten."

Oregon Journal
October 17, 18, 20,
21, & 22, 1927

DR. JOHN MCLOUGHLIN
Father of Oregon

Mrs. M. L. Myrick, who for many years lived at No. 595 Johnson Street in Portland, probably knew more about the old Hudson's Bay regime, from personal knowledge, than any other person in the West. She was the granddaughter of Dr. John McLoughlin, and when a girl served as his secretary. Her home was a veritable treasure house, from a historical standpoint. Mrs. Myrick was born at Yerba Buena on November 13, 1842. When I visited her recently, a few weeks before her death, she told me of her girlhood and of her experiences in the Oregon Country when many of the old-time Hudson's Bay employees were still living.

Her grandfather, Dr. John McLoughlin, was born on October 19, 1784, in Parish La Rivier du Loup, in Canada, on the St. Lawrence River. His father, John McLoughlin, was born in Ireland and drowned while her grandfather was a small boy. Her grandfather's mother, whose maiden name was Angelique Fraser, was born in the parish of Beaumont and died at the age of 83, the same year that Mrs. Myrick was born. Her father, Malcolm Fraser, was an officer in the Fraser Highlanders. When he retired from the army in 1763 he was a captain in the 84th regiment of the regular army of Great Britain.

Dr. John McLoughlin was one of seven children, of whom two were boys and five were girls. Dr. McLoughlin and his brother David were brought up by their mother's father. Their mother's brother, Dr. Samuel Fraser, was a lieutenant in the Black Watch regiment. he served in the Napoleonic wars from 1795 to 1803. After Napoleon's defeat in the battle of Waterloo, he settled in Paris, where he practiced medicine. Dr. John McLoughlin went to Scotland to study medicine. He enlisted as a young man in the Northwest Company. In 1821, when he was 37 years of age, he had charge of Fort William, at the mouth of Kaministiquia River on the north shore of Lake Superior. Fort William was the principal factory of the Northwest Company.

After the death of Alexander McKay on the Tonquin, his wife, with her son, Thomas, returned to Fort William. Dr. John McLoughlin met and married Mrs. McKay at this trading post. Dr. McLoughlin and his wife had four children. Eliza married Captain Epps, an officer in the British Army. John McLoughlin, Jr. was sent to take charge of the Hudson's Bay Company trading post at Fort Stikeen, in Alaska, where he was murdered in the spring of 1842. The third child was Eloisa. She married William Glen Rae at Fort Vancouver in 1838. Mr. Rae became chief trader of the Hudson's Bay Company and in 1841 was sent by Dr. John McLoughlin to Yerba Buena, in California, to care for the Hudson's Bay interests there. Mr. Rae died a violent death in San Francisco in 1844. Six years later his widow married Daniel Harvey. Mrs. Harvey died in Portland in October, 1884.

In 1824 Dr. John McLoughlin was sent to the Oregon Country as chief factor of the Hudson's Bay Company. He made his headquarters at Vancouver, where, from 1824 to 1846 he was virtual ruler of the Oregon Country. He was respected by the Indians and universally respected and esteemed by all those with whom he came in contact. The Indians called him "the white-headed eagle" and his employees referred to him as "the great white chief". From far-off Alaska to the shores of the Golden Gate, his influence was supreme.

Unlike other traders, he refused to sell liquor to the Indians. By 1839 he had established 20 trading posts in the Pacific Northwest. Officers of the British and American navies, missionaries, scientists, travelers, all were welcome at Fort Vancouver. Jason Lee, the Methodist missionary, and his party, Dr. and Mrs. Marcus Whitman, the Reverend and Mrs. H. H. Spalding and hosts of others made their home at Fort Vancouver until they could become established. Hundreds of emigrants in the 1840s who arrived in Oregon destitute were furnished livestock and supplies on credit by Dr. McLoughlin, and he himself absorbed the loss when they failed to pay.

Dr. McLoughlin located the town of Oregon City at Willamette Falls and gave generously to churches, schools, and others, not only furnishing them free lots, but also making generous donations, so as to enable them to put up buildings at Oregon City.

Oregon Journal
September 19, 1929

PETER SKENE OGDEN

Chief Factor, Hudson's Bay Company
Rescuer of the Whitman Massacre Survivors

Recently while walking down Third Street I passed a place where memorial stones and monuments are cut. Seeing a large gray stone, I stepped in and read the inscription, which was as follows:

"Peter Skene Ogden, 1794-1854. Born at Quebec. Died at Oregon City. Fur trader and explorer in old Oregon. Arrived Columbia River 1818. Clerk of the Northwest Company. Chief factor Hudsons Bay Company at Fort Vancouver. Rescued survivors of Whitman Mission 1847."

During the past 20 years I have interviewed a number of people who were personally acquainted with Peter Skene Ogden. A day or two ago I dropped in for a visit with Elizabeth Sager Helm and asked her to tell me what she remembered about Peter Skene Ogden.

"I saw Peter Skene Ogden first," said Mrs. Helm, "when I was ten years old. We were being held by the Indians as prisoners after the Whitman Massacre. Uncle Peter was a man you could not help liking. He was medium size but heavy for his height. He was a very merry, jolly man. I remember he teased us children and joked with us. After he had bought us from the Indians we started down the Columbia River for Fort Vancouver. There were four or five boatloads of us. In the boat in which I came down the river there were Peter Skene Ogden, Mr. Stanley, the artist, Mr. Charles, Gertrude Hall, now Mrs. O. H. Denny, and my sisters, Kate, Matilda, and Henrietta.

"Mr. Ogden, like many of the Hudson Bay employees, had an Indian wife. He treated her as respectfully as though she were white. I am glad, after all these years, that they are putting up a monument to him, for he certainly deserves it."

Peter Skene Ogden was the first white man to explore the region around the Great Salt Lake. The city of Ogden, Utah, was named for him, as well as Ogden Valley, Ogden Canyon and Ogden River.

(He) came of distinguished ancestry. His father, Isaac Ogden, was a judge and his god-father, Andrew Skene, was also a judge. In 1794 his father was appointed by the governor general of Canada one of the judges of the district of Montreal. In 1811, when Peter Skene Ogden was 17 years old, he secured a position as a clerk of the Northwest Company. Prior to going with the Northwest Company he had worked for a short time for John Jacob Astor. For some years he served as clerk on Isle a la Crosse, in the lake of the same name, located in southern Athabasca. While stationed at Isle a la Cross, Peter Skene Ogden married a woman of the Cree tribe. His first son, Peter, was born at the fort there on January 18, 1817. This son entered the Hudson Bay Company service as a young man and was employed by them at the time of his death in 1870.

When Peter Skene Ogden was 24 years old he came down the Columbia to Astoria. For the next year or two he was in charge of trapping parties operating between the mouth of the Columbia and the Puget Sound country.

His second son, Charles, was born in September, 1819, on the lower Columbia. In 1820 Peter Skene Ogden secured an interest in the Northwest Company and was placed in charge of the

Shuswap country. In 1821 the Northwest Company and the Hudson Bay Company merged. On October 27, 1824, Governor Simpson, Dr. John McLoughlin, Mr. McKay and one or two others arrived on the Columbia. In the spring of 1824 the directors of the Hudson Bay Company appointed Peter Skene Ogden chief trader.

During the next 25 years Peter Skene Ogden lived a life full of romance and adventure. He

---

"I am aware that many of your people have died, but so have others. It was not Dr. Whitman who poisoned them, but God who has commanded that they should die."

---

traveled all over the west, exploring new territory, became acquainted with most of the Indian chiefs in the Oregon Country as well as in northern California and Alaska. He had innumerable narrow escapes from death and was often reduced to eating horse meat or dog meat.

After the death of his first wife, Mr. Ogden married a wife from the Spokane tribe, a step-daughter of Francois Rivet of French Prairie, who had come to Oregon with Lewis and Clark. She died in 1886, aged 98 years.

Mr. Ogden rose to be chief factor of the Hudson Bay Company. He had charge of the Hudson Bay Company business on the Columbia River, being located at Fort Vancouver. He died at Oregon City on September 27, 1854, and was buried in Mountain View Cemetery there.

The rescue of the survivors of the Whitman Mission is but one example of his unfailing humanity, diplomacy, and courage. When a French-Canadian arrived at Fort Vancouver on December 6, 1847, with a letter from Captain William McBean of Fort Walla Walla, telling of the

massacre at the Whitman Mission, Peter Skene Ogden lost no time in adopting the course which he
knew would be the only effective one to free the
prisoners.

He started out next morning by boat for Fort
Walla Walla. On December 24 he assembled the Indians in council. The council lasted all day. Mr.
Ogden was the only white man present. When the
paration. I give you only advice and promise you
tell him what was said at the council, Mr. Ogden
reported that he said to the Indians:

"We have been among you for 30 years without
the shedding of blood. We are traders, and of a
different nation from the Americans, who are of
the same color, speak the same language and worship the same God as ourselves, and whose cruel
fate causes our hearts to bleed.

"Why do we make you chiefs, if you cannot
control your young men? Besides this wholesale
butchery, you have robbed the Americans passing
through your country and have insulted their women. If you allow your young men to govern you, I
say you are not men or chiefs, but hermaphrodites
who do not deserve the name.

"Your hot-headed young men plume themselves
on their bravery, but let them not deceive themselves. If the Americans begin war they will have
cause to repent their rashness, for the war will
not end until every man of you is cut off from
the face of the earth. I am aware that many of
your people have died, but so have others. It was
not Dr. Whitman who poisoned them, but God who
has commanded that they should die.

You have the opportunity to make some re-
paration. I give you only advice and promise you
nothing should war be declared against you. The
company has nothing to do with your quarrel. If
you wish it, on my return, I will see what can be
done for you, but I do not promise to prevent
war. Deliver me the prisoners to return to their
friends and I will pay you a ransom. That is

all."

To which Chief Tiloukaikt of the Cayuses replied: "Chief, your words are weighty, your hairs are gray. We have known you a long time. You have had an unpleasant journey to this place. I cannot therefore keep the families back. I make them over to you, which I would not do to another younger than yourself."

Five days later the captives were brought from Wai-il-at-pu to Fort Walla Walla. A day or two later Mr. Spaulding and the others from Fort Lapwai arrived and the entire party started down the Columbia on their five day trip to Fort Vancouver and Oregon City.

Oregon Journal
August, 1923

JOHN COLTER

Hunter, Trapper, Indian Fighter, Pathfinder

John Colter was buried on what is known as Tunnel Hill in the outskirts of St. Louis. Recently the railroad decided to abolish the tunnel, so they made an open cut. The old graveyard on Tunnel Hill had long been abandoned and most of the bodies of those buried there long ago went back to the dust from which they came. They used the dust and crumbling bones of John Colter and the others buried there to make a fill.

John Colter was a hunter, trapper, Indian fighter, pathfinder, and trusted member of the Lewis and Clark expedition. He was the discoverer of Yellowstone Park, having explored it in 1807. It seems sad to think that the dust of this heroic figure has been ruthlessly used to make a railroad fill.

A few days ago, while in Astoria, I interviewed Stallo Vinton, who was born in Indianapolis, Indiana, but who for many years has been a well-known counselor at law in New York City. He is the author of a recently published book entitled "John Colter, Discoverer of Yellowstone Park", published by Edward Eberstadt of New York City. Mr. Vinton received his LL.B. degree from Columbia College.

"The romance of the West has always appealed to me," said Mr. Vinton. "The more I read of the Oregon Country, of the adventures of Lewis and Clark, of Wyeth, of Bonneville, of Joe Meek, and of all the other Indian fighters, mountain men and trappers, the more anxious I was to secure

---

"When Colter, who had always been known as a trustworthy man, described the brimstone springs, the geysers shooting boiling waer high in the air, the deep canyons, the waterfalls, and what he called volcanoes spitting boiling water, he was branded an unmitigated liar."

---

more definite information about the lives of these early adventurers. In the course of my reading the name of John Colter constantly occurred. His life in the far west spanned but seven years, from 1803 to 1810, but he crowded that seven years full of adventure, perils and hardships. Not only did he discover Yellowstone Lake, but he was the first American to set foot in what is now Wyoming. He also discovered several passes through the Rocky Mountains. He stalks through history as a dim, shadowy, almost legendary figure. Originally, Yellowstone Park was known by the trappers as 'Colter's Hell'.

"John Colter is supposed to have been born in Virginia, and, while a boy, to have gone to Kentucky. He was born somewhere between 1775 and 1780. His father's grandfather, Micajah Coalter, whose people originally hailed from Scotland, came from the north of Ireland to Virginia about 1700. John Colter joined the Lewis and Clark expedition at Maysville, Kentucky, in 1803. Descendants of Micajah Coalter are still living at

Staunton, Virginia. Other members of his family live in Kentucky, Texas, and Mississippi.

"John Colter was a man of great strength and he had, like Daniel Boone, fitted himself to endure fatigue, privations, and perils. He was employed, while with the Lewis and Clark expedition, as a hunter. Captain Lewis was sent out to secure desirable men as recruits for the Lewis and Clark expedition to the mouth of the Columbia River. John Colter was one of the first men to be enlisted. He joined the expedition on October 15, 1803, as a private, at a salary of five dollars a month. If you will read the Lewis and Clark journals, you will find that his skill with a rifle, his reliability, his unfailing good nature, and his initiative made him a favorite not only with Captain Lewis and Captain Clark but with the other members of the expedition. A stream now known as Potlach Creek, a tributary of the Clarwater in Idaho, was originally named Colter Creek, in honor of John Colter, by Captains Lewis and Clark.

"On August 16, 1806, at the village of the Mandan Indians, John Colter asked permission to secure his discharge and to join some trappers on a fur trapping expedition. In describing this request, Captain Clark in his journal stated inasmuch as the offer was very advantageous for Mr. Colter and as he was disposed to be of service to one of the party who had performed his duty as well as Colter had, they agreed to his request, providing that no one else in the party would expect a similar favor, to which all of the other men agreed. Captains Lewis and Clark gave Colter some powder and lead and a few small articles for trade with the Indians.

"In the spring of 1807, Colter dissolved partnership with Dickson and Hancock, his fellow trappers, and started down the Missouri in a canoe for St. Louis. At the mouth of the Platte, Manuel Lisa, a fur trader of St. Louis, met him and persuaded him to join his brigade and go back up the river. Manuel Lisa's party went up the Yellowstone River to the mouth of the Big Horn, where he built a trading post named Fort Raymond, naming it for his son. However, the fort was usually called Manuel's Fort.

"John Colter was selected to visit the surrounding tribes and notify them that Manuel Lisa would welcome their trade. Colter, with a 30-pound pack, his long Kentucky rifle and powder and bullets, traveled 500 miles to where the Crow Indians were camped and told them of the newly

---

"The Indians decided to turn him loose and allow any warrior that could catch him to have his scalp."

---

established fort. He also visited other tribes.

"Colter visited the Stinking Water, the Absaroka Mountains, the Wind River Mountains, and located what is now known as Union Pass, which took him into the Jackson Hole Country. He also located what is known as the Teton Pass. He struck the Snake River above Jackson Lake, going up that stream to the center of the southern boundary of Yellowstone Park. From there he returned to Boiling Spring and went down the Stinking Water and the Big Horn toward Pryor's Gap. When Colter, who had always been known as a trustworthy man, described the brimstone springs, the geysers shooting boiling water high in the air, the deep canyons, the waterfalls, and what he called volcanoes spitting boiling water, he was branded as an unmitigated liar.

"In the summer of 1808, Colter and John Potts were captured by the Blackfoot Indians.

Potts was killed, Colter was disarmed and stripped naked. The Indians decided to turn him loose and to allow any warrior that could catch him to have his scalp. After running two and a half miles, the blood began gushing form his nostrils. One Indian only had been able to maintain the terrific pace. Colter stopped, and the Indian rushed at him with his spear. Colter seized the spear and pinned the Indian to the ground with it. He eventually reached the Madison River, pursued by the other Indians. Diving into the river he hid in a beaver's house till night. He traveled naked for 300 miles to Manuel's Fort on the Big Horn, living on roots and the bark of trees. In 1810 he settled at Charette, in Franklin County, Missouri, a few miles above the mouth of the Missouri River, where he died."

Oregon Journal
August 12, 1926

Bald Eagle

JIM BRIDGER

Pathfinder of the Overland Trail

E. A. Brininstool lives in Los Angeles. We
frequently exchange letters. He, like myself,
writes about early day life in the West. Recently
I sent him a marked article I had written about
an old-time Oregonian who had been an Indian
fighter, prospector, and scout. A few days later
I received a letter from him, in which he said he
was sending me a recent article he had written
for the Hunter-Trader-Trapper about Jim Bridger.
So many Oregon pioneers met Bridger while crossing the plains to Oregon and he was such an interesting and unique character that I am going to
quote his article in part.

"In the years between 1825 and 1870," says
Mr. Brininstool, "there were in the west a class
of men of a caliber, courage, determination,
pluck, fortitude and bravery whose like has never
since been seen. These were the
trail-blazers--the men who, with rifle and pack,
wandered into an entirely unknown wilderness.
With no knowledge of the country into which they
ventured, save what they learned from the Indian
tribes, they fared forth in their quest for ad-

venture and fur--and there was plenty of both to be had at that early day. These men were hardy, bold, fearless, and self-reliant, men 'with the bark on'. They were familiar with every phase of the rough, out-of-door life they had chosen. No obstacle was too great to surmount, no stream too dangerous to cross, no mountain too steep to scale, no section of the country too wild to refuse to penetrate its depths. In fact, the wilder and more dangerous the country, the more eager they were to venture into it, with the spirit for adventure luring them on.

"Among these hardy, self-reliant plains-men and mountaineers was one who stood unrivaled. And yet, he was one of the most modest and most unassuming frontiersmen of his time. His name was James Bridger, or, as he was more affectionately and familiarly called, 'Old Jim' Bridger. Born in Richmond, Virginia, March 17, 1804, he soon left that part of the country with his parents, who emigrated to St. Louis when the boy Jim was but eight years of age. There were three children in the family. The mother died in 1816, the father the following year. Jim Bridger's brother also passed away at an early age, leaving him with the care of a younger sister, and for a boy of 13 this was no small task.

"Bridger shortly thereafter started in to learn the blacksmith trade. In 1822 he joined a band of trappers under command of General William H. Ashley, who were bound for the fur-bearing section of the Rocky Mountains. Here Bridger found himself in his element. He took to the rough life of a trapper with the zeal and earnestness which soon attracted the attention of his older and more experienced companions. The Ashley party were under the direct command of Andrew Henry. On their way into the fur-bearing country, they encountered one misfortune after another. One of their boats, loaded with goods intended for barter with the Indians, was upset, en route

up the Missouri River, entailing a loss of some
$10,000. Their horses were stolen and the party
was so crippled that they were compelled to halt
near the mouth of the Yellowstone and 'fort up'
for the winter. In this wilderness they hunted
and trapped, making explorations in to the surrounding country, until the spring of 1823.

During the ensuing seven years, Jim Bridger
underwent the usual rigorous life of a fron-

"All through that country are geysers
that spout up to 70 feet high, with a hissing
noise, some of them spouting up at regular
intervals. There is a huge waterfall. The
river that empties out of the lake goes
through a deep, perpendicular canyon. There
are springs so hot that you can cook meat in
them. There are places where you can get
vermilion paint."

---

tiersman, developing into a keen, shrewd, courageous character, an unerring rifle shot, a
trapper of wonderful renown, and an Indian
fighter whose name was quickly spread through the
camps of the Blackfeet--then the most warlike of
the tribes in the Rocky Mountain section--as a
'holy terror'. It is to be greatly regretted that
there is so little actually known of Bridger's
wanderings in this period, as he had but little
education, and could neither read nor write, and
therefore kept no diary or account of his meand-
erings.

"It was during this period of his wander-
ing--probably about 1824 or 1825, that Bridger
first saw Great Salt Lake, being, so far as is
known, the first white man to gaze upon this vast
body of water. He thought--noting that the water

was salt--that he had discovered an arm of the Pacific Ocean, but upon making a tour of observation, it was discovered that the body of water had no outlet.

In 1830 Bridger had become so proficient in his calling and was considered so competent by the Rocky Mountain Fur Company, that he was sent with 200 men on a side scout for fur into the Big Horn Basin country. The party crossed the Yellowstone River and went north to about the present site of Great Falls, Montana. It is claimed that it was on this trip that Bridger first saw the Yellowstone Park section.

"The wonders of that marvelous section created such an impression upon Bridger that when he began to tell about the beauties and the almost supernatural features of it, he was not believed. His stories of hot water spouting hundreds of feet into the air, of boiling pools of water within a few feet of pools of ice cold water, and all the other wonderful features which are today one of our greatest tourist attractions, were not believed by his companions, and 'Jim Bridger's lies', as they were dubbed, were soon the talk of every trapper's camp. This so angered Bridger that in disgust, he began to invent 'real whoppers'. He declared that one day while out hunting he saw a fine elk feeding, apparently a couple of hundred yards away. Being out of meat, he drew up his gun, took careful aim, and fired. To his astonishment, the animal did not move nor pay any attention to the discharge of his rifle. Unable to account for such poor shooting, he again took more careful aim and fired. Still the elk remained undisturbed. Bridger, thereupon started a run toward the animal when, to his amazement, he plunged slap up against a solid mass of clear transparent glass, hundreds of feet in height, and it developed that he had been shooting at the elk on the opposite side of this glass mountain, several miles distant, instead of a few hundred feet which he supposed. Today this is known as the 'Obsidian Cliff'.

"Another of Bridger's yarns was his 'sure 'nuff idee' as to why ice cold water dropped into a pool instantly became boiling hot. He declared this was due to the friction produced by the rapid descent of the stream over the rocks.

"Bridger tried to have the wonders of the Yellowstone exploited, but could get no eastern newspaper editor to take any stock in his 'wild-eyed yarns'. It is said that the editor of the Kansas City Journal stated editorially in 1879 that Bridger had told him of these wonders full 30 years before and that he had really prepared an article for publication, but finally decided against it, fearing the ridicule to which he would be subjected if he printed any of 'Jim Bridger's lies'.

"In spite of the fact that Bridger talked about this wonderful region to everyone whom he met, he was simply laughed at, called 'just a little off', and unmercifully ridiculed. Bridger had described it as a place where 'hell literally bubbled up!' Such indeed is the Yellowstone Park section of today.

"Today it is well known that park visitors can catch trout in an ice cold stream, and, without moving from their tracks, can swing the fish about into a boiling pool. This was one of the stories which Bridger had so vehemently declared to be an actual fact. Yet he was mocked and derided and branded a liar of the first water!

"One of the great natural wonders along the Sweetwater River is the famous Independence Rock, a vast formation lying in a perfectly open country. Just how this great rock—nearly a mile in circumference and about 100 feet in height—came to be placed there, is best told by Bridger. 'That 'ere rock, when I fust come into this country, was jest a pebble on t' other side of the Sweetwater which I picked up one day and threw over to this side, and the soil is so darned prolific that it grew into this yere rock.'

"In one of Bridger's Indian battles in the Blackfoot country, he was wounded in the back by an arrow, the iron point of which remained firmly imbedded in the flesh for nearly three years. It was removed by Dr. Marcus Whitman, noted Oregon missionary, at that time en route to his station, who fell in with Bridger and his party at the annual rendezvous of trappers in 1835 at Pierre's Hole. No anesthetic was administered during the operation, and speedy relief was afforded from the extraction of the iron arrow point, which was nearly three inches in length.

"A volume could be written detailing the numerous adventures and hair-breadth escapes from savages and wild animals through which Jim Bridger passed during his years on the frontier as a trapper and mountain man. He often declared, when one of his friends was detailing him the marvelous yarns of Baron Munchausen, that some of his own adventures would sound 'just as reliable if writ into a book'.

"The historic Fort Bridger, located on Black's Fork of the Green River, was erected by Bridger in 1843, and this point became a most noted one during the years of overland travel to the Pacific coast states. The old Mormon Trail was close by, and the North and South Platte routes met near Fort Bridger, hence, the place became well known. Here Bridger's skill as a blacksmith--which had long lain dormant--came into play. He opened a shop, supply store, and trading post, and as the overland travel was heavy, he soon had more work on hand than he could possibly attend to. Most of the emigrants were fairly well supplied with money, and of course had to buy provisions and supplies and have their animals shod and their wagons looked over about the time they reached Bridger's post. As these transactions were mostly cash, Bridger soon acquired considerable money, and he did a lively business, although doubtless he did not spend all his time at Bridger's Fort, as history records that he made various trapping excursions into the mountains from time to time. However, Fort Bridger soon came to be looked upon as a veritable oasis in the desert, and he certainly exercised good judgment in locating his post at such a favorable spot.

"By 1857, however, overland travel had dropped off considerably from what it had been in previous years, and Bridger leased his property to the United States government for the sum of $600 per year. Uncle Sam never paid him a cent, however, and it was not until 30 years later that the government finally allowed him $6000 for the improvements he had made to the property, but not a cent for the land itself.

"Passing over many eventful years in the life of Bridger, we find him, in 1866, in the capacity of guide for Colonel Henry B. Carrington's expedition, sent into what is now the state of Wyoming, for the purpose of building forts and protecting the emigrants who were bound for the Montana gold fields and points on the Pacific coast. Carrington left Fort Kearney, Nebraska, May 19, 1866, under orders to enter the Powder River and Big Horn countries and build three forts. This was invading the very cream of what was then the hunting grounds of the Sioux--their last and best game section.

"The Carrington expedition was decidedly obnoxious to Chief Red Cloud, the great war chief of the Sioux, who declared in a press conference held at Fort Laramie, in June, 1866, that while he would not object to the government retaining Fort Reno along the Bozeman Trail, under no circumstances whatever would he allow the soldiers to penetrate further north into his hunting country, but that he 'would kill every soldier or white man who went north of Crazy Woman's fork'.

"At this conference, Jim Bridger was an attentive spectator and listener. He sat on a low seat with his elbows on his knees and his chin buried in his hands, watching every movement and listening to every fiery word which dropped from the lips of Red Cloud, who bitterly declared that the 'Great Father had sent soldiers to steal the road, whether the Indian said yes or no'. And when Red Cloud, with head erect and eye flashing fire, stalked haughtily out of the council, refusing to shake hands with any of the assembled government representatives, Bridger shook his head and declared 'hell will soon be a-poppin''.

"Bridger was right. No sooner had Carrington reached the point north of Fort Reno where he determined to commence the erection of the second fort, than hell was a-poppin for sure. Scarcely a day passed during the erection of the fort, but that skirmishes with the Indians occurred. In fact, during the two years of its existence, Fort Phil Kearney witnessed more than 50 distinct skirmishes and fights with the Sioux in the immediate vicinity of the post. The terrible Fetterman Massacre of December 21, 1866, when 81 men were drawn into an ambush and slaughtered to a man, was only one object lesson drawn by the wily Red Cloud.

"During most of these troubles Jim Bridger was acting as post scout for Colonel Carrington, who had, meantime, sent a detachment futher north to erect the third fort which was to serve as protection along the Bozeman Trail. This post was known as Fort C. F. Smith, and was built on the Big Horn River.

"During the time of the bitterest trial at Fort Phil Kearney, Jim Bridger was a source of the greatest comfort to the women and children of the post, to all of whom he was a faithful friend and adviser. His devotion and willingness to cheer them were greatly prized, and he was the one man in whom all placed implicit trust. No man was so keenly alive to the dangers about them, none so well knew Indian wiles and warfare.

"In August, 1868, the dangers along the Bozeman Trail had become such that the government determined to evacuate the country. This was exactly what Red Cloud was playing for. In vain had the government attempted to get him to listen to the appeals that a wagon road be opened into Montana. His only ultimatum was that the government abandon the forts and take every soldier out of the country--and Uncle Sam at length was compelled to listen to the great chief. The country was abandoned, the forts evacuated, and the Indians immediately burned the hated military posts to the ground.

"Much more could be said of Bridger's great value to the government. No important military expeditions were planned without employing him to guide them whenever possible. He was greatly respected and revered by all the old-time army officers, who paid the great frontiersman marked deference. Even the Indians regarded him with awe and wonder, and feared the magic power which he seemed to hold over them. And through it all he remained the same simple-hearted, unpretentious, plain prairie man who hated sham and braggadocio and detested anything which smacked of self-praise.

"But the greatest injustice which was ever done to Jim Bridger and his fame and notoriety, is that which is shown in a moving picture film entitled "The Covered Wagon". In this picture Bridger is represented as a whiskey-soaked, sodden, blear-eyed old sot who cannot make a move of any consequence nor remember past events, unless he is filled to the brim with whiskey. While Bridger doubtless liked his 'toddy', in common with most of the mountain men of his day and time, it is an indisputable fact that he was anything but a drunkard. It stands to reason that had he been such, the United States government never would have valued his services as a guide in their most noted expeditions, nor would Bridger have been respected and revered by all classes of men on the frontier--as he most certainly was. It is libel of the most underhanded sort, and places this grand old pioneer in a position which should call forth an indignant protest from those, at least, who are familiar with Bridger's history, his past life, and his valuable services to the United States government.

"There are several men living today who knew Jim Bridger intimately, among whom is Honorable John Hunton of Fort Laramie, where Bridger was stationed as post guide in 1868. Mr. Hunton was at that time in the employ of the post sutler at Fort Laramie, and Bridger slept in a bunk in the same room with Mr. Hunton and other employees, with all of whom he was on the most familiar terms.

"Dr. Gilbert E. Bailey of Los Angeles, head of the chair of geology of the University of Southern California, also knew Bridger intimately, having passed a winter with him in the latter '60s while a member of the surveying party who were putting the Union Pacific Railroad through. Dr. Bailey at that time was a youth of about 18, but distinctly recalls the noted frontiersman, who was acting as guide for the party, and whose quiet deportment and simple manners made a lasting impression upon young Bailey.

"Major A. B. Ostrander of New York City met and became acquainted with Bridger at old Fort Phil Kearney in 1866. At that time Ostrander was a youth of 19, who had left the headquarters of General Phillip St. George Cooke in Omaha, where he had been acting as confidential clerk to General Cook, to join his regiment, the 18th U. S. Infantry, at Fort Phil Kearney. He describes

Bridger as a man who would command a second glance from anyone; admired and respected by all his superiors, and of the strictest integrity and honesty, and far from the drunken sot which "The Covered Wagon" producers would foist on the American public, who--more shame to them--know little or nothing of the history of this great frontiersman, and doubtless believe the film-makers are showing up Bridger in his true light.

"There are other oldtimers who knew Bridger well enough to recall that he was not a drunken bum, but a gentleman, even though a diamond in the rough, who could fully and intelligently describe any country which he had once seen, and could make a map showing the streams, mountains, and other features absolutely correct, so that there was no trouble following it and fully understanding it.

"Bridger never made claims of knowledge of any country over which he had not traveled. In his little pamphlet on the life of Bridger, General Grenville Dodge says:

'He was a good judge of human nature. His comments upon people whom he had met and been with were always intelligent and seldom critical. He always spoke of their good parts, and was universally respected by the mountain men and looked upon as a leader also by all the Indians. He was careful to never give his word without fulfilling it. He understood thoroughly the Indian character, their peculiarities and superstitions. He felt keenly any loss of confidence in him or his judgment, especially when acting as guide, and when he struck a country or trail with which he was not familiar he would frankly say so, but would often say he could take our party up to the point he wanted to reach. As a guide, I do not think he had an equal on the plains. So remarkable a man should not be lost to history and to his country, and his work allowed to be forgotten.'

"Bridger married into two different Indian tribes. His first wife was a Ute, by whom he had two children, both of whom were educated in St. Louis. His second wife was also a Ute, by whom he had a daughter, who was likewise sent to school in St. Louis. His third wife was from the Snake tribe. Bridger did not have but one wife at a time, in spite of the representations of 'The Covered Wagon' that he employed 'Mormon Tactics' and had several wives at the same time.

"Bridger was 77 years of age when he died in 1881. He was buried on the Stubbins Watts farm, not far south of Westport, Missouri.

"In 1902, his friend General Grenville Dodge, builder of the Union Pacific Railroad, learned for the first time where the body of the noted old plainsman lay, and that his grave was neglected and forgotten. General Dodge felt keenly that this celebrated frontier character should be more prominently remembered, and with other admirers he interested the Mount Washington Cemetery Association of Kansas City in his plans, and they donated a prominent and beautiful burial site, where the remains of the noted old pioneer were removed, and on December 11, 1904, an imposing monument was unveiled.

"General Dodge further speaks of Bridger as follows:

'In person he was over six feet tall, spare, straight as an arrow, agile, raw-boned and of powerful frame; eyes gray; hair brown and abundant, even in old age; expression mild and manners agreeable. He was hospitable and generous and was always trusted and respected. He possessed in a high degree the confidence of the Indians. He was one of the most noted hunters and trappers on the Plains. Naturally shrewd and observing, he carefully studied the habits of all wild animals, especially the beaver, and he became one of the most expert of trappers. As a guide he was without equal, and this is the testimony of everyone who ever employed him. He was a born topographer; the whole West was mapped out in his mind, and such was his instinctive sense of locality and direction that it used to be said of him that he could smell his way where he could not see it. He was a complete master of plains and woodcraft, equal to any emergency, full of resources to overcome any obstacle, and I came to learn how it was that for months such men could live without food except what the country afforded. Nothing escaped the vision of these men--the popping of a stick, the breaking of a twig, the turning of the growing grass, all brought knowledge to them, and they could tell who or what had done it. A single horse or Indian could not cross the trail but that they discovered it, and could tell how long since they passed. Their methods of hunting game were perfect, and we were never out of meat. Herbs, roots, berries, barks of trees and every-thing that was edible, they knew. They could minister to the sick, dress wounds--In fact, in all my experience I never saw Bridger, nor any of the other voyagers of the plains and mountains, meet any obstacle which they could not overcome.'

"Such unstinted words of praise from a man who knew Jim Bridger so intimately should be sufficient to prove that this great man--this American--should be placed in the proper niche where he belongs, along with such men as Daniel Boone, Simon Kenton, Davy Crockett, Kit Carson, Uncle Dick Wootton, Lucien Maxwell and other re-nowned frontier characters."

Probably no man in the west has been as little understood or more maligned than James Bridger. The play "The Covered Wagon" did much to make people think he was a drunken squawman. He was far from that.

The Bridgers were of Scotch descent. Mrs. John Tyler, wife of the President of the United States, was a sister of James Bridger Sr., so President Tyler was the uncle, by marriage, of James Bridger, the trapper. Young Jim Bridger was only 13 when his father died, and he had a sister to support. He bought a flatboat ferry and ran the ferry to St. Louis. Later he was apprenticed to a blacksmith, but in 1822, when he was 18 years old, he landed a job with General W. H. Ashley, who was sending a party of trappers to the Rocky Mountains. This "fur brigade" of the Rocky Mountain Fur Company was commanded by Andrew Henry. They went up the Missouri to the mouth of the Yellowstone. The Indians stole their horses, and the boat, which was loaded with trade goods worth $10,000, was lost in the rapids. They built a fort and wintered at the mouth of the Yellowstone and spent the winter and spring in trapping. With the beaver pelts they had secured they went to St. Louis in the fall of 1822 and returned with more trade goods. On May 10, 1823, they were attacked by the Indians and more than half of the trappers were killed and the horses and baggage were captured by the Indians. Ashley and Henry joined the troops under Colonel Leavenworth.

Henry, with 80 men, one of them being James Bridger, started for the mouth of the Yellowstone in the summer of 1823. They had a fight with the Indians in which some of their men were killed and the Indians stole a number of their horses. The fort at the mouth of the Yellowstone was abandoned, and they established a camp near the mouth of Powder River. A number of the trappers, under Etienne Prevost, went to the Bighorn and Wind Rivers and thence to Green River in the late fall of 1823. Bridger was a member of this party. It was this party that discovered South Pass at the southern end of the Wind River Mountains, and it was the South Pass through which the Union

Pacific Railroad was built.

The Prevost party wintered on Bear River. Bridger and one of the other members of the party had a dispute about the course of Bear River, and to settle the bet Bridger struck out alone and followed Bear River to where it emptied into Great Salt Lake. When he returned and reported that Bear River emptied into salt water the men decided that Bear River emptied into the Pacific Ocean. Bridger was the first white man to visit Great Salt Lake. In the spring of 1825 they decided to visit this salt water and see if it was an arm of the Pacific Ocean. They made two skin boats and four men rowed completely around the lake and discovered that it had no outlet.

In the fall of 1824, Andrew Henry was succeeded by Jedediah S. Smith, who later became well known in Oregon. General W. H. Ashlen sold the Rocky Mountain Fur Company to Jedediah Smith, Jackson and Sublette in the summer of 1826. James Bridger trapped for them for the next three years. He spent the summer and fall of 1829 with Christopher Carson. He spent the winter of 1829-30 on Powder River, and in the spring of 1830 he and Jedediah Smith went to the Yellowstone River, thence to Judith Basin and from there to Wind River. Sublette, one of the partners of the Rocky Mountain Fur Company, in the spring of 1830, with 81 men and ten wagons, started from St. Louis and drove to the rendezvous of the trappers on Wind River, near the mouth of the Porporgie, which they reached on July 16. These were the first wagons to travel over what was later known as the Oregon Trail.

In the summer of 1830, when James Bridger was 26 years old, he became a partner in the Rocky Mountain Fur Company. The other members of the firm were Milton G. Sublette, John B. Gervais, and Henry Frack. James Bridger, with Milton Sublette and Fitzpatrick, enlisted 200 men to explore and trap the northern country. They went to the Bighorn Basin, crossed the Yellowstone River, continued on north to what is now Great Falls, Montana, went on up the Missouri to the Three Forks, and finally swung around to Great Salt Lake, where they met Peter Skene Ogden of the Hudson's Bay Company. They traveled 1200 miles and wintered on the Powder River. During this trip James Bridger visited Yellowstone Lake and the Geyser Basin. In describing Yellowstone Lake, Bridger said:

"The lake is 60 miles long. There are lots of wild horses around the lake. All through that country are geysers that spout up 70 feet high, with a hissing noise, some of them spouting up at regular intervals. There is a huge waterfall. The river that empties out of the lake goes through a deep, perpendicular canyon. There are springs so hot that you can cook meat in them. There are places where you can get vermilion paint."

Bridger's account of what is now Yellowstone Park was laughed at and everyone branded him as a liar, and yet he had discovered and described Yellowstone Lake, the Grand Canyon, Yellowstone Falls, the geysers, the Mammoth Springs and Cinnabar Mountain.

The competition of the American Fur Company caused Bridger and Fitzpatrick to abandon the country around Powder River and Green River and go westward to the forks of Snake River. In 1832 they met A. J. Wyeth, who had come out from New England and who had with him a number of free trappers and traders. While camped at Pierre's Hole on July 13, 1832, Bridger and his men, with a large number of free traders and trappers, in all about 300 white men, with several hundred Flathead Indians and some Nez Perce Indians, had a fight with the Gros Ventres. Five of the white men were killed and six wounded and the Gros Ventres left nine killed and carried some away with them. They admitted that they had lost 26 warriors. In the fall of 1832 the Blackfoot Indians attacked Bridger and his party on the Madison Fork, and Bridger was wounded in several places, one of the arrowheads which had been buried deeply in his back remaining there for the next three years, when at Green River in the summer of 1836, James Bridger met Dr. Marcus Whitman, who was on his way to Oregon. The arrowhead had buried itself in one of the vertebrae and was causing Bridger considerable discomfort, so Dr. Whitman had Bridger lie down on the ground and cut his back open and extracted the arrowhead, which was of iron and three inches in length.

It was Bridger who discovered the famous Two-Ocean Pass, which is 8150 feet above sea level and is about a mile long and a mile wide. Waters from this pass divide, part of the waters flowing into the Yellowstone and thence eventually to the Atlantic, and part to the Snake River and thence to the Pacific Ocean. James Bridger, following an old game trail, knowing that the animals would take the lowest and most feasible route across the mountains and the one with the least obstructions, was the real pathfinder of the overland trail, or, as we no know it, the Old Oregon Trail. This old buffalo trail over the mountains was also the trail used by the Indians in crossing from the great plains beyond the Rockies to the Pacific slope side.

Popular belief to the contrary notwithstanding, the first wheeled vehicle to travel over the Old Oregon Trail was a six-pound cannon taken out by General W. H. Ashley, founder of the Rocky Mountain Fur Company. This cannon was pulled by mule power from the Missouri River to Utah Lake, in the summer of 1826.

The first man to drive carts over this trail was Captain Benjamin L. E. Bonneville. Captain Bonneville was born in France in 1795. He came to America when a boy, graduated from West Point in 1815, was assigned to the construction of military roads and was promoted to captain of infantry in 1825 and from 1831 to 1836 traveled extensively throughout the Rocky Mountains, exploring and trapping. He died at Fort Smith, Arkansas, June 12, 1878. The next party to drive carts over the Old Oregon Trail was that of Dr. Marcus Whitman in 1836.

Bridger put in seven years between 1833 and 1840 with the American Fur Company. Most of this time he spent in the Big Horn River Country or in the country of the Snake River Indians, with whom he had many fights. In 1840 he became a partner of Benito Vasquez. These two men built Fort Bridger in 1843. James Bridger selected the site of Fort Bridger because it was on the overland trail as well as the Mormon Trail and, whether the emigrants came by the North Platte or the South Platte Road, both of these roads came together near Fort Bridger. Bridger bought the land from the Mexican government. Not only did he settle at Fort Bridger, but he lived there almost continuously from 1843 to 1857, at which time he leased the fort and the land surrounding it, for a rental of $600 a year, to the troops under command of General Albert Sidney Johnston, during the war against the Mormons. After the troops had moved in Bridger was told that his title was imperfect--that when Mexico had ceded their territory to the United States his title to the land had been extinguished.

They proceeded to build a military post on Bridger's claim and it was 30 years before the government finally paid $6000 to Bridger for his improvements, which did not begin to equal the money he had spent on the place. They refused to pay anything for the land. In writing to Pierre Chouteau at St. Louis from Fort Bridger on December 10, 1843, Bridger wrote:

"I have established a fort with blacksmith shop and a supply of iron on the road of the emigrants on Black Fork and Green River. In coming out here they are generally well supplied with money, but by the time they get here they are in need of supplies, horses, provisions and smith work. They bring ready cash from the states, and should I receive the goods ordered will have considerable business with them, and also establish trade with the Indians in this neighborhood, who have a good number of beaver. The fort has a beautiful location on the Black Fork of Green River, receiving fine fresh water from the snow on the Uintah Range. The streams are alive with mountain trout. The river passes the fort in several channels, each lined with trees kept alive by the moisture of the soil."

The fort was surrounded by a stockade which enclosed about two acres. It had large swinging gates in the center of the front of the fort.

On the Fourth of July, 1849, Bridger's second wife, a Ute squaw, died. He married a woman from the Snake tribe and moved his family to Jackson County, Missouri. He served as guide for the government troops during the Civil War in their Indian campaigns. In the spring of 1869 Captain Reynolds hired James Bridger to serve as guide in his exploration of Yellowstone Park. Bridger died July 18, 1881, and his friend, Major General G. M. Dodge erected a monument to his memory.

In speaking of Jim Bridger, famous scout and frontiersman, the Baker Democrat recently said:

"Bridger started his active career at old Westport, now Kansas City, when he was 18 years of age. His career as a trapper extended to the time when immigration across the plains made the use of guides necessary. As a guide Bridger had no superior...All the early plainsmen who afterward became guides first served as trappers and many of them started up the Missouri River from St. Louis or Westport. The evidence presented by old settlers convinced a writer in the Kansas

City Star that, while Jim Bridger drank whiskey, he was never a drunkard.

"Fort Bridger became a pioneer post a thousand miles west of the Mississippi River. After returning to his farm in Missouri, Bridger made frequent journeys to Fort Bridger and other points in the Far West. American life may not produce another Jim Bridger. It is such men who made the settlement of our frontier possible."

Oregon Journal
April 3, 4, 5, 1925
September 7, 8, 1928
one other, undated

JEDEDIAH SMITH
Trapper

In the spring of 1823 Jedediah S. Smith, later to become well known in Oregon, was a member of an expedition under General Ashley of the Missouri Fur Company to trap and trade for furs on the upper Missouri. The previous year the members of the Missouri Fur Company had had a brush with the Arikaras, killing two of them. The Arikaras had sworn vengence. General Ashley anchored his keelboats in the stream below the village of the Arikaras. He held a council with them and they professed to be friendly. He bought 40 horses to send to Major Henry to replace those that had been stolen by the Indians. Forty of Ashley's trappers, who were planning to go overland to join Henry, were camped on the river bank.

General Ashley very unwisely separated his force and camped in front of the village. It would have been the part of wisdom to have gone upstream a few miles and camped in a position that could have been defended from Indian attack. At daylight next morning the Indians attacked the 40 men who were camped on the river bank in front of their village. Many of these recruits were absolutely inexperienced in Indian warfare. Within a few minutes 13 of the trappers were killed and 11 wounded. Jedediah Smith and David E. Jackson fought until most of the horses were killed.

Meanwhile, General Ashley, in his keelboats, was urging the men to row the boats to where the fight was in progress to assist the men who were

---

"I am a long way from home and am anxious to get there as soon as the nature of the case will admit. Our situation is quite unpleasant, as we are destitute of clothing and most of the necessaries of life, wild meat being our principal substance."

---

being attacked, but the men in the keelboats were panic-stricken and when a number of the rowers had been wounded by arrows they refused to approach the shore. General Ashley called to the men on shore to swim out to the boats. Smith and Jackson, fighting as they retreated to the river's edge, succeeded in swimming out to the boats, in spite of the heavy fire directed at them by the Indians from the rifles that they had purchased from Ashley on the preceding day. The two keelboats dropped downstream and a landing was made in the timber on the opposite side of the river. General Ashley ordered his men to row up the river, past the Indian village, but the men mutinied and refused to go unless they were reinforced. He then called for volunteers to go onward, but only 30 volunteered, so, manning the Yellowstone Packet, he placed aboard it five of the men who were badly wounded and, placing one of his trusted men in charge, he directed him to go to Fort Atkinson, near Council Bluffs, a distance of about 450 miles down the river.

It was necessary to send a courier to Major Henry to ask him to send reinforcements. Not wishing to send a man to what looked like certain death, he asked for volunteers. Jedediah Smith stepped forward and volunteered to attempt to take the message through to Major Henry. An older man, a French Canadian, volunteered to go with Smith. General Ashley and his party dropped down the river with their keelboat to the mouth of the Cheyenne River, where they camped to await reinforcements from Major Henry. Smith and his French Canadian comrade made their way through a country infested with hostile Indians to where Major Henry was camped at the mouth of the Yellowstone River. Leaving 20 men in charge of the trading goods and the horses, Major Henry, with the rest of his force, came down the Missouri and joined General Ashley. The Yellowstone Packet reached Fort Atkinson on June 18 and that same day an express also came in informing Colonel Leavenworth that Immel and Jones, leaders of the Missouri Fur Company's party, with most of their men, had been killed by the Indians on the Yellowstone. Colonel Leavenworth sent six companies of the Sixth Regiment, with two six-pound cannon and supplies, in three keelboats, to escort General Ashley up the river and to meet and punish the Indians. Joshua Pilcher, with 60 men of the Missouri Fur Company and two keelboats, joined Colonel Leavenworth's force. At Fort Recovery they were joined by a band of Yankton Sioux and a few days later by about 200 more Sioux Indians.

General Ashley and Major Henry had moved their camp to the mouth of the Teton River. Colonel Leavenworth reached General Ashley's camp about the first of August. General Ashley had organized his trappers into two companies. Jedediah Smith was captain of one of the companies and Hiram Scott captain of the other. About the only real damage done in the fight that ensued was done by the Sioux Indians. They had joined the soldiers, hoping to see their old enemies, the Arikaras, thoroughly whipped, but when the Arikaras saw that they were being attacked by at least 1100 white men with a considerable number of Sioux Indians they decided to hold a council. Eleven of the Indians, with five of the army officers and General Ashley, signed a treaty providing that the Missouri River should be free and unobstructed and that the Indians should no longer attack parties of trappers coming up or down the Missouri. The Sioux Indians, who had stood the brunt of the fighting, withdrew in disgust.

General Ashley returned to St. Louis and Major Henry returned to the mouth of the Yellowstone to spend the winter.

It was a remarkable group of men who were gathered with Major Henry at the mouth of the Yellowstone. Among them were Edward Rose, Ezekial Williams, Louis Vasquez, James Bridger, William L. Sublette, Jedediah Smith, David E. Jackson, Thomas Fitzpatrick, Hugh Glass, and many others who later became famous.

It was a rough apprenticeship for many of the "enterprising young men" who had answered General Ashley's advertisement in the Missouri Republican. The Arikaras cut off, killed, and scalped two of the party. Later the Gros Ventres attacked them and killed four more of their men. The Blackfeet stole 22 of their horses, and Hugh Glass was so badly mangled by a grizzly bear that he was unable to travel.

Major Henry detached a trapper named Fitzgerald and a young man of 17 years of age to stay with Glass until he recovered so he could travel, or, if he died, to stay with him and bury him. Fitzgerald and the young man with him did not like the idea of staying with the wounded man, on account of the danger of having their scalps lifted. They did not have the heart to kill him, so, taking his rifle and powder horn and stripping him of his other belongings, they hurried on to overtake Major Henry's party, leaving Glass to die of his wounds, to be killed by Indians or to be eaten by the wolves.

Glass was unconscious when they left. When he came to, he crawled to a spring and, by eating berries near the spring and drinking the spring water, he recovered sufficient strength to be able to crawl. Finally, he walked and crawled nearly 100 miles to Fort Kiowa on the Missouri River. Here he found a party of trappers of the Missouri Fur Company who were bound for the Yellowstone. He could have gone on down the river to St. Louis, but he had sworn to have revenge on his two cowardly companions who had abandoned him to his fate, so he joined this party. He could not keep up with his companions. While he was making a short cut the Arikaras attacked the rest of the party, killing them. Glass struggled on and finally reached Fort Tilton. Some Arikara Indians recognized him as he was approaching the fort. He was too badly wounded to run, but two Mandan Indians on horseback, seeing the Arikaras were about to kill Glass, dashed past. One of them picked Glass up and swung him on his horse behind him and reached the fort in safety. They tried to get Glass to stay at the fort until he recovered from his wounds, but he refused and pressed on. For 38 days he traveled alone through a country infested by hostile Indians, finally arriving at Major Henry's camp. To his unspeakable disappointment he found that Fitzgerald, who had left him to his fate, had deserted the party and gone down the Missouri to Fort Atkinson. Instead of killing the 17-year-old boy who had been with Fitzgerald, he forgave him and started alone down the river to get the man who had deserted him. A book could be filled with the narrow escapes and adventures he had in making the trip down the river to Fort Atkinson, which he reached in 1824. Fitzgerald had enlisted in the army and had been sent elsewhere. Glass waited his opportunity, but was killed by the Indians in the winter of 1832.

During Jedediah Smith's first winter Major Henry sent out a party of 16 trappers in charge of Thomas Fitzpatrick and Smith to trap in the Crow country. Jedediah Smith did not seem to know what fear was. When a grizzly bear attacked him, instead of giving way he stood his ground and, before killing the bear, was badly slashed and mangled. Like Glass, he also had to be left behind, but before long he was joined by Colonel Keemle of the Missouri Fur Company and a number of his own men, and Smith, though his wounds had not yet healed, went on with them to the Big Horn.

The Crow Indians told Fitzpatrick of a pass across the Rockies, so in the spring of 1824 Fitzpatrick, Smith and their party of trappers went from the Big Horn to Wind River, crossed the South Pass, thence down the Big Sandy and on to Green River. Beaver were so abundant in this new country that they were able to secure large packs in a few weeks. Major Henry took the furs on hand down the Missouri to St. Louis, intending to return with additional supplies. He was not entirely satisfied with General Ashley's management, so instead of returning he retired from the partnership and General Ashley placed Jedediah Smith in charge of his trapping operations. Fitzpatrick returned by way of the South Pass to the Sweetwater, where he met Jedediah Smith enroute to the Columbia Basin. On the Sweetwater they made boats of skin and took their furs down the streams to the North Platte and thence into the Misouri. They were the first white men to navigate the upper waters of the Sweetwater and the North Platte. At the mouth of the Sweetwater the skin boats capsized. However, they were able to rescue part of the furs, which they cached. Fitzpatrick went with all haste to Fort Atkinson, where he secured horses, and, accompanied by Jim Beckwurth and Robert Campbell, went back to where he had left his men and furs and took them to

Fort Atkinson. Fitzpatrick was a free trapper. General Ashley furnished him his outfit and he sold his furs to Ashley.

During the summer of 1824 Jedediah Smith commanded one division of trappers and William Sublette the other. In Sublette's group of trappers was James Bridger. Smith, with his trappers, trapped around the headwaters of Green River and on the Lewis fork of the Columbia River. From there they went to the Clark Fork of the Columbia. Late that fall they ran across a party of Iroquois. They were trapping for Alexander Ross of the Hudson's Bay Company. The Snake Indians had stolen the traps and guns of these Iroquois and also part of their furs. Smith bought what furs they had left and promised to escort the Indians to Pierre's Hole, near the Three Tetons. However, while enroute to Pierre's Hole they met a search party sent out by Ross, which escorted the entire party to Ross' headquarters on Salmon River in what is now Custer County, Idaho.

As it was late in the season he decided to go with Ross to the Hudson's Bay Company's post in what is now Sanders County, Montana. They crossed the Bitter Root Mountains on November 1, passing through Ross' Hole and reaching Flathead Post toward the end of November. Smith was the first American to cross the continental divide north and west of the three forks of the Missouri since the days of Lewis and Clark. He was the first American to explore the Columbia River drainage in the upper Salmon River district since Andrew Henry had been there in 1810. At Flathead Post Smith met Peter Skene Ogden from Fort Vancouver on the Columbia River.

Next spring Ashley's trappers met near Great Salt Lake. There were three parties, under the leadership of Jedediah Smith, William Sublette and Etienne Provot. Johnson Gardner, a free trapper who worked for General Ashley, fell in with Ogden's trappers and induced 23 of them to desert Ogden and to sell their furs to him. General Ashley came out that summer and in place of having his men meet at some fort had them gather in a great Rendezvous. General Ashley was the first fur trader to institute these rendezvous, where the trappers and Indians met and spent several weeks in good fellowship and trading.

When Jedediah Smith entered the fur trade the furs were taken down the river in what were known as bullboats. These boats were made of buffalo skins stretched, while fresh, over a framework of cottonwood or willow. They were of very shallow draft and admirably adapted for use on the Platte and other shallow streams. Prior to 1831 the principal mode of transporting trading goods into the Indian country was by means of keelboats, which were either poled up the river or rowed with broad sweeps and at times propelled by sails. In swift water they were cordelled. These keelboats had a draft of about three feet, a length of 60 to 75 feet, and were about 15 feet wide.

In the spring of 1831 there was launched at Louisville a steamboat named the Yellowstone. It was commanded by Captain B. Young and was owned by the American Fur Company. Where boats could not be used conveniently the furs were taken to the river on pack animals. In 1826 General Ashley decided to see if wagons could be used, so he sent a six-pound cannon, mounted on wheels and drawn by mules, with the expedition of 1827. This was undoubtedly the first wheeled vehicle to make its way over the untracked desert as far as the Great Salt Lake.

In 1828 General Ashley realized $180,000 from the furs taken to St. Louis. The following year he sold his interest in the Rocky Mountain Fur Company to Jedediah S. Smith, Captain William Sublette, and David Jackson. The new partners in the Rocky Mountain Fur Company, in place of using pack animals to transport their furs, inaugurated the use of wagons. They brought their furs from their rendezvous on Wind River to St. Louis. They were pioneers in the use of wagons, being the first to bring furs from the trapping grounds by wagons.

Jedediah S. Smith was the first man to cross the continent about midway between the route taken by Lewis and Clark and the old Spanish trail on the south. Smith was not only a man of unquestioned courage and religious principles, but he was a man of vision. He prepared a number of maps showing the geography, in detail, of districts hitherto unknown. He also wrote rather extensively, but unfortunately his notebooks and maps disappeared. In the fall of 1824 Smith gave a report of the country he had traveled to General Atkinson, who embodied it in his report to the war department.

After General Ashley's retirement from the fur company he entered politics. He ran for United States Senator in 1829 but was defeated. In 1831 Thomas Biddle killed Spencer Pettis, the Congressman from Missouri, in a duel, and Ashley was elected to succeed Pettis. At the end of his term he was reelected and, in 1835, he was elected for the third time. He worked with Benton and Linn for the development of the west. In 1836 he ran for governor of Missouri but was defeated by L. W. Boggs. He died of pneumonia on March 26, 1838.

In the summer of 1826 Jedediah Smith with a party of 15 men started from their camp near the Great Salt Lake, on a trip of exploration through the southwest. They struck the Colorado River and followed its course until they came to a camp of Mojave Indians. After spending two weeks with these Indians, Smith and his party struck westward and arrived at San Diego in mid-October. The Spaniards were very suspicious of the Americans. They refused to sell Smith supplies or horses. Jose Maria De Enjeandio, who had been a lieutenant colonel in the Mexican army and served as professor of engineering in a college in Mexico City, was stationed at the Presidio. He was the second governor of California under Mexican rule. Smith secured from him permission to travel in California. In spite of this passport, the residents of California would have nothing to do with the American adventurer and obstructed his plans and refused to sell him supplies or deal with him. He appealed to the captains of some American vessels who were on the coast to secure cargoes of hides and tallow at Monterey and Yerbua Buena, and secured from them the following letter of recommendation to the residents of California:

"We, the undersigned, having been requested by Jedediah S. Smith to state our opinion regarding his entering the province of California, do not hesitate to say that we have no doubt he was compelled to do so for want of provisions and water, having entered far into the beaver country that lies between the latitudes of 42 and 43 degrees; that he found it impossible to return by the route he came, as most of his horses had perished for want of food and water. He was therefore under the necessity of pushing forward into California, it being the nearest place where he could procure supplies to enable him to return.

"We further state as our opinion that the account given by him is circumstantially correct and that his sole object was the hunting and trapping of beaver and other furs.

"We also examined the passports produced by him from the Superintendent of Indian Affairs of the government of the United States of America and do not hesitate to say that we believe them to be perfectly correct.

"We also state that in our opinion his motives for wishing to pass by a different route to the Columbia River on his return is solely because he feels convinced that he and his companions run great risks of perishing if they return by the route they came.

"In testimony whereof we have hereunto set our hands and seals this 20th day of December, 1826. William P. Dana, captain of the schooner Waverly; William H. Cunningham, captain of the ship Courier; William Henderson, captain of the brig Olive Branch; James Scott and Thomas Robbins, mates of the schooner Waverly; Thomas Shaw, supercargo of the ship Courier."

Jedediah Smith was the first white man to cross the Sierra Nevada Mountains on an overland trip from the east to the bay of San Francisco. With his certificate from the ship captains and his passport from the commandant of the Presidio he was able to secure supplies and to buy horses from the Spaniards. To quiet the apprehension of the priests he wrote a letter to Father Duran of the mission of San Jose in which he said:

"Reverend Father: I understand, through one of your Christian Indians, that you are anxious to know who we are. We are Americans on our journey to the Columbia River. We were in the Mission San Gabriel in January last. I went to San Diego and saw the general and got a passport from him to pass onward from that place. I have made several efforts to pass the mountains, but, the snows being so deep, I could not succeed in getting over. I returned to this place, it being the only point to kill meat, to wait a few weeks until the snows melt, so that I can go on. The Indians here being friendly, I consider it a most safe point for me to remain until such time as I can cross the mountains with my horses, having lost a great many in attempting to cross ten or 15 days since. I am a long way from home and am anxious to get there as soon as the nature of the case will admit. Our situation is quite unpleasant, as we are destitute of clothing and most of the necessaries of life, wild meat being our principal substance."

He wrote this letter from his camp near the headwaters of the San Joaquin and Merced Rivers. His unsuccessful effort to cross the mountains with his entire party caused him to decide to leave most of his men in camp there while he, with two men, seven horses and two mules, attempted to make his way back to the rendezvous on the Great Salt Lake. With his two companions he started on May 20, 1827. He passed through the Yosemite Valley and near the Sequoia Grove, where he lost two of his horses and a mule in the deep snow. It took him eight days to cross the mountains. Twenty days of hard travel brought him to the southwestern shore of the Great Salt Lake. The men were tougher than the animals in crossing the desert, for but two of the animals survived the trip. With his two comrades Smith reached the rendezvous on the Great Salt Lake in the middle of June.

He spent a month with his partners, Jackson and Sublette, and wrote a report to General William Clark of St. Louis, telling him of the country he had explored. This General Clark, by the way, is the Captain William Clark who with Captain Meriwether Lewis had made the trip from the Missouri to the mouth of the Columbia. On July 13 Smith, with Silas Gobel, one of the two men who had accompanied him from California, and with 17 other men and two Indian women, started back for California by the same route he had previously taken. Those in the party were Thomas Virgin, from whom Virgin River in California is named; Charles Swift, Toussaint Marshall, John Turner, Joseph Palmer, Joseph LaPoint, Thomas Dawes, Richard Taylor, David Cunningham, Silas Gobel, William Campbell, Francis Deramme, Boatswain Brown, Gregory Ortaga, John B. Ratelle, Isaac Galbraith, and Robiseau, Pale, and Polite. They passed through the country of the Utah Indians and through (the country of) various other tribes until they came to the Mojave Indians, with whom they had spent 15 days on their first trip. They laid over with this tribe three days, buying from them corn, melons, pumpkins, wheat and beaver skins.

The Spanish authorities had warned the Mojave Indians not to allow any more Americans to enter California. On the third day Smith bade them goodbye. When Smith's party was divided, some being on a raft on which they were crossing the river and the others on the river bank, the Indians, throwing off their air of friendliness, attacked them, killing ten of the party of 18 and capturing two squaws and most of the supplies and trading goods. They captured Smith's day by day journal and all of his papers. Two of his men were badly wounded. Smith and his company, by a forced march, reached San Gabriel Mission in nine and a half days. Thomas Virgin, one of the wounded men, was imprisoned at San Diego but was later released and allowed to rejoin Smith.

After all sorts of adventures, including being put in prison, Smith was finally able to give a bond signed by some American ship captains whose ships were anchored off Monterey and was allowed to proceed northward to the Columbia River. Smith and his party went up what the Spaniards termed the Buena Ventura River, but which we now call the Sacramento River. He wintered on the principal fork of this river, and this fork has ever since been known as the American fork. Twenty-one years later millions of dollars in nuggets and coarse gold were washed from the bars and the bedrock of the river on which Smith and his party spent the winter.

In April, 1828, they headed in a northwest direction and traveled till they reached the shores of the Pacific. They killed plenty of elk and deer and also varied their diet with trout, clams, strawberries and camas. When Smith started on his return trip from the Great Salt Lake, he brought with him a considerable quantity of butcher knives, looking glasses, beads, chisels, shawls, blankets, red ribbons, tobacco, awls, razors, combs, buttons, needles, dirks and hawk bells, but the Mojave Indians had captured most of his supplies. However, he was able to secure a considerable amount of furs, principally sea otter skins and beavers, from the Indians he met along the coast.

Toward the latter part of June they began having trouble with the Indians. On June 25 they found that three of their horses had been badly wounded with arrows. The next day one was killed by an arrow. On July 5, two Indians, who spoke the Chinook language, visited their camp and told them they were within ten days' travel of the head of the Willamette Valley. On the seventh of July about 100 Indians came into their camp to trade pelts and fish. The following day they came to the Coos tribe of Indians. An Indian who was dissatisfied with the price paid him for his furs shot five of their horses and three mules. The three mules and one of the horses died and the other four were badly wounded, two of them dying the next day.

On July 12 Harrison G. Rogers, whose journal was later recovered from the Indians by Thomas McKay, records that an Indian chief stole the only ax they had. They seized the chief and put a rope around his neck, telling them they would hang him if the ax was not returned. The ax was returned, but the party paid a fearful price for it. The Indian chief, smarting under what he considered a deadly insult, took his revenge the next day.

On the 13th of July the party was within two easy days' march of the head of the Willamette Valley. Smith decided to follow the north bank of the Umpqua River, which would have brought him out on a fork of the Willamette River not far from the present town of Drain, Oregon. On Monday morning, July 14, immediately after breakfast,

Smith started out afoot to find the best way for the party to march. As he was coming back to camp he met John Turner, who was running at full speed through the brush. Turner told him that a number of Indians had come to the camp, among them the chief who had been punished for stealing the ax. The men were off their guard because the Indians seemed friendly. Suddenly the chief gave the warwhoop and instantly the Indians fell on the men with knives and clubs, killing most of them before they could offer any resistance. Turner, who had served as cook that morning, was gathering up the cooking utensils, when the Indians tried to stab him. He grabbed a heavy limb from beside the fire and laid about him, killing several of the Indians. In the confusion, he escaped.

Arthur Black had been cleaning his rifle. He had just loaded it when the Indians attacked the party. Three of the Indians jumped on him but he succeeded in throwing them off and shooting one of them. He ran into the brush, pursued by several of the Indians. Black thought he was the only one who had escaped. He struck north until, weakened by hunger, he gave himself up to the Tillamook Indians, who fed him and took him to Fort Vancouver. Meanwhile, Smith and Turner made their way afoot, hiding by day and avoiding the Indians and living on berries and camas root till they also reached Vancouver.

Dr. John McLoughlin at once dispatched Tom McKay with a large party to the Umpqua country. When McKay arrived there he invited the Indians to bring their furs to trade. Sorting out the ones the Indians had captured from Smith's party, he told them that he was going to return these to Smith, for they had secured them by murdering the men in Smith's party. The Indians denied that they had been involved in the massacre. They said they had bought these furs from the Indians who had killed Smith's men. McKay told them that if

they had bought them from the murderers, to look
to the murderers for payment. The Indians who had
been in possession of the furs, smarting under
the loss of them, tried to make the ones from
whom they had bought them reimburse them for
their loss. This resulted in a fight in which the
Indians were more effectively punished than they
could have been by McKay, for the Indians knew
who had killed the white men, while McKay had no
way of determining the fact. McKay not only recovered the furs but also the horses and most of
the baggage, including the journals that had been
kept by Harrison G. Rogers. When the furs were
brought in Dr. McLoughlin purchased them at the
market price, giving Smith a draft on (a) London
(bank) for $20,000. Jedediah Smith and Arthur
Black spent the fall as guests of Dr. McLoughlin.

Smith released John Turner from his service
so that he could join a trapping expedition conducted by Alexander McLeod. This is the same Mc-
Leod for whom the McCloud River in California is
named, though they have misspelled his name.

On March 12, 1829, Jedediah Smith and Arthur
Black left Fort Vancouver and went up the Columbia River to Kettle Falls and from there to Fort
Caldwell and thence to Flathead House, from which
point they proceeded to the rendezvous of their
own company. They trapped on the Weiser and Pay-
ette Rivers and various tributaries of the Snake.

Smith, Jackson, and Sublette had a most di-
sastrous season in 1828. Samuel Tulluck, who was
in charge of a party of trappers for them, was
attacked by a party of Blackfoot Indians, who
killed three of Tullock's party and captured
$40,000 worth of furs, 44 horses, and most of the
trade goods they had with them. In addition to
the loss of Tullock's men and the men with Smith,
at the mouth of the Umpqua, another party of
trappers, while going from the Columbia River to
the desert country of central Oregon, lost four
men--Ephraim Logan, William Bell, James Scott,

and Jacob O'Hara. These four men had left the main party to see if they could see any beaver signs on a small stream, and they were never heard from again.

In spite of the known danger of the hostile Blackfeet, Smith took a party of trappers into their country in the spring of 1830. He trapped on the Tongue River and the Big Horn, as well as on Clark's Fork of the Yellowstone, the Musselshell and the Judith. That same summer they held their rendezvous on Wind River. William Sublette, one of the partners, made the trip from St. Louis in three months with ten wagons of trade goods, two Dearborn buggies and some cattle.

On August 4 Smith, Sublette, and Jackson sold their business to Jim Bridger, Milton Sublette, Thomas Fitzpatrick, Henry Fraed and Baptiste Gervais. Smith and his two partners, loading their furs in the ten wagons, drove back to St. Louis with one of the most valuable consignments of furs that had been brought out of the mountains.

Smith was now in a position to retire, for his share of the proceeds of the sale of the Rocky Mountain Fur Company, with his one-third interest in the ten wagonloads of beaver pelts at $4.25 a pound, had made him well-to-do. With this money he planned to help educate his brothers and sisters and to establish himself as a trader in St. Louis. When he reached St. Louis he found two of his brothers, Peter and Austin, who had been unsuccessful in raising any money to engage in the fur business, so he staked them with an outfit to go to Santa Fe. Milton Sublette, the brother of Smith's partner, had been trapping with Ewing Young in New Mexico two years before and reported that there was lots of money to be made in the Santa Fe trade. This is the same Ewing Young whose death in the Chehalem Valley in Yamhill County was one of the causes of the formation of the provisional government in Oregon.

Jedediah Smith, fearing that because his two brothers were inexperienced they might not make a success of their venture, decided to accompany them to Santa Fe.

The goods shipped for the Santa Fe trade consisted largely of silks, velvets, hardware and goods suitable for the well-to-do Spaniards. The goods were to be exchanged for mules or gold and silver bullion. In the spring of 1831 Jedediah Smith, with his former partners, William Sublette and David E. Jackson, his two brothers, and about 80 more men, started with their wagon train from St. Louis. At Lexington they were joined by Thomas Fitzpatrick, Smith's long-time friend and employee. They started from Independence, Missouri, on May 4. After crossing the Arkansas River there was a 65-mile stretch of waterless plain before they came to the forks of the Cimarron. The men as well as the animals became frantic for water. Jedediah Smith and his friend Thomas Fitzpatrick volunteered to scout for water. Fitzpatrick and Smith separated and finally Smith struck the dry bed of the Cimarron, where he found, here and there, small pools of water.

After he and his horse had drunk their fill he started back to guide the party to the live-giving water. Suddenly he was surrounded by a band of Comanche Indians. One of the Indians shot him through the shoulder. Smith, picking out the chief, fired at him and killed him. The other Indians shot their arrows at Smith but in spite of his many wounds he killed two more Indians before they succeeded in killing him.

Meanwhile, the wagon train had gone on, struck the Cimarron, and found water. They reached Santa Fe on July 4. Shortly after they arrived some Mexican traders came in and offered for sale a rifle and two silver-mounted pistols, which they had purchased form a war party of Comanches. The Indians were anxious to trade these weapons, because Smith had killed their chief with one of them and they felt it would be bad luck to keep them. Peter Smith recognized them as the property of his brother, Jedediah Smith.

Smith had left a number of maps and also his journals in St. Louis. Unfortunately, these were all destroyed.

Oregon Journal
February 4, 5, 6, 7, 8, 9, 1930

Fisher

"One of the places that will always stand out in the memory of those who took the Meek Cutoff is Stinking Hollow. The immigrants camped there three days, while the men folks were hunting for oxen that had taken the back trail...My father rode three horses till they were beat out, looking for water. Upon his return to camp he found three wagons had been placed facing each other in the form of a triangle, their tongues raised and tied together at the top, and that a group of sullen and angry men had put a picket rope around Steve Meek's neck and were about to hang him..."

STEPHEN H. MEEK

The Terrible Trail and The Blue Bucket Mine

If Homer were still in the land of the living, what a narrative he could recite about the wanderings and adventures of Stephen H. Meek, mountain man and trapper, scout, guide, and Indian fighter, prospector and hunter, wagon train master and freighter, one-time resident of Vancouver, Champoeg, Linn City, and Yreka. Some day some historian will gather the isolated facts we have about his life in the Oregon Country and write a book that will give the generation of today a picture of the long-gone days.

Yreka, the county seat of Siskiyou County, is intimately associated with Oregon. Lane Gulch is named for General Joseph Lane, Oregon's first territorial governor, who, with a party of Oregonians, mined here in the early '50s. I spent this afternoon with Minnie R. Hearn, who was born on Oregon Street here in Yreka, October 28, 1858, and her sister, Mrs. Isobel Martin, who was born in Yreka, September 9, 1860. Miss Hearn showed me files of early-day newspapers published in Yreka in the '50s, and also early-day photographs of men who later became famous. Among these old-time photographs was one of Stephen H. Meek, taken at Fort Jones, 18 miles from Yreka.

Stephen H. Meek was born in Washington County, Virginia, on the Fourth of July, 1807.

When he was 20 years old he was hired by William Sublette, trader and fur trapper, to work in his warehouse. His job at first was to "rum beaver pelts". In those days it was the custom to sprinkle the pelts with raw rum to keep the moths out. In 1829, when he was 22, he went to Lexington, Missouri, and worked for his brother, Hiram Meek, who owned a store at Lexington. Hiram Meek moved to California not long after the discovery of gold in Sutter's Mill Race, settling in Amador County, and was still hale and hearty in the early '80s, though he had passed his 90th milestone.

In 1830 there were four rival companies trading with the Indians for furs. The most powerful was the Hudson's Bay Company. Then came the American Fur Company, the Rocky Mountain Fur company, and a company of free trappers and mountain men having a loose organization. William Sublette and Robert Campbell sent out a number of trappers, one of the number being Stephen Meek. Meek trapped on the Lewis Fork of the Columbia River, his winter quarters being located on Blackfoot Lake. In 1831 he was still employed by Sublette & Campbell, his field of operations being in the Black Hills, near where Fort Laramie was later located. He wintered on the Powder River. Next spring he wandered far, trapping on the Yellowstone, Wind, and Musselshell Rivers, going through Jackson's Hole to the rendezvous on the Popyoisa River. The next year, 1832, he and Jim Bridger trapped in the Blackfoot Country. They crossed the Yellowstone and Powder Rivers and traveled up the Missouri to Three Forks. They followed the left hand fork to the head of the Big Gray Bull River, thence to Green River, wintering on Snake River where Fort Hall was later built.

In the spring of 1833 he trapped on the Salmon and Port Neuf Rivers, and while on Green River he met Captain B. L. E. Bonneville, who hired him as a guide to go with Joseph Walker and a party of 34 men who were to explore the country in the vicinity of the Great Salt Lake. On this trip they discovered and named the Truckee, Carson, and Walker Rivers, Donner Lake and Walker Pass. They established their winter camp on the shores of Tulare Lake. In December Joseph Walker with a party of ten men made his way to Monterey. Returning in March, they bore south to the Colorado River, which they followed up to where the Bear River enters it. Here they found Captain Bonneville. That fall, 1834, Meek accompanied Captain Bonneville with a party of 22 men on a trapping expedition to the Snake River. They visited Fort Walla Walla and trapped on the John Day, the Malheur, Owyhee and Powder Rivers.

In the spring of 1835 Meek started for Champoeg and French Prairie, in the Willamette Valley, but at Fort Walla Walla he was hired by the factor of the Hudson's Bay Company, and he wintered at Fort Vancouver, working under Dr. McLoughlin. In the spring of 1836 he and Tom McKay made their way by the old Hudson's Bay Trail to northern California. They had fair success at trapping on the Scott River, Klamath River and the Sacramento. They took their furs to Yerba Buena, as San Francisco was then called, and sold them to Mr. Ray, the Hudson's Bay agent. They spent the next few months trapping on the American, Yuba, Feather, Pit, McLeod and Shasta Rivers, catching some beaver but overlooking the vast deposits of placer gold found a few years later. They returned to Fort Vancouver, where Meek spent the winter.

In the spring of 1837 he had good success trapping in the Rocky Mountains. He sold his catch to Jim Bridger, whom he met on Green River. He went to the Black Hills and trapped on the streams there, and also on the Sweetwater and Platte. He wintered at Fort Laramie, which had just been put up by William Sublette. In the

spring of 1838 he drifted south as far as Kit
Carson's home at Taos, New Mexico, gradually
working back into his old stamping ground by way
of the Arkansas and Platte Rivers. Andrew Sublette had built a trading post at the mouth of
Cherry Creek, near where Denver was later located. He named it Fort Robert, for Robert Campbell. Here Meek wintered, and from Fort Robert he
started the following spring on horseback for
Independence, Missouri, to carry the yearly express. While waiting for the westbound express to
be prepared he visited his brother Hiram and his
sister at Lexington, Missouri. Returning to Laramie with the express he joined the spring hunt
as a member of Frapp's brigade. In July he was
given the job of wagon master and sent in charge
of the wagon train to take the season's catch of
furs to St. Louis.

In the spring of 1840 McGoffin Brothers hired him as wagon master and sent a wagon train of
supplies in his charge on the Old Santa Fe Trail
to Santa Fe and Chihuahua. He wintered at Chihuahua. The Mexican governor of Chihuahua employed an American, James Kirker, to kill roving
bands of Apaches, and agreed to pay $2.50 each
for all horses or cattle captured form the Indians. Kirker hired Meek to help him clean up the
Apaches. They and their American comrades drove
the Indians out of the district and captured and
turned over 15,000 head of stock to the governor
of Chihuahua.

He wintered in New Mexico and next spring
went to Independence and was hired as guide to
take a party of emigrants with 17 wagons to Oregon. He guided them as far as Green River, where
they joined the Fitzpatrick brigade, with whom
they traveled to Fort Hall. The wagons were
abandoned at Fort Hall and the emigrants went
with pack horses by Sublette's Cut-off, thence
down the Snake River, down Burnt River and up
Powder River to Grande Ronde Valley, crossing the

Blue Mountains at Lee's encampment and following the Umatilla to where it flows into the Columbia. They followed the Columbia to Wishram at The Dalles of the Columbia and went down the Columbia to Fort Vancouver and up the Willamette to Oregon City.

He would start out on a trapping trip to travel through a country infested with hostile Indians, and during the season would cover hundreds of unpathed miles. Some beaver traps, his gun, some powder and lead and a little salt and he was provisioned for a six months' trip. Once a year, when he made his way to the rendezvous to dispose of his furs, he would experience the luxury of eating bread, for at such times the free trappers were usually furnished five pounds of flour each.

In 1842 he was hired as guide to bring a small party of emigrants from Independence, Missouri, to Fort Hall. He continued on to the Willamette Valley and secured work from L. W. Hastings, carrying a chain to survey lots and streets on Dr. John McLoughlin's land claim at Oregon City. When "Falls City", as Oregon City was then called, had been surveyed he wintered in Washington County and on French Prairie, and in the spring of 1843 was hired as guide to take a party of emigrants who were dissatisfied with the Willamette Valley to Sutter's Fort, where free land was to be had and where they could secure work from Captain Sutter. While guiding the emigrants to California by way of the old Hudson's Bay Trail he met, not far from the present city of Medford, Captain Joe Walker, bringing a band of California cattle to the Willamette Valley.

Meek took his party to Sutter's Fort and he himself went to Monterey, where he wintered. At Monterey he met Captain Smith of the vessel George and Henry of Baltimore. Captain Smith induced Meek to go with him on a trading trip which would take them along the coast, to the Sandwich

Islands, thence to China to dispose of their furs for tea, silk, and spices, and back to New York, Boston, or Baltimore. Captain Smith received advices at Valparaiso which required his return to Baltimore, so he and Meek made their way northward to Panama. At Gaquille, Columbia, Meek was stricken down with yellow fever and came near to crossing the great divide. They caught a ship at Panama and arrived in New York City in July, 1844. Meek visited his old home in Virginia, which he had not seen for 17 years. March, 1845, saw him in New Orleans. From there he went up the Father of Waters to St. Louis, where he renewed his long-time friendship with Sublette, Fitpatrick, Campbell, and other fur traders for whom or with whom he had trapped.

He visited the Oregon-bound emigrants who were camped at the rendezvous waiting for the grass to get "strong" enough to graze their oxen. He was hired as a guide, and on May 11, 1845, the westward trek was begun. The day they started Meek met a young woman in the wagon train, Elizabeth R. Schoonover by name, and the 38-year-old lover made such ardent love that she capitulated and they were married just a week from the day they had met.

At Fort Hall William B. Ide and his party decided to take the southward trail for Sutter's Fort, so, with Greenwood as their guide, they left the party. The rest of the party were undecided whether to continue to the Willamette Valley by way of the Snake and Columbia Rivers and The Dalles, or to take Meek's advice and go by way of an old Hudson's Bay trail, since known as Meek's cut-off. The party divided, a large number of the emigrants accompanying Meek. While trappers or mountain men could have made the trip by this cut-off without difficulty, slow-going oxen, whose feet grew tender on the sharp rocks, and women and children, could not stand the forced marches between water holes, so they refused to follow Meek any longer, and wandered in the country around the upper waters of the Malheur and John Day till many of the party died. Meek was told to leave the party or he would be killed. He hurried on, and sent help to them. It was while wandering around seeking for a way to The Dalles that what is known as the Blue Bucket Mine was discovered. It is thought the rich strike at Canyon City, made some years later, may have been the so-called Blue Bucket Mine.

Meek and his wife settled at Linn City, just across the Willamette from Oregon City. He lived here from the fall of 1845 till the spring of 1848, when, with his wife and child, he went to California.

October, 1848, found him in the gold diggings at Coloma. He ran a butcher shop that winter and made money. In the summer of 1849 his wife and child returned to Linn City, on the Willamette, and in December, 1850, Meek joined them.

Next spring he started for the newly discovered gold diggings of Yreka, in northern California. He washed out $6000 in dust on a claim at Yreka, which he invested in a stock of goods. He sold his goods at a good profit and went to Santa Cruz and opened a butcher shop. He had become wealthy by now, so he invested his stake, amounting to $34,000 in a Mexican land grant near Watsonville. Other heirs of the estate turned up and Meek lost the claim and the money he had paid for it. He tried to recoup his losses by going to the Fraser river diggings in 1858, but came back poorer than he went. He mined in Amador County, California, till 1865, when his wife died and he took to the hills, hunting and trapping.

In the spring of 1867 he served as wagon master for a train of 22 wagons loaded with machinery for a stamp mill. He piloted this wagon train from Sacramento, California, to the Boise Basin in Idaho. In many places he had to build his own roads through or across the mountains. In the winter of 1867 he wintered with his brother, Joe Meek, on Tualatin Plains, near Hillsboro. In 1868 he was employed as a guide for a party of 30 men who went from the Willamette Valley to the headwaters of the Malheur in search of the Blue Bucket Mine. During the Bannock War he was employed by the government as wagon master to keep the troops supplied with provisions. For months the soldiers had been trying to locate the hostile Indians. General Crook found that Meek was trustworthy, so he employed him as a scout, and Meek guided the soldiers to Sugar Loaf Crater, where the Indians were located and defeated.

When the Bannock War was over Meek went to Silver City, Idaho. Later he went to Winnemucca, Nevada, and on to Sacramento. In the fall of 1871, finding his funds had run low, he went to Red Bluff and purchased traps and, with his son George, he resumed his old-time trade as trapper. They trapped on the Sacramento, Pitt, Scott, McLeod and Trinity Rivers. Josiah Doll had a ranch in Scott Valley and here Meek and his son made their headquarters. Eastern sportsmen began coming into northern California to hunt grizzlies or deer, and Meek found his services in demand as guide to the "Big Bear" country. He died as he lived, simple, trustful, friendly, a lover of nature.

Oregon Journal
April 16, 17, & 19,
1927

During the last 25 years or more I have attended most of the pioneer reunions in Portland as well as numerous other celebrations at Champoeg. I have also attended numerous gatherings of various clans, and other pioneer meetings. Rarely have I heard the pioneers speak of the hardships of the trip across the plains. The perils and hardships are forgotten, and as they look back at the six months' journey they remember only the friendships formed, and have only happy memories of the journey. Recently I interviewed Pierce Parker, who lives in Portland and was born on his father's donation land claim, east of Salem, where the penitentiary is now located. His father, Sam Parker, was captain of a wagon train that crossed the plains in 1845. On August 24 they took what is known as Meek's cut-off. I am going to copy a few extracts from the diary Captain Parker kept.

On August 24, Captain Parker writes: "Took Meek's cut-off. Mrs. Best took sick this day.

"August 25. Traveled over hills all day. Came to Malheur by night.

"August 26. Rocky and hilly. Camped on small stream. Made 14 miles."

For the next week his comments are largely confined to how bad the road was and a discussion of broken wagons. On August 30 he writes: "Rock all day. Poor grass. More swearing than you ever heard." The record for September 1 reads: "Worst road you ever saw. Five wagons broke. Mrs. Best worse." He continues:

"September 2. Went to small creek, down the worst you ever saw a wagon go."

On September 8 they stopped to bury a child who had died. On September 10 his record reads: "Traveled all day and all night. Struck a small spring in the morning. Cursing and swearing. 150 wagons. September 11. Traveled five miles. Laid here four days. Couldn't find water. From 10 to 20 and 30 men out hunting water. Some came in to camp and couldn't speak.

"September 16. Left at 3 o'clock p.m. Traveled all night. Came to water at sunrise. Mrs. Best no better. Wagons in company, 198; 2299 loose cattle; 811 head of oxen. All these cattle to get water for.

"September 21. Some of the company didn't get in till after dark. Swearing without end. Coming in all night.

"September 23. Buried four persons here.

"September 24. Traveled all day and all night; 25 miles. Many couldn't get to water and water had to be taken to them. Here we buried six persons.

"September 29. All day getting up the hill. Camped without water. Buried three here.

"September 30. Traveled all day until into the night and came to water. Some straggled in all night. Five buried here.

"October 2. Got to Deschutes River. Mrs. Best died this day. My wife and child and second daughter sick.

"October 3. Crossed the Deschutes River in the wagon body. Took the wagons apart. This day my two small boys took sick, Gideon and George; also Susan, my fourth girl. Six of my family sick.

"October 5. Here we buried Mrs. Best and three more.

"October 7. This morning nothing to eat. Got to the Methodist mission at dark. Got in the Methodist mission house with my family. Got something to eat. This was the first day we had done without something to eat. Some of our company had been without bread for 15 days and had had to live on poor beef. Pen and tongue will both fall short when they try to tell the sufferings the company went through. My wife and baby Virginia died.

"I left on November 3 for Oregon City in a large canoe with four Indians. The wet weather has set in. I didn't expect to get to the city with my four children. I thought my second girl would die any time. I took my seat in the canoe by her and held her up, and the same at night. At the Cascade Falls we had to make a passage of three miles. I put my sick girl in a blanket and carried her and only rested once that day. Made the portage with the help of the four Indians, my oldest boy and my oldest girl, neither of whom had been sick one minute on the road.

"November 8. Landed at Oregon City, wet, hungry, and almost worn out, with my family most all sick. The three youngest soon got well, but it was 19 days after I landed till my second daughter could stand alone."

Oregon Journal
March 30, 1935

(A son of Job McNemee recounts the misadventures of the party of immigrants who in 1845 were misled by Stephen Meek, of "Meek's Cut-off" fame. As an incident there always attaches the story of the Blue Bucket Mine, which Mr. McNemee tells just as his father told it to him. There will be more from this same narrator in this space tomorrow.)

"When my father, Job McNemee, moved to Portland there were only three houses here," said Andrew Jackson McNemee, when I visited him recently at the home of his niece, Mrs. C. A. Morden, in East Portland. "My father built the fourth house in Portland, a good-sized log cabin. I was born here in Portland, 76 years ago last spring.

"I was born in a cabin made of split boards--shakes, we called them then--located at the southwest corner of Yamhill and Front Streets. My people spent the winter of 1845 on Dick Richards' place, at Linnton. Boiled wheat and salmon formed their staple diet that winter.

The next spring Father bought a couple of lots of A. L. Lovejoy in his newly laid out townsite--Portland. Father put up a log cabin and brought the family from Linnton to Portland. He traded his two thin oxen for a fat young steer, which he killed. With this meat he started the first butcher shop in Portland. People going from Vancouver to Oregon City usually tied up their canoes at the clearing on the river bank near our house, so Father sold the meat to these travelers as well as to the settlers in the vicinity of Portland. Father also started the first hotel in Portland. He called it the Ohio House, for his native state. Father made the first pumps in Portland. He bored a hole through the center of a log and fixed up a handle and a plunger. Later he took the contract from Mrs. Pentland to make pipes for Portland's first water system. I helped him bore the holes in the logs for the water pipes. Later my father worked for Leonard & Green when they bought the city water department.

"When gold was discovered in California, in 1848, every able-bodied man in Portland went to the gold diggings. My father was among the first to go. My oldest brother, Francis, who was not yet 12 years old, chopped the wood for most of the women who were left husbandless. I was a baby in arms at the time. Mother had no money to buy feed for our cow, so she took the straw from the ticks on our beds and mixed some flour with it and fed it to our cow, so the cow would give milk for me and the other children. Father made big money in the mines, but invested it in other mining claims, so he came back broke. Later he went into the stock business and became well-to-do, having at one time over 100 Durham cattle.

"My father was born near Columbus, Ohio, October 14, 1812. My mother, Hannah Cochrane Mc-Nemee, was born near Chillicothe, Ohio, January 29, 1815. Her father, David Cochrane, was born in Virginia, but went to Kentucky with Boone and Kenton and the other pioneers of Kentucky. He moved from Kentucky to Ohio. Father was 21 and

Mother 17 when they were married. They struck out for themselves, going at first to Indiana and later to St. Joe, Missouri. Father bought 160 acres of land on the edge of St. Joe. When he took the Oregon fever he traded his quarter section for $400 in cash and eight horses. Today his farm is in the heart of the best residence district of St. Joe.

"Fred Waymire married my mother's sister. Fred's brother George was elected lieutenant of the wagon train when my people came across the plains in 1845. Colonel W. G. T'Vault was captain of the wagon train. Dr. Elijah White, who was on his way east, met the wagon train of which my mother was a member and told them of a more direct route. The T'Vault wagon train, with others, swung south to take this cutoff. Stephen Meek, a brother of Joe Meek, said he could guide the immigrants to the Willamette Valley by this cutoff. Mountain men and Hudson's Bay trappers, in former days, had crossed the Cascades by this cutoff and he was confident he could follow the old trail. He became confused and bore off too far south. They struck the desert country south of central Oregon, where the cattle suffered severely from lack of pasture and, particularly, from lack of water. In place of saving 200 miles, as they had expected, and having an easier way, they suffered severe hardships, lost three weeks, and finally made their way to The Dalles.

"Meek had guided them by the old trail for some time, but when they got into the foothills of the Malheur Mountains, all signs of the old trail disappeared. The alkaline water was the cause of many of the immigrants becoming sick with mountain fever. My sister Emaline, who was a babe in arms, died and for three days they carried her body in our wagon, until they could find a place to bury her. Wolves and coyotes followed the party, and while the wagons were still in sight, they could be seen fighting over the bodies of oxen that had been abandoned. They also dug up the bodies of members of the party that had been buried in shallow, rocky graves. The cattle became restless and tried to take the back track. The wagon train would have to halt while the immigrants searched for the hungry and thirsty cattle.

"While Dave Herron was out looking for his lost cattle he noticed in the bed of a stream a piece of metal that looked like copper or brass. He picked it up and put it into his pocket and took it with him to the camp. Another member of the party also brought a piece of dull yellow metal to camp. They were unable to determine whether it was gold, copper or brass. This was in 1845, before the discovery of gold at Sutter's Mill in California, so they knew nothing about gold in the form of nuggets. One of the nuggets was given to Mr. Martin, who hammered it flat with a hammer on his wagon tire. He threw it into his tool chest and paid no more attention to it.

"The immigrants were more interested in finding the lost trail to the Willamette Valley and in securing food and water for their hungry and thirsty children and grass and water for their cattle than in gold, so no attention was paid to the stream on which the nuggets had been found. The stream ran in a southwesterly direction, but whether it was a branch of the Malheur River or not the immigrants did not know. A few years later, when gold was discovered in California, the finding of these nuggets was recalled. When my brothers went to the Orofino Mines in Idaho, my father said he believed he could guide them to where the gold had been found, in what was called the Blue Bucket Mine. The reason for giving this name to the location was that one of the immigrants, when asked about it, said, 'I could have picked up my blue bucket full of nuggets if I had known it was gold.'

"When an ox is all in, he quits. An ox will stay with it as long as he can, but when he finally gives up it is almost impossible to persuade him to get to his feet again.

"One of the places that will always stand out in the memory of those who took the Meek Cutoff is Stinking Hollow. The immigrants camped there three days, while the men folks were hunting for oxen that had taken the back trail. They had a limited supply of water in their barrels and kegs, so the women and children as well as the men were on short rations of water.

"My father rode three horses till they were beat out, looking for water. Upon his return to the camp he found three wagons had been placed facing each other in the form of a triangle, their tongues raised and tied together at the top, and that a group of sullen and angry men had put a picket rope around Steve Meek's neck and were about to hang him. My father, pointing his gun at the men, said, 'The first man that pulls on that rope will be a dead man. Steve Meek is the only man who has ever been in this part of the country before. If you hang Meek we are all dead men. If you give him a little time he may be able to recognize some landmark and find a way out'. The men agreed to give Meek three days. Meanwhile, the emigrants took the back track and reached the old immigrant road and started for The Dalles. Meek left during the night and made his way to The Dalles, where he appealed to the missionaries for help. The missionaries there were either unwilling or unable to do anything, so Mose Harris, or the 'Black Squire', as he was usually called, an old mountain man and a companion of Joe Meek, procured supplies from the Indians and started out with relief for the lost immigrants.

"The party did not reach The Dalles till the middle of October. More than 20 of the immigrants had died from mountain fever during their three weeks of wandering on the headwaters of the Malheur and in the Malheur Mountains, in search of the cutoff. My father, having no money to hire a bateau, cut some trees near the river bank and made a log raft upon which he put the family and our household goods and on which they floated down the Columbia River to Fort Vancouver.

"At Fort Vancouver he bought a bateau and plied for the next few months on the river, transporting passengers and freight from The Dalles to Fort Vancouver. Dr. John McLoughlin furnished wheat and salmon to my father on credit, and on this they lived during the winter of 1845 while staying at Linnton.

Oregon Journal
October 10 & 11,
year illegible

JOE MEEK

Mountain Man

(The career of one of Oregon's most notable
and most popular characters is here sketched by
Mr. Lockley who approaches the main subject
through a brief interview with a son of this
old-time maker of Oregon history.)

Some time ago, when I was at Hillsboro, I
ran across a man who looked as if he was an
old-timer, so I stopped to pass the time of day
with him. After we had talked for a few moments I
said, "By the way, you failed to tell me your
name."

"My name is Joseph Lane Meek," he answered.

I smiled and said, "Well, you picked out two
good names while you were picking. General Lane
and Joe Meek are two of Oregon's best known and
best loved pioneers."

"My father, Joe Meek, was a great admirer of
General Lane," he responded, "so he named me for
him. I was born October 6, 1855, about four miles
north of Hillsboro. I now live on a wheat ranch
45 miles east of Lewiston. I met some old Nez
Perce Indians up around Lapwai who told me about
my mother's people. My mother was a member of the
Nez Perce tribe. Her father, whose name was

Tau-you-le-nim, was a chief, and he is remembered even to this day for his skill as a buffalo hunter.

"I went to school at the old Jackson School, north of our donation land claim. A man named Campbell was my first teacher. I was a very bashful little boy. He told me to stand up and say my a-b-c's. I shook my head. He thought I was disobedient, but really I was bashful. He said, 'I'll teach you to mind me when I give an order,' and he gave me a severe whipping, which I did not think I deserved. My mother wanted us to learn her native tongue, Nez Perce, but we boys wouldn't do it.

"No, I never was much to hunt and fish. I preferred working on the place. I was always a great hand with horses. You can do more with a horse if you try to understand it. Many a horse that is said to be mean or balky is perfectly willing to do what you want it to, but it doesn't know what you want, and, of course, the more you jerk and whip it and raise your voice the less it knows what you want.

"In 1895 I left Washington County and went to Idaho. I own 360 acres and rent 320 acres of Indian land. I raise wheat and oats. Steve, my brother, lives here. Olive Meek Riley, my sister, lives in Lane County. My sister Jennie lives at Volmer, Idaho."

I have met scores of pioneers who knew Joe Meek intimately, and whenever his name is mentioned their eyes soften and they smile reminiscently and usually tell me some comical adventure of this hardy, courageous and lovable "mountain man". Joseph L. Meek was a Virginian, born in Washington County, Virginia, in 1810. He did not "get around" to going to school till he was 16 years old. His teacher printed his a-b-c's on a broad wooden paddle and told him to learn them.

Joe knew a lot about hunting and woodcraft, but
he had but little patience with learning to tell
one letter from another, and when the teacher
decided to increase his love of learning by the
use of the rod he hit his hot-tempered,
bald-headed teacher over the head with the wooden
paddle on which the a-b-c's were printed, and
decided he had had all the schooling he could
make use of, so he quit then and there. He did not

There was a moment of hesitation, when
Joe Meek called out, "Who's for a divide? All
in favor of organization follow me."
He led off and for a moment it looked
like a tie, till F. X. Matthieu and Etienne
Lucier joined with the Americans, making the
vote 52 to 50 for the provisional government.

---

take to manual work, for at that time slaves were
supposed to do the work while their masters directed them.
When he was 18 he struck out for himself, as
his stepmother held views different from his as
to the desirability of his going to work. In the
spring of 1829 he fell in with William Sublette
at St. Louis and enlisted his company of fur
hunters and adventurers. They started from St.
Louis on St. Patrick's Day, 1829, and for the
next few weeks traveled through wind-driven sleet
and rain storms, sleeping at night in their wet
clothes, a process well calculated either to kill

or harden new recruits. There were 60 in the party and they were a hard-drinking, hard-fighting, fun-loving, big-hearted outfit. Their rendezvous that year was on a tributary of the Big Horn River. Arriving there, they were met by scores of free trappers and hundreds of Indians. For the next 30 days horse racing, drinking, gambling and fighting was the order of the day and Joe Meek was initiated into the reckless fraternity of mountain men.

Meek put in the first season hunting in Jackson's Hole. Within the next year he had been engaged in numerous fights with the Blackfoot Indians, had lived for days on snow in lieu of other food while dodging Indians who had cut him off from his comrades, had become a proficient trapper and hunter and in their winter camp had not only learned his a-b-c's from a fellow trapper but had spent his leisure time reading and rereading worn copies of Shakespeare and the Bible, the only two books carried by Sublette. The next year, with Jedediah Smith as leader and Jim Bridger as guide, Meek and his fellow-trappers made their way into Judith Basin and to the country of the Snake Indians, to share the beaver trapping with the trappers of the Hudson's Bay Company, who claimed that territory. They lived on beaver, buffalo, mountain sheep and antelope, and when game was scarce they ate porcupines or killed a horse.

For the next ten years Meek traveled all over the west, having many hair-breadth escapes and suffering much hardship. In 1838 he married a Nez Perce girl, whom he named Virginia, for his native state. She belonged to the Salmon River band of Nez Perces, whose head chief was Kow-e-so-te, and she was a sister of Dr. Robert Newell's wife.

By 1840 the trappers and mountain men were out of an occupation, for not only were the beaver becoming scarce, but silk was being used in the manufacture of plug hats in place of beaver, so they were compelled to turn to some other pursuit. Meek was 28 years old and had nothing to show for his 12 years of starving, wading in ice-cold streams and fighting Indians and grizzly bears, except an Indian wife and two children, so when his comrade, Dr. Newell, proposed that they give up their wandering life and settle in the Willamette Valley he fell in with the plan. They secured two wagons left at Fort Hall by Dr. Marcus Whitman and Meek with his Nez Perce wife and their two babies started for the Willamette Valley, with Newell, Craig, and Nicholas. Meek had four half-broken Indian cayuses and a mule hitched to his wagon. Newell drove four horses on the other wagon. Meek and Newell finished what Whitman had started, and drove the first wagons from Fort Hall to the Columbia River. With almost incredible difficulty they finally made their way across the mountains to Waii-lat-pu, where Dr. Whitman had established his mission. When they went on, after a pleasant visit with the Whitmans, Joe Meek left his little girl, Helen Mar, the daughter of his first Indian wife. The wagons were left at what is now known as Wallula, and the rest of the journey was made by pack horse. The next spring Dr. Newell returned and drove one of the wagons to his place on the Tualatin Plains.

Meek and his fellow mountain men put in an uncomfortable and hungry winter on Tualatin Plains. The next summer he landed a job as guide to Commodore Wilkes.

That fall he applied to the Methodist Mission for a cow on credit. He was told that he should pray for one. He said, "All right. I'll get down on my knees and pray for half an hour if you will see that my prayer is answered and I get a cow on credit." They agreed, so Meek, kneeling in the muddy trail, prayed for 30 minutes, after which he marched home leading a cow.

Meek soon became one of the most popular men in the valley, for he was always willing to give a helping hand to those in need. He was a natural leader. This was exemplified at the "wolf meeting" at Champoeg on May 2, 1843, when the settlers had met to take measures for the civil and military protection of the colony. A motion that a provisional government should be formed was voted on and lost. G. W. LeBreton, being in doubt as to the vote, made a motion that the meeting should divide, all in favor of such an organization stepping to the right and those opposed to the left. There was a moment of hesitation, when Joe Meek called out, "Who's for a divide? All in favor of an organization follow me." He led off and for a moment it looked like a tie, till F. X. Matthieu and Etienne Lucier joined with the Americans, making the vote 52 to 50 for the provisional government.

The meeting came once more to order and elected a supreme judge, a clerk of the court, a sheriff, four magistrates, four constables, a treasurer, a mayor, a captain, and nine members of a legislative committee. Meek was elected sheriff, and proved just the man for the job, being utterly fearless and possessing a great deal of tact. He arrested moonshiners, broke up bootlegging, took the census, collected the taxes and performed innumerable other duties. It was said that Joe Meek held more offices and made less out of them than anyone else in Oregon. He it was who had wished on him the dangerous and unpleasant duty of serving as messenger of the provisional government of the United States. Resigning his seat in the legislature, he started on January 4, 1848, for a winter journey overland to Washington D. C. On his way he stopped at the Whitman Mission and buried the bodies of Dr. and Mrs. Whitman, his little daughter Helen, and the others whose bodies had been dug up by the wolves. With one or two hardy mountain men as his companions, he went on snowshoes through a country full of hostile Indians, living on what they could shoot, which at times happened to be skunks. Hungry, ragged, ill-fed, without a cent, he made his way in record time to the nation's capital. Returning from Washington, he served as guide to General Joseph Lane, the newly appointed territorial governor. Meek became United States Marshal after Oregon became a territory, and to the day of his death he was one of Oregon's most popular officials.

While at Champoeg recently I fell into talk with Edith Tozier Weatherred, who told me many interesting details of her old-time neighbor, Joe Meek, who, with his Nez Perce wife and his family, lived in Washington County from the days of its early settlement...He was related to President Polk. Living with a stepmother who had strict ideas of discipline did not appeal to Joe Meek, so he struck out for himself. With Robert Newell and George W. Ebberts he left St. Louis on St. Patrick's Day, 1829, with a company of trappers under the charge of Sublette. Curiously enough, these three young men later helped make history in the Oregon Country. All three of them settled on the Tualatin Plains in the 1840s. Ebberts--better known to old-timers of Oregon as "Squire" Ebberts, or "the Black Squire"--was born in Kentucky, January 22, 1810. He was 19 years old when he made his first trip to the Rocky Mountains, trapping beaver. Robert Newell--better known as "Doctor" Newell--took up a place near Champoeg. He was born near Zanesville, Ohio, March 30, 1807. He died at Lewiston, Idaho, November 14, 1869. Joe Meek served as Oregon's first federal marshall, and, as such, executed the Indians at Oregon City for killing Dr. Marcus Whitman and his wife and others in the fall of

1847 at the Whitman Mission. Joe Meek died June
20, 1875, at the age of 65.

Oregon Journal
January 7, 1933
January 15, 1934

Turkey

JOHN BALL
Oregon's First School Teacher

John Ball was Oregon's first school teacher. He came across the plains to Oregon with Nathaniel J. Wyeth in 1832.

When he was born, in 1874, the United States
claimed a population of approximately 4,000,000.
He was born on a rocky hill farm in New England,
and was the tenth child. Sarah, his oldest sister, was 20 years his senior. He spent his boyhood working on the farm. There was never any
spare time, for whenever there was no farm work
to do the children picked up the stones in the
plow field and carried them to the border line of
the farm to be used in making fences. To wring a
living for a large family from the granite hills
of New England meant that as soon as the children
were old enough they went to work. Only two hol-
idays were celebrated in those days--the Fourth
of July and Thanksgiving Day. Christmas was regarded as a pagan holiday and was not celebrated.

Mr. Ball's father had but little education,
but his mother was fond of reading. John Ball
picked up a large part of his education from the
Bible, Watts' Hymns, Webster's Spelling Book,
Morse's Geography, and Adams' Arithmetic. Each
winter the children went to school for a few

weeks. Once a year his father took butter, cheese and other products of the farm to Boston to barter for the year's supply of groceries.

At that day most of the living came from the farm and consisted of Indian bread, rye bread, pork and beans, pumpkin and apple pie and game. The clothing was made on the farm, the wool being spun on a large spinning wheel, while the linen was made on a little foot wheel. The yarn was woven on a hand loom. The women of the household bleached the linen, making sheets, shirts, tablecloths and towels. When a family could afford it, they had a traveling tailor come to the house to make clothing from the woolen cloth for the men.

The family belonged to the Congregational Church. They were strong partisans of Reverend Page, the preacher, until, at the time of Jefferson's election, he preached a sermon commending Mr. Jefferson. This gave great offense. One of the leading members of the church voiced the sentiment of many of his fellow members when he said, "Mr. Page, we employ you to preach Jesus Christ and him crucified, but you preach Thomas Jefferson and him justified."

As was the custom at that time, Ball's father claimed the services on the farm of all the children till they reached their 21st birthday. Mr. Ball attended a private school kept by a Reverend Rolph at Groton. This school was four miles, by the bridle path over the mountain, and he went daily all of one fall and winter.

Mr. Ball at first taught a writing school, but later taught district schools in Vermont. After teaching for a year or so he went to Salisbury Academy, at Franklin, New Hampshire, where he studied Latin and Greek. The principal of the academy recommended him as a fit student for college, to President Brown of Dartmouth College. In those days the president of the college traveled throughout New England to meet and examine the students who desired to go to Dartmouth College. President Brown passed favorably upon Mr. Ball, in spite of the fact that he had only attended school four years altogether.

For the greater part of the time he was at college, Mr. Ball bached, as he could not afford to board. His roommate, Jasper Newton, often took him home with him to give him a change from his own cooking. The Newton family consisted of ten sons, none less than six feet tall, and six daughters. Jasper was six feet, four inches, tall.

After graduating, Mr. Ball read law for two years and then went to Darien, Georgia, where he spent the winter of 1822-23 teaching school. In the summer of 1824 he was admitted to the bar and shortly thereafter was made justice of the peace. On account of the death of his brother-in-law, who owned an oilcloth factory, he gave up the law and took charge of the factory. Leaving the foreman in charge of the factory, he became traveling salesman for the oilcloth, traveling all over New England and the South.

When his sister took a partner in the oilcloth business, Mr. Ball wrote to Nathaniel Wyeth of Boston to see if he could accompany Mr. Wyeth to Oregon the following season.

On February 10, 1832, Wyeth replied as follows:

"Your favor of February 8th is at hand. What Mr. Kelly tells you is not the truth. It is true that I once proposed to join his expedition, but I relinquished the idea when they joined their two expeditions into one, for I consider it impracticable and inhuman to attempt passage across the continent with a party composed of men, women, and children. The undertaking is enough for men. Your observation in regard to salmon fishing is good and a strong effort will be made to arrive in season, to avail ourselves of it, to procure food for the winter. I see no probability that Mr. Kelley's party will move at present. They have made no preparation as yet, nor do I believe that they can ever make provision for moving such a mass as they propose. My party will leave Boston early in March. We have now nearly enough men, but any number of suitable persons will be received on the conditions named in my letter to Mr. Bache. Please use this letter as one of introduction to Charles Wyeth of the firm of Wyeth and Norris, merchants in Baltimore. He is my brother and has some general knowledge of my plans. This gentleman will leave Baltimore for New York about the 25th inst., after which time he may be found at Messrs. Cripps & Wyeth in Pearl Street. Leonard I. Wyeth of the last named firm would also give you information on this subject which he may possess. He is also a brother of mine. If you conclude to join our expedition, please give me early notice. Bear in mind that there will be no avoidable delay in setting out."

They arranged to meet the next spring, 1832, at Baltimore. That winter he visited New York City to learn all he could from the employees of John Jacob Astor about the Oregon Country. Here he had met Mr. Seaton, who had helped establish Astoria, and also Ramsey Crooks, who had been in charge of the overland expedition to the mouth of the Columbia River, for Mr. Astor.

At Washington, D. C., he met Colonel Ashley, who had been in the fur trade for many years and was familiar with the country between the Missouri River and the Rocky Mountains. General Ashley had sold out his fur business to William Sublette of St. Louis, and had been elected a member of Congress.

Mr. Ball went to Baltimore, where he joined Nathaniel Wyeth and his party. They traveled from Baltimore on the Baltimore & Ohio Railroad, which was operated by horse power. The length of the road was 60 miles, and at that time, it was the longest railroad in the United States. At Frederick they left the horse power railroad and started westward on foot, to Monongahela, where they took a steamboat for Pittsburgh. At Pittsburgh they took a steamer for St. Louis. On their trip down the river he and Reverend Lyman Beecher and Nathaniel Wyeth had many long and interesting talks. They stopped for a while at Cincinnati, which at that time was but a village with a few wooden buildings.

At St. Louis they took a boat up the river to join William Sublette. On this steamboat were a large number of soldiers going up the Mississippi to fight Black Hawk. Mr. Ball joined Mr. Sublette at Independence, Missouri. Campbell's party, from St. Louis, also joined Sublette at Independence, so that when they were ready to start for the Rocky Mountains there were 80 men and about 300 horses. The last white settlement they came to was a settlement of Mormons, who had settled there a few months before. The last white man they saw, aside from members of their own party, was a man acting as gunsmith among the Indians on the Kansas River, about where Topeka was later built.

Shortly after leaving the prairies of Kansas, they overtook Captain Bonneville, who had obtained a leave of absence from the army and was on a trapping and trading expedition. Early in June they reached the forks of the Platte River, where they came across the first buffalo, on which they were to depend for food for the greater part of their journey.

The camps were always made in the form of a hollow square, of which the stream formed one side. The horses were hobbled, turned loose, and just before dusk Mr. Sublette would call out, "Ketch up, ketch up," and the horses would be brought in and tied to stakes. They were guarded all night.

At daybreak Mr. Sublette would call out,

"Turn out, turn out," and the horses were allowed to graze until the men had eaten breakfast, after which the horses were caught, saddled, the packs put on, and those who were ready first formed the head of the line. They crossed the Laramie River at about where Fort Laramie was later built. They crossed the Rocky Mountains by the South Pass.

On the Fourth of July they struck the headwaters of the Columbia, at least, of one branch of the Columbia. They camped at Pierre's Hole to await the arrival of the mountain men and trappers. Here were gathered Sublette's trappers, also some traders and trappers of the American Fur Company and also two large companies of Nez Perce and Flathead Indians. They had brought with them about 600 horses and a large amount of furs to trade. Sublette and his party purchased a number of strong, fat Indian ponies, the price being a blanket and a knife for each pony. There were about 200 white men and several times that number of Indians who spent two weeks together at Pierre's Hole. Ball was struck with the fact that the horses they had bought from the Indians would get away and join the Indian herd of horses, but each time the Indians would catch the horses they had sold and return them to the white men.

Captain Nathaniel Wyeth, who was one of the first settlers on Sauvies Island, came with William Sublette across the plains.

Sublette took back to St. Louis with him 70 large packhorse loads of beaver, worth about $50,000 in the New York market. Most of Mr. Wyeth's party, who had never before been far from Boston, decided to return to Boston, so he was left with the twelve men of his original party. Milton Sublette, with a party of trappers, half-breeds and Indians, planned to trap far to the westward, so Wyeth, Ball and their party joined them.

Shortly after they had started, Antoine, a half-breed with the Sublette Party, went out to meet a party of Blackfeet. Antoine's father had been killed by the Blackfeet, so he watched his chance, and while talking to the Blackfoot chief he killed him and rode back full speed to he camp.

The Blackfeet attacked Sublette's party and in the course of the fight six white trappers and a number of friendly Indians were killed while others were wounded. They camped near where Fort Hall was later built. Sixteen free trappers in the party decided to trap down the Humboldt River, while Frapp and the other trappers in Sublette's party turned back.

Wyeth, with John Ball and the ten other members of the Wyeth party, turned northward, leaving Milton Sublette on August 28. They were heading for the Lewis River, which they planned to follow to the junction of the Columbia. Meeting a band of Shoshone Indians, they traded awls and knives for salmon. One of the Indians made a map with his finger in the sand, indicating trails and rivers and showing the exact location of Walla Walla. When they came out of the Blue Mountains they were out of food, so they killed one of the thin old horses to eat. Wyeth with four of the men, mounted on the best horses, started for Walla Walla, while the rest of the party came on more slowly. They arrived at Fort Walla Walla, which at that time consisted of a stockade of upright timbers about 15 feet high.

At Fort Walla Walla they secured a boat and hired two Canadians to take them down the Columbia to Fort Vancouver. Some friendly Indians on the banks of the Columbia gave them a young horse which they killed and ate for supper. At The Dalles they found the Indians mourning over the death of many of their people from fever. They stopped overnight at the Hudson's Bay sawmill, which was run by a member of the Astor party.

The following day, on October 29, they arrived at Fort Vancouver. Wyeth, Ball and the rest

of the party were received in the most hospitable
manner by Dr. McLoughlin and invited to make Fort
Vancouver their home. Some of the party, including Ball, paddled down the Columbia to Fort Astoria. Here Ball was particularly struck with the
tremendous height and size of the trees. From
Astoria he went to Clatsop Point, where he
reached the broad Pacific, the end of his journey.

The members of Nathaniel Wyeth's party had
lived on meat almost exclusively for many months
and when they reached Vancouver and were given
green vegetables, one of the men ate so heartily
that he took the colic and died before morning.
Wyeth and Ball were invited by Dr. John McLoughlin to eat at his table and to occupy rooms in
the fort.

In speaking of his reception at Fort Vancouver,
Ball says: "We were received at the fort as
guests, without talk of pay. Not liking to live
gratis, I asked the doctor, as he was called,
being a physician, for some employment. He told
me I was a guest. He did not expect to set me to
work, but after further urging he said, if I were
willing, he would like to have me teach his son
and other boys about the fort. I, of course,
gladly accepted the offer, so he sent the boys to
my room to be instructed.

"They were all half-breed boys, of course,
for there was not then a white woman in Oregon.
The doctor's wife was a Chippewa from Lake Superior. Then there was a Mrs. Douglas, a
half-breed woman from Hudson Bay. I found the
boys docile and attentive and they made good
progress, for they are precocious. The old doctor
used to come in to see the school and seemed much
pleased and well satisfied. He said, 'Ball, anyway, you have the reputation of teaching the
first academy in Oregon.'

"The gentlemen in the fort were pleasant and
intelligent, a circle of a dozen or more usually

at the well provided table, where there was much formality. They consisted of partners, clerks, captains of vessels and the like. Men waited on the table and probably cooked. We saw nothing or little of their women except on horseback rides, at which they excel.

"The boundary had not then been settled beyond the mountains and the papers claimed that the Columbia River would be the boundary and they called the country south of the river the Ameri-

---

"They were all half-breed boys, of course, for there was not then a white woman in Oregon."

---

can side. The fur trade was their business. If an American vessel came to the river or onto the coast for trade, they would at once bid up on furs to a ruinous price, ten times their usual tariff.

"They got a bull and seven or six cows from California. In seven years they had about 400 cattle. They had turned the prairies into wheat fields and had much beyond their wants and they made good flour. Salmon was so abundant that men would throw it away to get imported salt beef, for they had not killed any of their own raising. The wheat was green all winter. There was no snow. The summers are so cool that harvest did not come till the last of July or the first of August.

"Next spring Wyeth and two of his men returned home across the mountains. The other members of Wyeth's party went into the employ of the Hudson's Bay Company.

"I wrote to my friends in New Hampshire and

New York, sending the letters by the Hudson Express that leaves Fort Vancouver in March, goes up north by the main branch of the Columbia to about 52 degrees of latitude, thence by men on snowshoes over the mountains, for about two weeks, to where they take bark canoes on the La-Bashe, that flows into the Arctic Ocean. Descending that a distance, they make a short portage to Fort Edmonton and to the Saskatchewan and down that to Lake Winnipeg and by its outlet to Nelson, to Hudson Bay, thence to Montreal, from which place my letters were sent to my friends, so that they got them in September.

"Though urged by Dr. McLoughlin to continue the school, I determined to go to farming, believing that others would come soon to settle. When I learned that some of the company's men had turned farmers and settled on the Willamette River, I went there to see the country, and I found it very inviting. When the doctor found I was bent on going to farming, he kindly told me he would lend me farming utensils, seed for sowing, and as many horses as I chose to break in for a team. I took seeds and implements by boat, getting help up the Willamette to the Falls, where Oregon City now is, passing the site where Portland stands.

"I at first stopped at one of the settlers, with two wives. His name is J. B. Desports. Yes, he had two wives, seven children, and cats and dogs numberless. I caught from the prairie a span of horses only used to the saddle. I made a harness for them and put them to work. I stuffed some deerskin, sewed in due form, for collars, fitted crooked oak limbs around the collars for hames, tied top and bottom with elkskin strings. To these I tied straps of hide for tugs, which I tied to the end of the stick for a whiffletree, to the center of which I tied a drag made from the crotch of a tree. On this crude contrivance I drew out logs for a cabin, which, when I had laid up and put up rafters, I covered with bark peeled from cedar trees. The bark covering for my roof was secured by poles tied with strings made of willow withes. From split plank I made a bedstead and a table, and so I dwelt in a house of fir and cedar. With the aid of my neighbors and their teams I broke a large field of rich prairie land and closed the same with fencing and sowed and planted my farm. My farm abutted for half a mile on the river.

"My family consisted, for a part of the time, of Mr. Sinclair, one of my mountain companions, and a young wild native, to catch my horses. I got meal from the fort to make my bread. My meat was venison or salmon from the falls. I found it a lonely life and, not seeing when it was likely to be less so, no emigrants arriving. I began to think I might as well leave.

"The Willamette Valley is a fine country, being a valley watered by a stream of that name. The valley is 50 miles wide by 150 miles long, with the Coast Range on the west and the towering Cascade Range on the east, crowned by Mount Hood, which, on the bright summer days, is ever in sight. I was near the river, handy for a bath, and but a short distance from my house was a fine, cool spring, from which I got my water.

"The Company being about to send a vessel to the Bay of San Francisco and the Sandwich Islands, I exchanged my crop for a passage on their boat. On the 20th of September, 1833, I quit my home on the Willamette, with something of regret. When I got down to the Falls I asked the chief of the band for two of his men to row me to the fort, but he told me that all his men were either sick or dead, so Mr. Sinclair and I had to wearily paddle our own canoe.

"After some delay at Fort Vancouver, the ship Dryad made sail down the Columbia, with Mr. Douglas, a botanist, Also Mr. Finlayson, myself, Mr. Sinclair, and two others of Nathaniel Wyeth's party. We stopped at Astoria, or Fort George as they call it, for some time. On October 18, we sailed from Astoria, and on November 4 entered what is now known as the Golden Gate. A mile or two beyond and back from the bay was a mission called Dolores Mission, consisting of adobe buildings. On the opposite side of the bay were some farms."

From the Golden Gate, Mr. Ball went to the Sandwich Islands, where he took passage on the whaling ship Nautilus, which was bound for New Bedford. They left on January 6, 1834. They stopped at the Society Islands, made the trip around the Horn and put in at Rio de Janeiro, where Mr. Ball secured a position as a clerk on board the man-of-war Boxer, which mounted ten guns and was commanded by Lieutenant Farragut, who later became Commodore. A day or two later the Boxer sailed for the United States and 37 days later it came to anchor in Hampton Roads.

Returning to New York, Mr. Ball was restless, so, shortly thereafter, he went to Detroit, where he was shortly thereafter nominated and elected as representative to the legislature. He resumed his practice of law at Grand Rapids, devoting a good deal of his time to land matters. Mr. Ball died on February 3, 1884.

Oregon Journal
April 11 & 13, 1928

DR. MARCUS WHITMAN

Pathfinder and Patriot

Dr. Marcus Whitman was born at Rushville, New York, September 4, 1802. His father, Beza Whitman, was born at Goshen, Massachusetts. In 1799 he moved to Hopewell and from there to Gorham, later known as Rushville, where he ran a hotel. He died on April 6, 1810. Mordecai Lincoln, the son of Samuel Lincoln, who came from Norfolk County, England, in 1637, settled in Salem, Massachusetts, and married a granddaughter of John Whitman, who settled in Weymouth, Massachusetts, in 1638. Mordecai Lincoln was the great-great-grandfather of President Lincoln.

Dr. Whitman's father was a tanner and currier. Shortly after his father's death, when Marcus Whitman was eight years old, his grandfather, Deacon Samuel Whitman, who lived at Plainfield, Massachusetts, took Marcus to his home. He did not see his mother again for four years, and then only for a brief visit. At Plainfield he studied Latin under the Reverend Moses Hallock. Later the Reverend David Page was his instructor. He wanted to become a minister, but his brothers, Augustus, Henry and Samuel, objected so strenuously that he decided to become a doctor. He studied medicine for three years under Dr. Ira Bryant of Rushville, receiving his diploma in 1824. This same year he joined the Congregational Church at Rushville. Nine years later he joined the Presbyterian Church, in which he became a ruling elder.

On February 2, 1836, he received his letter of dismissal from the Presbyterian Church at Wheeler to "where the providence of God may cast his lot". His lot was cast with the Mission Church of Oregon, which he joined in 1838.

From 1824 to 1828 he practiced medicine in Canada. His brother Henry owned a sawmill and needed help, so Dr. Whitman upon returning from Canada helped operate his brother's sawmill, near Potter's Center. Being disappointed in his desire to study for the ministry, he wrote to the American Board of Commissioners for Foreign Missions at Boston, under date of June 3, 1834, asking to be sent to a mission field among the Indians, saying: "I am willing to go to any field of usefulness, at the direction of the American Board. I will cooperate as physician, teacher, or agriculturist, so far as I am able."

The Mission Board had been so much interested in the Oregon Country that they had sent a missionary from the Sandwich Islands to visit Oregon and report on the prospects for missionary work among the Indians. His report was favorable. Meanwhile, the Reverend Samuel Parker at Middlefield, Massachusetts, wrote to the American Board of Commissioners for Foreign Missions offering to go as a missionary to the Indians of Oregon.

Mr. Parker was born at Ashfield, Massachusetts, April 23, 1779, and was the son of Elisha and Thankful Marchant Parker. His great-grandfather was a freeman of Barnstable, Massachusetts, in 1634. Samuel Parker graduated at Williams College in 1836. After teaching school for a year at Brattleboro, Vermont, he studied theology under the Reverend Theophilus Packard of Shelburn, Massachusetts. For a while he served as home missionary, after which he attended Andover

Theological Seminary, being a graduate of the first class at Andover. He became financial agent of Auburn Theological Seminary, in which position he served for 15 years. The mission board accepted his services, but when Mr. Parker reached St. Louis he found he had missed the annual fur caravan that left for the Rocky Mountains in the spring of 1834. He returned to New York and spent the winter lecturing on Oregon.

"I am willing to go to any field of usefulness, at the direction of the American Board. I will cooperate as physician, teacher, or agriculturist, so far as I am able."

He interested Dr. Whitman, who was accepted by the board and commissioned to go with Mr. Parker, whom he joined in St. Louis in April, 1835. They left St. Louis on April 8, going by steamer to Liberty, Missouri, where they joined the caravan of the American Fur Company. When they reached the fur traders' rendezvous on Green River on August 18, Jim Bridger, learning that Marcus Whitman was a doctor, asked him to extract an arrowhead three inches long that had been shot into his back three years before, in a skirmish with the Blackfoot Indians. This was before the days of anesthetics, but the fur traders and trappers had learned stoicism from the Indians, so, no matter how serious the operation, they rarely showed any indications of pain. After successfully operating on Jim Bridger, Dr. Whitman then extracted an arrowhead that had been buried for several years in the shoulder of one

of the other trappers. Having proved his skill
his services were in frequent demand thereafter.

In those days people knew nothing about
germs, and apparently suffered very little from
them. In talking with an old pioneer some years
ago, he told me of a surgical operation that had
taken place in the wagon train of which he was a
member. A herd of buffalo had run through the
wagon train, causing the oxen to stampede. One of
the men was thrown from the front seat of his
wagon. The heavily loaded wagon passed over him,
breaking his leg just above the knee. One of the
members of the wagon train who had been a butcher
volunteered to cut his leg off. The man with the
broken leg was placed on the ground. His arms and
legs were spread out, and three men were detailed
to sit on him, one on each arm and one on his
uninjured leg. A fire of sagebrush was built in
which the endgate rod of his wagon was heated
until it was cherry red. The butcher cut off his
leg, sawed the bone off with a meat saw, seared
the bleeding arteries with the redhot endgate
rod, and with a sack needle and some twine sewed
the flesh up so that the bone wouldn't project.
Six weeks later they made some crude crutches for
him and before they reached Oregon he was hob-
bling around very successfully on a peg leg.

(From the fur rendezvous) Mr. Parker sent
Dr. Whitman back to New York to enlist additional
workers for the mission field, while he himself
accompanied the Nez Perce Indians who were going
down the Columbia River. He decided to visit Fort
Vancouver to investigate the mission field. After
spending the winter at Fort Vancouver, Mr. Parker
returned to New York State and did not see his
associate, Dr. Whitman, again until Dr. Whitman
came back from the Oregon Country to visit New
York in 1843.

Dr. Whitman took with him on his trip east,
two Indian boys, promising to return them alive

and unharmed to their tribe, agreeing to allow the Indians to kill him if he failed to do so. He reached St. Louis in November and went home to Rushville, New York, arriving late one Saturday night. Next morning he walked with his two Indian boys into the church of which he had been an elder, creating tremendous interest, for his friends supposed that he was in the Oregon Country. The two Indian boys attended school that winter and accompanied Dr. Whitman back to Oregon next spring.

Dr. Whitman spent the winter traveling and lecturing on Oregon in the various churches and schoolhouses. He secured as additional missionaries the Reverend H. H. Spalding and his wife, who had been appointed to the Osage Indian Mission, and also William H. Gray of Utica, New York. And, by the way, Dr. W. H. Gray's daughter, Mrs. Jacob Kamm, at the age of 90, is still a resident of Portland. The missionary board told Dr. Whitman it would be expedient for him to go as a married man rather than a single man as missionary to the Indians.

At Angelica, New York, Dr. Whitman met Narcissa Prentiss, who was born at Prattsburg, New York, March 14, 1808. She was the daughter of Judge Stephen Prentiss, who was a descendant of Henry Prentiss, who had come to Cambridge, Massachusetts, in 1637. Narcissa was the third of a family of nine children. She was a member of the Congregational Church, having united with the church when she was 11 years old. Narcissa Prentiss was educated at Miss Willard's seminary at Troy, New York, and later attended Franklin Academy. After graduating from Franklin Academy, she and her sister Abigail established a school for infants at Bath. Before meeting Dr. Whitman, she had written to the board of missions asking to be sent as a missionary to the Indians. In her letter to the board she said, "Feeling it more my privilege than duty, to labor for the conversion of the heathen, I respectfully submit myself to your direction."

Dr. Whitman and Narcissa Prentiss were married in the church at Angelica in February, 1836, shortly before their departure for the rendezvous of the fur traders on the Missouri River. The wedding ceremony was performed by the Reverend Everett Hull. From Angelica Dr. Whitman and his bride went by sleigh for a part of the journey and thence by stage to Pittsburgh, where they took a steamer for St. Louis.

At Cincinnati they were joined by the Reverend H. H. Spalding and his wife. Mr. Spalding was born at Prattsburg, New York, November 26, 1803. He received little or no education until he was 21, at which time he went ot Franklin Academy, where he worked for his board. He was converted when he was 22. He graduated from Western Reserve College, in Ohio, at the age of 30. On October 12, 1833, he married Eliza Hart of Trenton, New York, who was born in Berlin, Connecticut on July 11, 1807. At the age of 30, Mr. Spalding entered Lane Theological Seminary at Cincinnati, and in August, 1835, was ordained by the Bath Presbytery, New York. After going to the Oregon Country, Mr. and Mrs. Spalding worked with the Nez Perce Indians at Lapwai. The first printing ever done in the Oregon Country was the printing of booklets in the Flathead, Nez Perce, and Spokane languages, at Lapwai, in the spring of 1839. After the Whitman Massacre, Mr. and Mrs. Spalding moved to the Willamette Valley, where they lived for many years. Mrs. Spalding died at Calapooya on January 7, 1851, and in May, 1853, Mr. Spalding married Rachel I. Smith, who was born at Boston on January 31, 1808. Mr. Spalding died at Lapwai, Idaho, on August 3, 1874.

When Dr. and Mrs. Whitman and Mr. and Mrs. Spalding reached St. Louis they visited the officials of the American Fur Company, who promised their protection to them in crossing the plains. At Liberty Landing they were joined by W. H. Gray. Mr. Spalding, with two wagons and the horses and cattle, drove from Liberty Landing to Council Bluffs, leaving Dr. Whitman with his wife and Mrs. Spalding and the goods to come up the Missouri on the boat of the American Fur Company. The trappers did not want to be burdened with a missionary party, so they did not stop at Liberty Landing but continued on up the river to Council Bluffs. When the missionaries reached Council Bluffs they found that the trappers had gone on. Dr. Whitman, in charge of the four-horse wagon; Mr. Spalding, driving the two-horse wagon, and W. H. Gray, with the two Indian boys on horseback, hurried on and late in May overtook the fur trappers on Loup Fork. From here they traveled in company to Fort Laramie.

No wheeled vehicle had traveled beyond Fort Laramie, but Dr. Whitman believed that a wagon could be driven through to the Columbia River. The fur company loaned Dr. Whitman one of their two-wheeled carts and he also took his own light wagon along. The first day the cart was upset twice and the wagon once. Two of the trappers were detailed to help Dr. Whitman, and he went ahead and broke the road across the sagebrush, a road that later became the Great Medicine Trail of the whites--the road to Oregon.

Dr. Whitman had purchased for the trip across the plains two wagons, eight mules, 12 horses, and 16 cows, as well as blacksmith tools, a plow, seeds and other equipment to start his mission. Although urged by the others to abandon his wagon and the cart, he did not want to leave the plow and other equipment behind, so, selecting the best road possible, he continued to go forward with the wagons. After crossing the Laramie River the country was very much broken, making it difficult to drive. They crossed the Platte River near the present town of Casper,

Wyoming.

Mrs. Whitman and Mrs. Spalding were the first women to make the trip overland to Oregon. They broke the trail across the sagebrush for the road followed by thousands a few years later, whose slow plodding oxen and prairie schooners made the Old Oregon Trail.

Dr. Whitman's party followed the Sweetwater up to Independence Rock where they had a very narrow escape from losing their stock and possibly their lives. The caravan was strung out about two miles in length. From behind a nearby hill a herd of buffalo suddenly emerged and charged in a lumbering gallop toward the train. Instantly the trappers dashed at the head of the herd, shooting down the leading buffalo and trying to turn the herd. Soon the bulls leading the herd of buffalo and the stock of the caravan were mingled in hopeless confusion. Finally the trappers turned the bulk of the herd, which swept on to one side, while other buffaloes broke through the caravan.

On July 4 they entered South Pass. An express was sent forward to the rendezvous at Green River and that evening a group of Nez Perce and Flathead Indians, after a hard ride, arrived in camp to welcome the missionaries. At the head of the delegation of the Nez Perces were Tak-ken-sui-i-tas, or, to put his name in English, Rotten Belly, and Is-hol-hol-hoats-hoats, the Indian term for lawyer. They brought with them a letter from the Reverend Samuel Parker in which he spoke of the kind reception the Indians had given him the year before. The Indians were as much delighted to meet the Nez Perce boys that Dr. Whitman had taken with him as the boys were to return to their people.

Two days later they reached the rendezvous on Green River, where they found more than 2000 Indians and trappers assembled. A large delegation of Nez Perce Indians had journeyed to the rendezvous to welcome Dr. Whitman and his fellow missionaries. They found here also Nathaniel J. Wyeth, who had just sold Fort Hall to the Hudson's Bay Company and was on his way east. They also met John McLeod and Tom McKay, the latter the stepson of Dr. McLoughlin. Among the Indians who had come there to trade were Snakes, Bannocks, Flatheads, Cayuses and Nez Perces.

The two white women created a great sensation--not only among the Indians, but among the four or five hundred trappers and mountain men, many of whom had not seen a white woman for years. On the third day after their arrival the Indians, in honor of the mssionaries, gave a grand review. The Blackfoot Indians, stripped to the buff and fantastically painted, mounted on their horses which were also as well decorated with paint as their owners, led the parade. They were followed by the Nez Perces, decked in all the finery of beaded buckskin, eagle feathers, elk teeth, bear's claws and wampum. They engaged in a sham fight. Inasmuch as representatives of 15 tribes were at the rendezvous it took several days for each tribe to exhibit their war tactics and their dances and to express their welcome.

Jim Bridger was delighted to greet Dr. Whitman again and promised to send his half-daughter, Mary Ann, to Dr. Whitman's mission as soon as it should be started, which promise he later kept. Tom McKay and John McLeod volunteered to take the missionaries under their wing and help them for the rest of the journey.

Practically everyone advised Dr. Whitman to leave his wagon at Green River, as they felt it would be impossible to take the wagon through the Bear River Mountains. The Indians thought it could be done. Tom McKay said if Dr. Whitman wanted to try it he would go ahead and select the easiest grades and help him in every way possible. On the advice of Tom McKay the wagon was cut down into a two-wheeled cart, the extra wheels and the axletree being carried along on the cart. Everything was lashed on the cart securely, for it was realized that it would undoubtedly tip over frequently, which it did. In fact, in crossing the Snake River, both the cart and the mules had a narrow escape from being lost entirely. Tom McKay swam out to where they were struggling in the swift water, got his rope around the neck of one of his mules and, telling two of his men to swim their horses to the rear of the cart, they steadied it and finally got it ashore. Dr. Whitman, when the cart overturned, was caught in the cart and was rescued from drowning by Tom McKay.

At Fort Boise Dr. Whitman was told that it would be impossible to take the cart farther, as the trail over the mountains in many places was a narrow ledge along the edge of the precipice, and that if he took the cart it would have to be taken to pieces and carried over the mountains on the backs of mules. Dr. Whitman decided to leave the wagon at Fort Boise, and, after he had located his mission, to come back and get it.

Mrs. Spalding, eating buffalo meat pretty steadily, had become sick and refused to eat. The Indians brought biscuits made of dried camas roots, which she was able to eat, and also brought her salmon, and Captain Drips found a cupful of dried apples, which she greatly enjoyed. Mrs. Spalding had had several narrow escapes while crossing the plains. In the Bear River Valley a mule team her husband was driving became frightened and he was unable to stop them. They ran into Mrs. Spalding's horse, knocking it down and mules and cart ran pell-mell over Mrs. Spalding and her horse. Both Mrs. Spalding and the horse were somewhat indignant, but neither of them was hurt. The day after they left Fort Hall her horse stepped into a wasps' next and bucked Mrs. Spalding off and her foot caught in the stirrup. Thomas McKay, who was always on hand in an emergency, rescued her from this predicament. She also had a rather narrow escape in fording the Snake River.

They arrived at Fort Walla Walla, a Hudson's Bay post, on September 2. Pierre C. Pambrun, the Hudson's Bay factor at the post, gave them a royal welcome. In place of pemmican and the usual pounded buffalo meat he served them venison, brant, potatoes, corn, melons and bread. He furnished them boats and Indian oarsmen, who took them down to Fort Vancouver. Dr. McLoughlin, always hospitable, did everything in his power to make their stay with him pleasant. Dr. McLoughlin invited them to make Fort Vancouver their home as long as they desired.

After staying at Fort Vancouver two weeks, Dr. Whitman, Mr. Spalding and W. H. Gray started up the Columbia River, accompanied Pierre Pambrun, to look for a site for their mission. Dr. Whitman and Mr. Spalding left their wives at Fort Vancouver. Dr. Whitman and Mr. Gray chose The Dalles as a site for one of their two missions, but Mr. Spalding objected so violently that they yielded to his wish to locate the missions farther inland. Later the Methodists established a mission at The Dalles and when they gave up their work among the Indians they sold their mission property at The Dalles to Dr. Whitman for $600.

Dr. McLoughlin forwarded the orders of Dr. Whitman and Mr. Spalding for all goods needed, to England, accepting drafts on the American Board of Missions and when the goods arrived at Vancouver, Dr. McLoughlin saw that they were sent up to the missions at Lapwai and Waiilatpu, and at very little expense.

Dr. Whitman chose his station at the mouth of Mill Creek, about six miles from where the city of Walla Walla was later built. He adopted the Indian name for the place, Wai-i-lat-pu, meaning, "the place where the rye grass grows".

While at Fort Vancouver, Mrs. Whitman went on board the Hudson's Bay Company's vessel, the Neriade. This was the first ship Mrs. Whitman had ever seen. Dr. Whitman saw to it that Mrs. Whitman and Mrs. Spalding were furnished gentle horses, and they spent much of their time riding over the country. On September 14, Mrs. Whitman recorded in her journal:

"We rode 15 miles this afternoon. We visited the barns and stock. They estimate their wheat crop at 4000 bushels this year, peas the same, oats and barley between 1500 and 1700 bushels each. The potato and turnip fields are large and fine. Their cattle are numerous and they have swine in abundance, also sheep and goats. We find hens, turkeys and pigeons, but no geese.

"You will ask what kind of beds they have here. The bedstead is in the form of a bunk with a board bottom, upon which are laid about a dozen Indian blankets. These, with a pair of pillows covered with calico cases, constituted our beds. There are several feather beds here, made from the feathers of wild ducks, geese, and cranes. There is nothing here suitable for ticking; the only material is brown linen sheeting. The Indian ladies make theirs of deerskin. Could we obtain a pair of geese from any quarter, I could think much of them.

"Every day we have something new to see. We went to the stores and found them filled above and below with the cargo of two ships, all in unbroken bales. They are chiefly Indian goods and will be sent away this fall to the several different posts of the company in the ship Neriade. We have found here every article for comfort and durability that we need. Visited the dairy, where we found butter and cheese in abundance. We saw an improvement in the manner of raising cream. Their pans are large but shallow, flaring a little and are made of wood, lined with tin. In the center of the pan is a hole with a long plug. When the cream has risen they place the pan over a tub, removing the plug so the milk runs off, leaving only the cream in the pan. They milk between 50 and 60 cows. On visiting the mill we find it goes by horsepower and has a wire bolt. This seemed a hard way of getting bread, but better so than no bread or to grind by hand. The company have a mill at Colville that goes by water.

"It is five days' ride from Walla Walla, from whence we expect to obtain our flour, potatoes, and pork. Dr. McLoughlin promises to loan us enough to make a beginning. All the return he asks is that we supply other settlers in the same way. He appears desirous to afford us every facility in his power. No person could have received a more hearty welcome or be treated with greater kindness than we have been since our arrival."

On September 18, Mrs. Whitman records in her journal:

"Mr. Beaver held two services in a room in Dr. McLoughlin's barn today. Enjoyed the privilege much. The most of the gentlemen of the fort are Scotch Presbyterians. The great mass of the laborers are Roman Catholics, who have three services during the Sabbath, one of which is at this house, at which Dr. McLoughlin officiates in French. He translates a sermon or a tract, reads a chapter in the Bible, and a prayer. The singing in Mr. Beaver's Episcopal Church is done by the children, some of their tunes having been taught them by Reverend Samuel Parker, and others by Mr. Cyrus Shepherd of the Methodist Mission.

"There is such a variety of eatables here I know not where to begin. For breakfast we have coffee or cocoa, salt salmon and roast duck, with potatoes and bread and butter. For dinner we are treated to a dish of soup, which is very good. All kinds of vegetables are taken, chopped fine and, with rice, boiled to a soup. Tomatoes are a prominent ingredient and usually some fowl meat--duck or other kind. After our soup dishes are removed comes a variety of meats. After selecting what we care for we change plates and try another if we choose, so with every new dish we have a clean plate. Roast duck is our every-day dish. Boiled pork, tripe, trotters, fresh salmon, sturgeon--yea, all articles too numerous to mention. When they are set aside, a pudding or an apple pie is introduced, after which a water or muskmelon make their appearance. Last of all cheese, bread, or biscuits and butter are produced.

"I sing about an hour every evening with the children, teaching them new tunes, at the request of Dr. McLoughlin. The Montreal Express came this afternoon and a general time of rejoicing it is to everyone, bringing news from distant friends."

After selecting a site for what has always been known as the Whitman Mission, Dr. Whitman, Reverend Spalding, and W. H. Gray built a house to serve as a residence and schoolhouse for Dr. and Mrs. Whitman. Leaving Mr. Gray in charge, Dr. Whitman and the Reverend Spalding went to the country of the Nez Perces to select a station there. Leaving Reverend Spalding with the Nez Perce Indians, Dr. Whitman returned to Vancouver, where he purchased from the Hudson's Bay Company's store, clothing, blankets, nails and hardware for building; Indian trade goods, hoes, rakes and spades, medicines and other material for his mission.

The Nez Perce Indians furnished Reverend and Mrs. Spalding a large lodge made of tanned buffalo hides, in which they lived until their house was built. They moved into it the day before Christmas. Mrs. Whitman moved into the house at the Wai-i-lat-pu mission on December 10. Dr. Whitman and Mr. Gray had built a house with a good chimney and fire place, but as yet it had no doors or windows. Blankets were used until doors and windows could be made. Mrs. Whitman's nearest white neighbors were the Spaldings, who were 90 miles distant. Her next nearest white neighbors were at Fort Vancouver and Reverend Jason Lee, Daniel Lee, P. L. Edwards and Cyrus Shepherd at the Methodist mission in the Willamette Valley, about 350 miles distant.

The Nez Perce Indians, where Reverend Spalding had his mission, were among the most intelligent, the most numerous and were undoubtedly the strongest and most friendly Indians in the Pacific Northwest. There were about 2500 Nez Perce Indians when the Reverend Spalding started his mission there in 1836. The Cayuse Indians, where Dr. Whitman had his mission, had intermarried among the Nez Perce Indians and most of them understood the Nez Perce language. They were one of the wealthiest tribes, for their numbers, in the west. Though small in number, consisting of not over 300 in all, they had great influence with the other tribes.

A letter from Dr. Whitman, written in September, 1843, gives a good picture of the life at the Whitman Mission. In speaking of his charges, the Cayuse Indians, he says:

"Their migrations are much on the following order: The spring return is the most general and uniform. During this period the congregations on Sabbath are from 200 to 400 and from 20 to 50 on weekday evenings. Planting commences about the middle of April, which is also the period for commencing the rausch harvest. To obtain this farinaceous root, known to the travelers and traders as the biscuit root, they disperse along the streams coming out of the Blue Mountains. Some of these streams are not more than ten to 15 miles from the station, while others are 30 or 40. This root forms the great staple of native food and will be likely to continue such for a long time. From six to eight weeks are spent in gathering, drying, and depositing this root. During this time, and from the 10th to the 15th of May, the salmon arrive and some fruits are ripe, which receive their share of attention. At this season all the smaller tributaries of the Columbia are barred by a wicker-work of willows, for taking salmon. The skill of the natives is favorably displayed in this simple contrivance and their toil is amply repaid by the quantity taken. While thus occupied, they visit the mission station to attend to the cultivation of their crops.

"The latter part of June is the usual period for buffalo hunters to set out on their expedition. A migration of from 40 to 60 miles takes them across the Blue Mountains into the Grand Ronde. The river of the Grand Ronde is well supplied with fish and the mountains abound with bear and deer. The wheat harvest, which begins the latter part of July, and the care of their other crops, bring many to the station, who remain till the first of October or until the potato harvest is past. During this period there are more in the neighborhood of the station than at any other period except the spring. Our congregation averages from 50 to 200. During this period their attention is divided between their crops and herds, hunting, fishing, and preparing dried fruit. Soon after the potatoes are secured they disperse to their winter quarters. From 50 to 60 remain during the winter.

"Their belief is that the present race of beasts, birds, reptiles and fish were men who inhabited the globe before the present race. Though doomed to their present state, their language is still retained, and these beasts, birds, reptiles and fish have the power to convey this language to those people into whom they see fit to pass. To obtain this boon, boys are required to leave the lodge and repair to the mountains alone and there to stay for several days without food, in order to be addressed by some of these supernatural agencies. Some return without any assurance of the kind. Others believe themselves to be addressed and are free to communicate what was said to them, while others profess great secrecy and claim great reverence on account of their mysterious possession. At these times they profess to be told what is to be their future character and in what way they may secure honor, wealth and long life--how they will be invulnerable and, if wounded, by what means they will be healed. The surgical knowledge imparted generally consists in directions how to cast off the extravasated blood and then to sit in a stream of water and sing, according to certain rules. At these times they believe that one person becomes possessed of power to shoot another with an invisible influence or arrow, so that disease and death will follow. This is the foundation of a system of sorcery, as seen in the so-called medicine men. Most of their efforts to cure the sick consist in obtaining one medicine man to counteract another who is supposed to have caused the sickness.

"The sorcerer employed to cure the sick calls to his aid a number of persons who sing and beat upon sticks, making a terrific noise, while he himself sings, talks, and practices sundry contortions, using at the same time incoherent expressions, supposed to be the language of the former race of men as delivered to him by beast, bird, reptile or fish, which is helping him in his conjurations. When he sees a prospective death he often points out someone who he says is causing the sickness and declares the other to be possessed by a more powerful agent than himself, so that he cannot overcome him. Should death occur, they watch the dying person to see if any expression of his fastens suspicion upon the person named. All are careful to remember if any hard words had passed, or any cause whatever confirms the supposition. Very often, in cases of this kind, nothing can save the conjuror. The number and horror of such deaths that have come under my observation have been very great.

"In the same way, individuals arrogate to themselves power over the wind, the clouds, the rain, the snow--in short, all or every desirable object is sought for from this source. Some of the Indians are losing their confidence in such things, while others are yet strong in the belief of their reality.

"A young man shot himself through the body last July in order to convince his countrymen of the strength of his supernatural protecting agent. The ball entered the abdomen a little to the right and below the umbilicus and came out by an oblique line near the spine on the same side. This occurred 60 miles from my house at Grand Ronde. The third day after he encamped near me for the night. I saw him and examined his wound in the morning. He was walking about and making preparations to depart. Soon he rode off on horseback. This was the second trial of his strength, he having shot himself through in much the same way two years before. He will now be regarded as a strong mystery or medicine man."

On March 4, 1837, which was Mrs. Whitman's 29 birthday, their daughter, Alice C. Whitman, was born. Alice was baptized in November, 1837, at the same time Eliza Spalding was baptized. On Sunday, June 23, 1839, when little Alice Clarissa was about two years and three months old, she took a cup from the table and went down to the river to get a drink. She fell into the water and was drowned.

In 1838 Mrs. Whitman copied a schoolbook, translating into the Nez Perce language, to be sent to Honolulu to be printed on the mission press there, but the following year E. O. Hall and his wife came out from Honolulu with a press and type to print books in the Nez Perce and Spokane languages. The press was set up at Lapwai among the Nez Perce. The first books to be printed in the Oregon Country were issued from this press. The first book consisted of 20 pages and was in the nature of a primer. The next book consisted of 52 pages, of which 800 copies were printed. In 1840 a book of eight pages of laws was printed, probably the first law book to be printed on the Pacific Coast. A translation of the book of Matthew, a hymn book and Nez Perce and English vocabulary were also issued. In 1842, Messrs. Walker and Eells, who were stationed in what is now the state of Washington, prepared a 61-page book in the Spokane language, which was printed on the press at Lapwai. This old press is now in the rooms of the Oregon Historical Society in Portland.

It was two years and four months after Mrs. Whitman left home before she received the first letter from home. On September 25, 1838, Mrs. Whitman wrote to her sister:

"When the contemplated railroad over the Isthmus of Darien shall have been opened, which is expected to take place within two or three years, I hope communications shall be more frequent than they are at the present time."

In the spring of 1837 W. H. Gray went east to obtain additional missionaries. He returned in 1838 with his bride, and also with the Reverend A. B. Smith, Elkanah Walker and Cushing Eells and their wives and Cornelius Rogers, an unmarried man. So much friction developed between Mr. Gray and Reverend Spalding and they became so critical of Dr. Whitman that he decided to resign and allow them to carry on the mission work. The death of his little daughter caused him to forgive his fellow laborers for their needless and frequent harsh criticism, and he went on with the work.

In the fall of 1838, Vicar General F. N.

Blanchet and Reverend M. Demers came to Fort Walla Walla, celebrated a mass, and baptized three converts. Pierre Pambrun, who was in charge of Fort Walla Walla, was killed by a horse in 1841 and he was succeeded by Archibald McKinley, a Scotch Presbyterian.

In the early 1840s, practically everyone who came to the Oregon Country stopped at the Whitman Mission. Among others were T. J. Farnham, who, in his book, "Travels Across the Great Western Prairies, the Anahoac and Rocky Mountains", gives a graphic picture of life at the mission in the fall of 1839. He describes his meeting with Dr. Whitman, E. O. Hall, the printer from the Sandwich Islands, Mr. Munger, and others. After describing the mission premises he says:

"At last we came to the grist mill. It consisted of a spherical wrought iron burr four or five inches in diameter, surrounded by a counter-burred surface of the same materials. The spherical burr was permanently attached to the shaft of a horizontal water wheel. The surrounding surface was firmly fastened to timbers in such a position that when the water wheel was put in motion the operation of the mill was similar to that of a coffee mill. It was a crazy thing, but for it the doctor was grateful. It would, with the help of himself and an Indian, grind enough in a day to feed his family for a week, and that was better than to beat it with a pestle and mortar. It appeared to me quite remarkable that the doctor should have made so many improvements since the year 1836, but the industry which crowded every hour of the day, his untiring energy of character and the very efficient aid of his wife in relieving him in a great degree from the labors of the school, are perhaps circumstances which render possibility probable that in three years one man without funds for such purposes, without other aid for that business than that of a fellow missionary for short intervals, should fence, plow, build, plant an orchard and do all the other laborious acts of opening a plantation in that distant wilderness, learn an Indian language and do the duties meanwhile of physician to the associate stations on the Clearwater and Spokane.

Oregon Journal
March 24-29, 1930

EWING YOUNG

The Cause for Law in Oregon

A few days ago I stood on the porch of John U. Smith's farm house four miles northwest of Newberg and looked out over the beautiful rolling hills and prairies of the Chehalem Valley. Pointing to a symmetrical oak about half a mile away, Mr. Smith said:

"That tree grew from an acorn planted by my mother when she was a girl. She planted it on the grave of Ewing Young. It was the death of Ewing Young that was one of the leading causes for the establishment of civil government in Oregon. He died intestate and the settlers felt there should be some legal way of disposing of his property.

"My father, Sidney Smith, who came to Oregon in 1839, worked for Ewing Young. Young was an old-time mountain man and trapper who finally settled in the Chehalem Valley. He brought a lot of cattle from California. he took up a claim here in the Chehalem Valley. In those days the Willamette Valley was unsettled, so he claimed the valley from Wapato Lake to the river east of Newberg, and from the summit of Chehalem Mountains on the north to the Handley Hills in the south. When Father was working for Ewing Young this whole valley was covered with a luxuriant growth of wild grass so high that a man could ride through it on horseback and be completely hidden from sight. My father was with Ewing Young when he died. Young had suffered for many years with indigestion and the medicine which he took for his indigestion ate through his stomach.

"I have heard Father tell how he went barefoot for lack of moccasins and how he worked for six bits a day, living on boiled wheat and deer meat, and how he finally bought a couple of yards

---

"When Ewing Young died the settlers who attended the funeral didn't know what to do with his property, so his death indirectly led to the formation of the provisional government."

---

of Hudson Bay flannel, cut a hole in the middle through which he put his head, and laced the edges together with buckskin thongs, which made a very durable if not very stylish shirt. He hired an Indian woman to make buckskin breeches. Father worked for a little while for the Methodist Mission, rafting logs from Mission Bottom to Oregon City.

"When Ewing Young died my father bought his squatter's right as well as his brand, and the horses and cattle that were out in the hills, agreeing to pay $500 as the purchase price. Father built a log cabin and before long he was well to do in the wealth of the country, which at that time consisted of cattle."

Mary Jane Heater Judy:

"When I was a little tot I attended school at the old Ewing Young Schoolhouse. We lived on the Ewing Young place from the time I was seven till I was 16 years old. There is a fine big old oak tree on that farm under which Ewing Young built his cabin, and this oak tree now shades his grave. Ewing Young came to Oregon in 1834. He died on February 15, 1841. He was born in Tennessee and came out to California in 1834 with Hall J. Kelly. When Ewing Young died the settlers who attended the funeral didn't know what to do with his property, so his death indirectly led to the formation of the provisional government."

When Ewing Young was buried, under the old oak tree on his own farm, a meeting was organized immediately after the funeral was concluded. The Reverend Jason Lee was chosen chairman. The Reverend Gustavus Hines, who came to Oregon with the "Great Reinforcement", was chosen secretary. George W. LeBreton, who came to Oregon with Captain J. H. Couch aboard the Maryland in 1840 and who later served as secretary of the "wolf meeting" at which the provisional government of Oregon was organized, was added to the committee to attend to the disposal of Ewing Young's effects. This committee appointed a committee of seven to draft laws for the settlement south of the Columbia River.

Next day the committee met at the home of David Leslie and appointed the Reverend David Leslie chairman. The committee chosen to draft laws consisted of the following persons: The Reverend David Leslie, the Reverend F. M. Blanchet of the Catholic Church, the Reverend Jason Lee and the Reverend Gustavus Hines of the Methodist Church, David Donpierre, whose grave I have seen in the churchyard at St. Paul, Oregon; M. Charlevon and Robert Moore, who came to Oregon in 1840 and who had served in the War of 1812 and in the Missouri legislature in 1822. Robert Moore was Oregon's first territorial printer. When he was appointed territorial printer in 1850, he was the owner of the Oregon Spectator, at Oregon City. Reverend J. L. Parrish, whom I knew as an old man at Salem, was also a member of this committee, as was Etienne Lucier, who came to Oregon with Hunt's overland party in 1812 and was the first man to settle on a farm in Oregon. He took up a place in what is now East Portland and in 1827 moved to French Prairie. In 1829 he built three cabins at Oregon City for Dr. John McLoughlin. William Johnson was also a member of this committee. He was an old-time sailor, having served on the Constitution in the War of 1812. In 1843 he was living on part of what is now Portland.

At this meeting Dr. Ira L. Babcock was appointed supreme judge with probate powers ot administer the estate of Ewing Young; George LeBreton was named clerk of the court and public recorder, and William Johnson was apointed high sheriff. Dr. Babcock was instructed by the committee to act according to the laws of the state of New York until regular laws should be adopted for Oregon.

Oregon Journal
March 15, 1932 &
one other, undated

EUGENE SKINNER

Founder of Eugene City

"My father, Eugene Franklin Skinner, was born in Essex County, New York, September 13, 1809," said Mrs Phoebe Skinner Kinsey when I spent a recent evening with her at her home at 831 Overton Street. "His father, Major Joseph Skinner, was born at East Windsor, Connecticut, on March 25, 1775. My father's mother died when father was three months old, so he was taken by his aunt Betsy Warren, who lived at Plattsburg, New York. He lived with his Aunt Betsy till he was 14 years old.

"When he was 14 something happened which profoundly affected his whole life. Their home was near the lake, and my father was an expert skater. He took smallpox in school and was lying in bed in an upper room. He got out of bed to see if the boys were skating on the lake. When he saw that they were, the temptation was too much for him, so he dressed, got his skates, slipped out of the house and went skating. He was so weak, however, that he soon came back to the house, undressed and went to bed. When Aunt Betsy went up to his room she found he was having a congestive chill. All of the men of the Skinner family

were large, robust men, but Father, from that day
to the day of his death, was frail physically and
was slight in stature. He was never able to do
hard physical work. This same year he went to
Wisconsin to visit relatives, and later returned
to Plattsburg, where he lived for some years.
From Plattsburg he went to Hennepin, Illinois.

"Father and Mother were married on November
28, 1839, in Illinois. My mother's maiden name

"As they swung northward, my father
saw what is now known as Skinner's Butte.
They stopped and Father looked the land
over and decided to take it up as his
donation land claim."

---

was Mary Cook. She was born at Augusta, Oneida
County, New York, on February 7, 1816. While my
father was serving as sheriff in Putnam County,
Illinois, he read law.

"My father had heard such good reports of
the opportunities to get ahead in the west and
also of the healthful climate in California, that
in the spring of 1845 he joined a company bound
for California. Father spent the winter of 1845
at Sutter's Fort. Captain Sutter urged the settlers to stay, offering them free land, but father, believing that Oregon would offer better
opportunities, came, with a number of his old
neighbors, northward to the Willamette Valley.
They sold their oxen and wagons to Captain Sutter, bought horses, and came north by the old
trappers' trail.

"My father and mother went to what is now
Dallas, in Polk County. In June, 1846, my father,
Captain Felix Scott, William Dodson, and Elijah

Bristow started from Polk County toward the head of the Willamette Valley to locate claims. They went on horseback, traveling on the west side of the Willamette River and finding no settlers between La Creole and what is now Eugene.

"Elijah Bristow, as they passed over one of the rolling hills between the coast fork and the middle fork of the Willamette River, seeing it was well timbered with oak and fir trees, and seeing also that there was a beautiful view from the crest of the hill, was reminded of his old home in Virginia and decided to take up his claim. He named it Pleasant Hill. They camped beside a spring, cut some fir trees, and put up a cabin to hold the claim. Mr. Bristow blazed a number of the trees to inclose his square-mile claim. William Dodson took the claim just south and east of Mr. Bristow's and Captain Felix Scott took the one joining Mr. Bristow's on the west. Later he abandoned this claim and took up one on the McKenzie River just opposite the mouth of the Mohawk. As they swung northward, my father saw what is now known as Skinner's Butte. They stopped and Father looked the land over and decided to take it up as his donation land claim.

"My sister Mary Elizabeth was born at Dallas on December 2, 1846. She died on October 4, 1860, not long before her 14th birthday. Father and Mother had lost three children in Illinois--all girls--Harriet, Clara, and Amelia. My sister Leonora was born on our place within what is now the city limits of Eugene, on September 2, 1848. She died in Portland on August 29, 1862, and was buried on her 14th birthday.

"After taking up his claim Father returned to Polk County, and the next spring, the spring of 1847, he took a man with him, returned to his claim and built a log cabin on the west slope of Skinner Butte. My sister Leonora was the first white child born in Eugene. I was the next member

of the family, and on November 17, 1851, my brother, St. John B. L. Skinner, was born. My sister
Amelia, who was named for her sister Amelia who
had died in the east, was born on April 6, 1855.

"My father served as clerk of the court at
Eugene and was also postmaster there for many
years. In 1854 Father built a new house to take
the place of the old log cabin. This was the
first frame house to be built in Eugene. He used
part of the logs from the first cabin for the
building of our second home.

"My mother was the first white woman to
settle in Eugene. Among the early pioneers who
settled in Lane County were Elijah Bristow, Isaac
and Elias Briggs, Prior Blair, Charles Martin,
Cornelius Hills, Charnel Mulligan, Wickliff Gou-
ley, Benjamin Davis, John Akin, H. Noble, A.
Cargell, Ben Richardson, John Brown, Jacob
Spores, J. N. Hendricks, Caswell Hendricks, Robert Callison, Michael and Harrison Shelley,
William Bowman, Calvin T. Hale, and Abel, William, and E. L. Bristow. All of these settled in
the vicinity of Eugene prior to 1849.

"On December 10, 1864, my father took a
heavy cold, which turned into pneumonia, and he
died five days later. Two years later Captain N.
L. Packard, a retired sea captain came to Eugene
on business. He and Mother met and they were
married on his 50th birthday, February 7, 1867.
My father was ambitious for me to secure a good
education, so he sent me to the Sacred Heart
Academy at Salem. I started in the summer of 1864
and attended for two years. My seatmate was Mary
Scott, now Mrs. Plamondon, for many years a resident of Salem, but now a resident of Portland."

When it was decided to locate a county seat
in Lane County, there were four contenders for
the honor of having the county seat located on

their claim. These were Charnel Mulligan, Prior Blair, Eugene Skinner, who had platted the town between the east end of Skinner's Butte and the Willamette River, and a settler near the present town of Springfield. An election was held in June, 1853, to decide on which of these four sites the county seat should be located. The site offered by Prior Blair received 105 votes. Charnel Mulligan's site received 134 votes, and the other two places received a total of 155 votes. As a result of the canvass of the votes the board of commissioners located the seat of justice for Lane County on the Mulligan donation land claim, which joined that of Eugene F. Skinner. Charnel Mulligan and Eugene F. Skinner executed a bond in the sum of $5000 binding himself to deed the county 40 acres from the northeast corner of his claim. Among the records to be found in the courthouse at Eugene is an interesting document that reads as follows:

"Know all men by these presents, that I, E. F. Skinner, of the county of Lane and Territory of Oregon, am held and firmly bound unto the board of county commissioners of said county, in the sum of $5000 to be paid said board of county commissioners of said county, to which payment well and truly to be made, I do bind myself, my heirs, executors and administrators, firmly by these presents. Sealed with my seal, this 14th day of June A. D. 1853.

"Now the condition of this obligation is such that if the above bound E. F. Skinner for like consideration in like manner and like condition as expressed in the conditions of the above within bond of Charnel Mulligan to make a good and sufficient warranty deed to the board of county commissioners of the said county for Lane, for the use of said county for 40 acres of land out of his land claim and lying north and adjoining said donation of Mulligan, in a square form, and

"Furthermore, said Skinner agrees to ferry over the west branch of the Willamette River at his ferry, all citizens living north of said stream in Lane County when crossing on county business, free, as foot men, or half price as horsemen, then this obligation to be void. Otherwise to remain in full power and effect.

"In witness whereof I have hereunto set my hand and seal on the day and year first above written. E. F. Skinner."

On July 5, 1853, a survey of this 80-acre

"...said Skinner agrees to ferry over the west branch of the Willamette River at his ferry, all citizens living north of said stream in Lane County when crossing on county business, free, as foot men, or half price as horsemen..."

---

tract was ordered and it was further ordered that the lots were to have a frontage of 80 feet and to be 160 feet in depth, that alleys 14 feet wide should be located at the center of each block and that the streets should be 66 feet wide. The county commissioners also authorized the county clerk to employ a workman to build a courthouse 16 by 20 feet in size and one story high. This building, which was to be used for county purposes, was placed on a block bounded by Willamette, 9th, Oak and 10th Streets. On account of the small size of the building, when cases were tried the jury, in charge of a deputy sheriff, were taken out to sit on the ground under an oak tree to pursue their deliberations.

On January 15, 1855, the county commissioners decided to build a new courthouse, 40 by 60 feet in size and two stories high. On April 3, 1856, the contract was awarded for the building of the courthouse, at a cost of $8500. The adherents of Eugene F. Skinner wanted it built on the Skinner donation, while Mulligan's friends wanted it built on his side of the line, so, to prevent bad feeling, the courthouse was located on the line that divided the claims of Skinner and Mulligan. The board of county commissioners sold lots at five dollars each to the Methodist Episcopal and the Cumberland Presbyterian Churches, and they also sold to the school district and to the Episcopal Church lots at a nominal price. They also directed that Martha Jane Mulligan should be allowed to select any lot in Eugene City not located on the public square, as a donation from the county commissioners, and they donated a lot in a like manner to Mary Skinner.

The courthouse had been built in the center of 8th street, between Pearl and Oak. In this position it blocked all traffic, so it was decided to move the courthouse from the middle of the street. After a rather strenuous campaign by opposing factions it was finally ordered to be moved on the north side of the street.

In 1855 Thomas Holland and W. Burton started a store in Eugene. This same year J. L. Brumley also opened a store at the corner of Oak and Fifth Streets. On October 17, 1862, the legislature incorporated Eugene City. On October 22, 1864, the title of the city was changed to the City of Eugene. The first election to be held in the city was on the first Monday in April, 1865.

When I visited Mrs. Pheobe Skinner Kinsey, at her home in Portland, she said:

"My father visited Portland in the spring of 1846, when there were only two or three cabins in Portland.

"I have seen my father's old donation land claim become one of the most beautiful cities in

Oregon--the university city of the state--a city of schools and churches, of culture and prosperity. What pride my father and mother would have taken if they could have lived to see their dream of a great city at the head of the Willamette Valley realized."

Oregon Journal
March 28 & 29, 1929

DR. WILLIAM KEIL

Founder of the Aurora Colony

Midway between the metropolis of Oregon and the capital city is the picturesque old town of Aurora. There are two Auroras. The stranger passing through the city on the smooth and well-kept highway sees but one Aurora. That is the Aurora of today--the modern Aurora, represented by concrete garages and modern bungalows; but there is another Aurora there. It is of this other Aurora that I am going to write--the Aurora which is a bit of the old world, transplanted to the western shores of America.

You cannot visit the land of yesterday unless you are in the mood for it. It is like the mirage, which vanishes as you approach. The gateway to the land of yesterday is not easily found. You must have spiritual vision, sympathy with the viewpoint of the past, and a real interest in the lives of the people of that vanished era.

Back from the main street of Aurora you will see substantially built buildings whose roofs are thick with the accumulated moss of more than half a century. You will see old houses, set far back from the street, whose wide porticos are shaded by trees and whose paths are bordered with violets and jonquils.

To reach the magic land of yesterday you must travel the paths and byways, not the highways. You must sit on the back steps of the old farm houses and listen with infinite leisure to

---

"No one was ever in want, for every member of the colony had a right to have the colony tailors make them suits, to have the colony hat factory make them hats, and also a right to draw supplies of every kind from the colony store..."

---

the myths, the traditions, the unwritten history of the community. You must go into the parlors and look at the old-fashioned pictures in the family albums and hear the story of those who have long since departed for the land of the hereafter. You must sit with the village cobbler and hear the gossip of today and yesterday. You must go through old attics and revisualize the past from the old spinning wheels and home-made furniture that is covered with the dust of the vanished years.

Rummaging among a lot of old books I ran across some maps of Champoeg, Butteville, St. Paul, Gervais, St. Alexcie and Aurora. The old Oregon and California Stage Road is shown passing through Aurora. The lands of the Aurora colony are shown, and here, too, are shown the farms of Samuel Burkholder, who may still be seen wearing his old-country wooden shoes as he visits his long-time cronies about Aurora. Here are the farms of Fred Keil, William Keil, Charley Keil, and the other children and relatives of Dr. William Keil, the founder of the colony. Here are the farms of Jacob Miller, John Stauffer, John Scheurer, J. Schwander, Jacob Giesy and Dr. Fink. Here lies Peter Fellers' farm, between the farms of F. X. Matthieu and Willard H. Rees. Every name on the map is reminiscent of the past and, like the faint odor of incense in a cathedral, carries a subtle suggestion of the days that are no more.

I dropped into the village shoe shop, where Captain William Miley sat at his bench, half-soling a pair of shoes. For nearly 60 years Captain Miley has been a part of the community life of Aurora. In the old days he was the village drayman and expressman, making deliveries with his trusty ox-team. He was county commissioner of Marion County at the time the courthouse at Salem was being built. As he hammered home the tacks he told me of his boyhood days in Iowa where he was born 78 years ago. He was one of a family of 11 children and was 19 years old when he crossed the plains in 1863 to join the Aurora Colony.

"Dr. William Keil, the founder of our colony, was a man of dominating personality," said Captain Miley. "His last surviving son, Emmanuel, died January 18, 1922--only a few weeks ago. Dr. Keil was a physician as well as a preacher. His word in the early days was supreme, but the young people became restless about the marriage restrictions and other regulations, so the colony was finally disbanded and the lands allotted in severalty to colony members."

Sitting on the back porch of his farmhouse, Elias Keil told me, as he fixed a doubletree, of the early days of Aurora.

"I was only a little chap when my grandfather, Dr. William Keil, died, in 1877," said Mr. Keil, "so, of my own knowledge and observation I cannot tell you much about him. (He had) nine children. Their names were Amelia, Aurora (after whom this community is named), Glorianda, Louisa, Elias, August, Emmanuel, Fred and William. Six of these children, including my father, Fred, are buried here in Aurora. One is buried in Missouri and one at Willapa. My father, Fred Keil, had six children, three of whom are living. We five are the only grandchildren left.

"My grandfather was born in Prussia, March 6, 1812. His wife, whose maiden name was Louisa Ritter, was also born in Prussia, strangely enough, on the same day as her husband. While he worked at his trade as a tailor he studied medicine. He practiced his profession at Pittsburgh, Pennsylvania, a while, and then went out to Missouri as a missionary of the Lutheran Church. He founded a colony at Bethel, Missouri, in 1843, the rules of which were that, as in the days of the disciples, all things should be held in common. They were each for all and all for each, and none should be rich and nor should any be poor.

"In the '40s and '50s Missouri was the starting place for emigrants to Oregon. Dr. Keil heard so much about the wonderful country by the shores of the Pacific that he decided to send some members of the colony to the Oregon Country to spy out this land, flowing with milk and honey, and bring back a report. He sent eight men. Their report was favorable, so in the spring of 1855 the colony started from Bethel, with 35 wagons and about 140 members of the Bethel Colony. Willie, my father's brother, was 16 years old. He was enthusiastic about going to the land of promise beyond the desert. He made his father promise that whatever happened he should not be left behind. Some of the colony were to remain at Bethel until later. Willie died just before the party were ready to start for Oregon. They had promised he should go with them, so they made a water-tight coffin, and, putting the body into it, they filled it with alcohol to preserve the body and brought it with them across the plains. It took them six months to make the journey with their ox teams.

They settled on Willapa harbor. There they buried Willie by the shores of the Pacific. The next year the colony moved to the Willamette Valley and settled here at Aurora.

Dr. William Keil, who founded Aurora in 1855, was a man of great magnetism and ability. He was born at Erfurd, Prussia, March 6, 1811. He learned his trade as a tailor in Prussia and there he became interested in communistic societies. He was deeply religious, and his study of the Bible determined him to found a colony of the old patriarchal type. He settled at first in Pennsylvania, where he gained a number of converts who went with him to Missouri, where they founded a colony at Bethel, where all things should be held in common.

In 1853 Dr. Keil sent out a delegation from Bethel to investigate the conditions on the Pacific coast. Among those sent on this mission were Christ Giesy, Joseph Knight, Michael Schaefer, John and Hans Stauffer, Adam Schuele, and some others. They settled on Willapa Bay. In 1855 four more parties started westward. Two of these parties came overland, one consisting of six wagons and another of 20 wagons, while the other two parties came by way of the Isthmus of Panama.

Dr. William Keil was captain of one of the wagon trains, and as 1855 was a bad year, he was advised not to make the attempt. They met a party of Indians on Green River and Dr. Keil invited them to the camp, fed them, and gave them a present of a quantity of tobacco. The next morning five cattle were found to be gone. Dr. Keil refused to become excited or send his men out to punish the Indians. Presently a band of mounted

Indians rode into camp with the missing cattle
and said they found them wandering away and were
afraid the doctor might think they had stolen
them. They refused to take any payment for
bringing the cattle in, and promised to pass the

"The skirts that we girls made and
wore in those days would make dresses for a
large family of girls today. The girls of
today wear as little as their conscience will
allow and some of them don't seem to have
much conscience."

---

word along to the other tribes so that Dr. Keil's
wagon train would not be molested.

The Keil wagon train had no trouble with the
Indians in spite of the fact that the settlers
were forted up at The Dalles and on Fifteen-Mile
Creek and that the Indian War of 1855-56 was in
progress. Dr. Keil and his party went to Willapa
Harbor, but decided it was too isolated, so he
went to Portland, from which place he traveled
around the country looking for a good location.
He practiced his profession as a physician and
surgeon in Portland during the winter of 1855.

In the spring of 1856 Dr. Keil purchased for
$1000 a half section of land on which the town of
Aurora is located. One of the quarter sections
was owned by George White, the other by George
Smith. Twenty-five members of the colony moved
into a small log cabin on the White place that
had been built in 1849. In addition to the 320
acres of land and the cabin, there was a small
sawmill and a grist mill with a set of burrs.

Among those who settled with Dr. Keil at
Aurora in 1856 were David Fischer, Henry Schnei-

der, his son Charles, Moses Miller, George Rauch, Henry Barkholder, Daniel Snyder, Jacob Engel, Henry Allen, Herman Bonser, George Ling, and A. Metzger. Dr. Keil bought the half section of land and the mills for $1000, but was unable to pay in cash, so gave notes for it. The lumber manufactured by the colony was sold and the indebtedness on the place paid.

The men were divided into working gangs of four. One of the rules made by Dr. Keil was that no gang of four should have breakfast until they had cut down a tree, unless there was no meat on hand, in which case they must kill a deer before they ate breakfast.

The census of 1870 showed that the Aurora colony had a population of 320 and that their property at Aurora and vicinity was assessed at $80,000, while their property in Clackamas County was assessed at $40,000. Although this property was all in the name of Dr. Keil, he served as trustee only, for at his death in 1877, the property was divided among the members and it was decided no longer to conduct the colony as a communistic enterprise.

Charles Snyder of Aurora is the only surviving member of the original Aurora Colony. He came to Aurora in 1856. When I visited him recently I asked him to describe Dr. William Keil, the founder of the colony. He said:

"Dr. Keil was a large man, fleshy, with a gray beard under his chin, a goatee, and lots of long, curly hair. He was a very decided man. His wife was small, slender and quiet."

As Mr. Snyder was talking, Mrs. Snyder came in from the barn. She had her apron full of eggs. She shook hands with me cordially, and said: "As soon as I put up these eggs I will come right back."

She was back in a moment or two, and I asked

her, "Are you a member of the Aurora Colony too?"

She shook her head, and said: "No more. I was, but don't you ever join a colony. When I was a girl my husband here wanted to marry me. But Dr. Keil, the head of the colony, and the elders, used to decide who should marry each other, so when we wanted to be married they shook their heads. We went to the school teacher, Carl Ruche. He was a justice of the peace. He married us. But they made us live in a little shack in the woods.

"Dr. Keil would not let any girl in the colony marry outside the colony, for he said if we brought in ungodly members the colony would soon be broken up. He would not let any young man in the colony marry an outside girl. He wanted to choose the different young people who should be married to each other, but the young people liked to choose for themselves. The village elders could not pick out a girl and say, 'You shall love this young man or that young man.' He might be just as good or better than the one she would pick out for herself, but she wanted to do the choosing.

"Father"--that is what she called him--"and I have lived together more than 50 years. We celebrated our golden wedding some years ago. We have had three pairs of twins, besides other children. We were married November 9, 1865. My maiden name was Christine Schuele. I drove a mule team across the plains in 1867. We were part of the reinforcement to the colony. My husband was 78 on February 16. I was 75 on January 27.

"You remember the old church that stood on the hill? My husband helped build that church. He worked two years on it. None of the men received any pay. They belonged to the colony. Dr. Keil and the elders decided what kind of work each member of the colony should do. All the work in the old church was hand-made. There were no nails used in it. The framework was fastened together with wooden pins. The boards were dovetailed together. The tower was 114 feet high. We had three bells hanging there. In the tower was an observation gallery, where our band of 60 members used to gather to play.

"There were many good things about the colony. No one was ever in want, for every member of the colony had a right to have the colony tailors make them suits, to have the colony hat factory make them hats, and also a right to draw supplies of every kind from the colony store. No man could have more than he needed. We had no divorces. We had no lawsuits. We had singing schools, church services, a park, a colony band. But even with all that, when Dr. Keil died the members of the colony, particularly the young people, preferred to work for themselves and not to give all they made to the colony, nor let the elders tell them what to do.

"The young women spun, carded, and wove the cloth. Do you see this petticoat? I made it more than 50 years ago. It is of pure wool and is very finely woven. The dye which was madder, I raised in my own garden. Here is an overskirt of soft blue, brown, and gray. That also is pure wool. I made it before I was married.

"The skirts that we girls made and wore in those days would make dresses for a large family of girls today. The girls of today wear as little as their conscience will allow and some of them don't seem to have much conscience.

"Wait here and I will go upstairs and bring you some blankets and bedspreads that I made when I was a girl. They don't make any like them any more. We used only the finest wool and we did not hurry to do the work. We did the work so our children and our grandchildren would be proud of it. Do you see this woolen blanket? It was made by a relative of mine, and here in the corner she wove her name and the date--1840. In those days we did not use gay colors, as the girls use today. We wore soft colors. For green we used peach leaves, for brown we used walnut hulls, and for red we used madder. Most of our dyes were vegetable dyes.

"Our colony here in Aurora was founded in 1857. We built the church ten years later, and ten years after that, in 1877, Dr. Keil died. The final settlement of the affairs of the colony was made ten years later, in 1887. The colony property was worth over $1,000,000. There was no lawsuit. It was decided that each person should accept the share that was considered just. Some were given 40 acres, some 80 acres, and others 160 acres. Others, who did not care for land, were given money, $1000 and up, depending on how long they had been members of the colony and how old they were.

"Almost all the old colony people are gone. The famous band has long ago been disbanded. The children who went to school to Carl Ruche are now grandfathers and grandmothers. When our colony here in Aurora was disbanded the mother colony at Bethel also went out of existence and the property was distributed.

Oregon Journal
April 11, 1922

GENERAL JOSEPH LANE
Oregon's First Territorial Governor

(In a sketch that will appear in three installments, a niece of General Joseph Lane reviews the career of that notable character. The first is devoted to his early life and his record in the Mexican war and as a servant of the people of Oregon in high official stations.)

Miss Kate Lane, whose uncle, General Joseph Lane, was Oregon's first territorial governor, lives at the Patton Home, in Portland. When I visited her recently she said:

"My father, Reverend Jesse Lane, was born in North Carolina in 1799. His brother Joseph was born December 14, 1801. My twin sister Winifred and I were born in Kentucky, December 29, 1839. My father died when I was five years old. Mother lived on a farm near Evansville, Indiana. General Joseph Lane also owned a farm in 'the pocket' of Indiana. I wish you could have known my Uncle Joe. He was one of the most lovable men I ever met. In 1816, when he was 15, they moved to Warwick County, Indiana, where he worked as a clerk in a store. He was elected to the legislature in 1822, when only 21.

"At the breaking out of the Mexican War he enlisted as a private in the Second Regiment of

Indiana Volunteers, and a few weeks later became colonel of the regiment. Before long he was promoted to brigadier general. At the Battle of Buena Vista he was wounded. Not long after, at the Battle of Humantla, he won the love of his troops

---

"General Lane reached Oregon City on March 3, issued a proclamation organizing the Territory of Oregon, and assumed his duties as governor of that territory."

---

and a brevet as major general for his gallantry. He was in command at Atlixco. In November, 1847, he took Matamoras and in January, 1848, captured Orizaba.

"President Polk wanted to have Oregon organized as a territory under his administration, so he asked my uncle if he would accept the governorship and start for Oregon at once. Congress passed the bill organizing the Oregon Territory August 14, 1848. My uncle, accompanied by Joe Meek and a small escort, started overland for Oregon by way of New Mexico and Arizona. They arrived in San Francisco in February, 1849, at the height of the gold excitement. He and Colonel J. W. Nesmith came to Astoria together on board the Indian brig Janette. As there was no ship at Astoria coming up to Oregon City, and as time was pressing, my uncle bought a small boat and helped row from Astoria to Oregon City, where he arrived one day before the end of Polk's term of office.

"General Lane reached Oregon City on March 3, issued a proclamation organizing the Territory of Oregon, and assumed his duties as governor of the territory. He had promised President Polk that Oregon Territory should be organized under his administration, and he kept his promise, though he had but a day's leeway, as Polk went out of office the next day, March 4.

"One of the first things General Lane had to attend to was the pursuit, capture, trial, and execution of the Indians who had murdered Dr. Marcus Whitman and his wife and the others at the Whitman Mission in November, 1847.

"It is a rather curious thing that when he issued his proclamation organizing Oregon Territory on March 3, 1849, it was printed in the Free Press at Oregon City, of which George L. Curry was editor and publisher. He, like my uncle, later became governor of Oregon.

After about a year and a half in office, General Lane resigned as governor and went to northern California, where he worked on a placer claim during the winter of 1850-51. In 1851 he was elected Oregon's delegate to Congress and continued to serve until Oregon became a state, when he was elected United States Senator. He took his seat as one of Oregon's first two United States Senators on February 14, 1859. Delazon Smith was the other senator.

"Under the system of dividing the whole body of United States Senators into three classes, with overlapping terms, the terms of the two Oregon senators fell into the two classes expiring March 3, 1859 and March 3, 1861, respectively. The longer term fell to General Lane. The next year he was the candidate for vice president on the ticket headed by Breckenridge.

"While living at Umpqua, Oregon, in the summer of 1853, he organized a force of volunteers and had a fight with the Indians and was shot through the shoulder in the same place he had received a musket ball while charging the Mexicans at the head of Lane's Brigade during the Mexican War. The battle with the Indians occurred on August 24. On September 4, he and a few white men met the Indians at Table Rock and made a treaty of peace. In 1849, shortly after he had become governor, with Colonel J. W. Nesmith he explored the Siletz country and the Yaquina Bay District. He and Nesmith went out over the bar at Yaquina in an Indian canoe to sound the channel to see what depth there was at low water.

"When my uncle's term as senator had expired, on March 3, 1861, he returned to Oregon. He had written to my twin sister Winifred and myself to come to Washington prepared to go to Oregon with him. We reached Washington in time to see President Lincoln inaugurated. My uncle always thought that if President Lincoln had been able to have his way the Civil War, with all its bitterness, would never have occurred, for President Lincoln wanted to buy the slaves and colonize them in Africa. But there were too many hotheads, both North and South, so we had to suffer four years of fratricidal strife.

"We went by steamer from New York to the Isthmus of Panama. We had to land on the sand at Panama City, as the depot had recently been burned. After crossing the Isthmus we went aboard the steamer Golden Gate for San Francisco. We left New York City about April 1 and arrived at San Francisco about three weeks later. When we went ashore at San Francisco one of the first things we were told was that Fort Sumter had been fired upon and war between the North and South had been declared. From San Francisco we came to Portland, where we visited a few days with Uncle Joe's daughter, Mary, who had married Aaron Shelby.

"My uncle bought a carry-all here in Portland and a good team of horses. From Portland we drove to Corvallis, where we visited Nat Lane, whose son, Dr. Harry Lane, later was United States Senator from Oregon and also served as mayor of Portland. My uncle's son Lafayette came with us from Washington. His son John, at West

Point, resigned as soon as war was declared in 1861 and became a colonel in the Confederate Army, serving on General Robert E. Lee's staff. When Lee surrendered, John wired to his father at Roseburg for money to come out to Oregon. He and his brother Simon mined in the beach mines at Gold Beach, in Curry County. Later Colonel John Lane studied law with his brother Lafayette. He died at Wapio, Idaho, while serving as superintendent of the Indian agency there.

"Winifred and I went from Corvallis to Roseburg in a mud wagon. The roads were hub-deep in places. General Lane, with the carry-all, came on by way of Siuslaw. His daughter Melissa, who had married Andy Barlow, lived on the Siuslaw.

"Uncle Joe hired an Irishman to drive the team. Near Drain the carry-all got stuck in the mud. While Uncle was helping lift it out of the mud his revolver dropped out of its holster and was discharged and shot him through the shoulder. He had been shot through the shoulder with a musket ball in the Mexican War. In the Rogue River Indian War he was also shot through the same shoulder.

"The driver was terrified for fear General Lane would die and he would be blamed for killing him. He said, 'Hurry up, General, and write a paper saying I didn't shoot you.'

"Just then a man on horseback came along, so my uncle stopped him and said to him, 'For the peace of mind of my driver, I want you to know he didn't shoot me. I was shot accidentally. This man had nothing to do with it.'

"They went on to Drain where my uncle had his wound dressed, and where he stayed several days. The bullet severed a tendon, so my uncle was never thereafter able to lift his arm.

"Shortly after we reached my uncle's place, near Roseburg, my sister Winifred secured a school on Deer Creek. General Lane's sons, Lafayette and Simon, drove a bunch of cattle to the mines in eastern Oregon to sell.

"General Lane's daughter, Mrs. Barlow, on the Siuslaw sent word for her mother to come at once, as she had been accidentally shot. Mrs. Barlow's son was riding a wild horse. He had been out hunting. He called to his mother to come out and get his rifle. His mother took the gun and put it on the bed. Her baby crawled along the floor, pulled itself upright and in some way pulled the trigger, discharging the gun. The bullet shot Mrs. Barlow through the knee. My aunt went to be with her daughter, so this left General Lane and me alone on the farm. His wounded shoulder prevented his milking the cows. They were Spanish cattle and rather wild. Uncle drove them into a narrow chute and I had to do the milking. We kept house together and did all the farm work for two weeks before he was able to get a man to help on the farm.

"I secured a school at Galesburg. Mr. Levins ran a store there and kept the stage station. Passengers stopped there for breakfast. Four families hired me to teach their children. I boarded with Mrs. Levins. I taught there two years. From there I went to Rock Point, in Jackson County, to teach. This also was a stage station and hotel. It was about 12 miles from Jacksonville. I boarded with Mrs. Birdseye. She and Nat Lane's wife were sisters.

(From a granddaughter of General Joseph Lane Mr. Lockley obtains data for a sketch of that remarkable leader of men, who was a hero of the Mexican War and of Oregon's Indian wars and Oregon's first territorial governor and one of Oregon's first United States Senators.)

Winifred M. Lane lives at 271 Knott Street, in Portland. She was born at Empire City, the one-time county seat of Coos County. "My father, Colonel John Lane, was the fifth son in a family of ten. His father was General Joseph Lane, first territorial governor of Oregon." said Miss Lane. "Simon Lane, now more than 90 years old, who lives at Roseburg, is the only child of General Joseph Lane now living. Colonel John Lane, my father, was a graduate of the military academy at West Point. At the breaking out of the Civil War Father joined the Irvin Guards, of Virginia, an artillery organization.

"On Christmas, 1878, Father married Harriet Sherrard, my mother, whose home at that time was near Empire City. Her father crossed the plains in 1853, settling near Eugene.

"At the close of the Civil War my father came to Roseburg, going from there to Randolph, near Bandon, where he was engaged in gold mining in the black sand on the beach. My father was assessor two years and sheriff four years, after which he came to Roseburg and practiced law nine years with his brother LaFayette. He was appointed special Indian agent by Grover Cleveland and later became inspector. Resigning at the end of Grover Cleveland's term, he went to Lewiston, where he practiced law four years. He died December 24, 1914, at Lapwai, Idaho.

"My grandfather, General Joseph Lane, was born in North Carolina, December 14, 1801. While still a small child he went with his parents to Kentucky, where he spent his boyhood. He moved from Kentucky to Indiana, where he was elected to the state legislature. At the breaking out of the Mexican War he raised a company of volunteers, and, as you know, served with distinction in the Mexican War. The position of governor of Oregon Territory was offered Abraham Lincoln, but his wife did not care to come out to Oregon, so Lincoln declined, and the position was then offered to my grandfather, who accepted it and started at once for Oregon. He was commissioned August 18, 1848, and came to Oregon overland, by way of New Mexico, Arizona, and California.

"He reached Oregon City March 3, 1849. One of his first official acts was taking a census, which showed there were in Oregon at that time

---

"One of his first official acts was taking a census which showed there were in Oregon at that time 8785 American citizens."

8785 American citizens. He resigned as governor June 18, 1850. He was elected Oregon's delegate in Congress June 2, 1851...."

Miss Lane loaned me her grandfather's scrap book, which is a regular storehouse of early-day history, as it contains letters written by General Scott in 1851 on the slavery question and many other issues that were live questions in that day, as well as letters from many of the well-known politicians of Oregon of the early '50s. It also contains muster rolls of the Mexican War and other interesting miscellany.

A correspondent of the Salem Statesman gives an interesting picture of General Joseph Lane, whom he visited at the time he made the peace with the Indians near Table Rock. The Indians had begged "Tyee Joe" Lane not to fire his "hyas rifle", as they called the cannon. They said it took a hatful of powder and it might kill them all. In describing his visit to General Lane the correspondent of the Salem Statesman said:

"Never having seen General Lane, my curiosity prompted me to visit his camp. Having seen generals in the states, togged out with epaulets, gold lace, cocked hats and shining swords, I expected to find something of the kind here, but fancy my surprise on being introduced to a robust, good-looking middle-aged man with his right arm in a sling and his shirt sleeve slit open and dangling, bloody, from his shoulder, his legs encased in a pair of old breeches, the upper end of them being supported by buckskin straps in place of suspenders, his head ornamented with a forage cap—this composing the uniform of 'the hero who never surrendered'. His quarters were in keeping with his garb—a rough log cabin with a hole in one side for the door, and destitute of floor and chimney. In one corner lay a pile of sacks filled with provisions for the troops. In the opposite corner was a stack of guns of all sorts and sizes from old French muskets to fancy silver-mounted sporting rifles. In the third corner were a camp kettle, a frying pan, a coffee pot minus a spout, four packsaddles, and a dozen tin cups, while in the remaining corner lay a pair of blankets—the general's bed. In the center of the quarters was a space four feet square, for the accommodation of guests and other visitors."

Oregon Journal
February 5, 6, & 7,
1926
one other, undated

JOHN WHITEAKER

First Governor of the State of Oregon

(A daughter of the first governor of the state of Oregon tells Mr. Lockley of her father's first introduction to office holding. Mr. Lockley then takes up the tale and relates the story of Oregon's attainment of statehood...)

Miss Ann Whiteaker is a daughter of John Whiteaker, first governor of the state of Oregon. I visited Miss Whiteaker recently at her home in Eugene and she told me of her early days and also of the political service of her father in Oregon.

"My father was born in Dearborn County, Indiana, May 4, 1820," said Miss Whiteaker. "My mother's maiden name was Nancy Jane Hargrave. She was born in Missouri, September 17, 1828...

My father left home when he was 16 years old and worked at carpentering in various parts of Illinois until the fall of 1846, when he moved to Missouri. On August 22, 1847, he and my mother were married. They lived at Lancaster until the spring of 1849, when my father went to the California gold fields, while my mother stayed with her parents. After spending a year or more in California, he went back to Missouri in the summer of 1851. The next spring, with a group of his neighbors, he started with his family for Oregon. Because of his knowledge of traveling on the plains, he was elected captain of the train.

215

"My father and mother spent their first winter in Yamhill County. In the spring of 1853 they moved to Lane County. Father took up a donation land claim of 320 acres just south of Spencer Butte. A few years later he sold this claim and bought a farm from John T. Gilfrey, near Pleasant Hill.

"My sister Frances was born May 24, 1852, while crossing the plains. She died and was buried near Cascade Locks. My brother John was born April 20, 1854. For many years he was a practicing physician here in Eugene. He died in the fall of 1888. I was born on our farm at Pleasant Hill when Oregon was still a territory, so I can qualify as a pioneer.

"In 1854 the county court appointed my father a justice of the peace. This, by the by, was his introduction to politics. In the summer of 1856 he was the Democratic candidate for probate judge of Lane County and was elected. The next spring he was the successful candidate on the Democratic ticket for a seat in the territorial legislature."

I am not going to attempt to quote Miss Whiteaker further, but will summarize her story of the exciting political events during the closing days of the territorial government in Oregon and the early days of our state government. On the second Monday in November, 1857, a vote was taken by the electors of Oregon on the acceptance or rejection of the state constitution. Over 10,000 votes were cast, of which more than 7000 were in favor of the constitution. An election was held on the first Monday of June, 1858, to elect the members of the first state legislature as well as a representative in Congress. It was further provided that the state legislature should assemble on the first Monday of July, 1858, to elect two United States Senators.

The legislature, elected in June, 1857, met

December 17, 1857. Hugh D. O'Bryant was elected president of the council and Ira F. M. Butler speaker of the house. The legislature elected territorial officer and adjourned January 5, 1858. At the election in June, 1858, the Oregon Democrats nominated LaFayette Grover for Congress and John Whiteaker for governor, while the National Democrats headed their ticket with Colonel James K. Kelly for Congress and E. M. Barnum for governor. The Republicans nominated John R. McBride for Congress and John Denny for governor. As the election drew near it was seen the Republicans had no chance, so they swung their votes to the National Democratic candidates, voting for Kelly for Congress and Barnum for governor. L. F. Grover received 5859 votes, while James K. Kelly, his opponent, received but 4190 votes. Whiteaker received 5738 votes for governor and Barnum 4214, so Grover won for Congress and Whiteaker became the first governor of the state of Oregon.

At this election Mathew P. Deady, Riley E. Stratton, R. P. Boise and Aaron E. Wait were elected justices of the Supreme Court. The recently adopted constitution provided that the state legislature should meet July 5, 1858. At the meeting of the legislature Joseph Lane and Delazon Smith were elected United States Senators. On July 8, three days after the legislature met, John Whiteaker was inaugurated the first governor of the state of Oregon. It was supposed at that time that the state would be admitted at once, but as a matter of fact, Oregon did not become a state until February 14, 1859. The legislature met December 6, 1858, and on January 22, 1859, the last territorial legislature adjourned. Meanwhile, our two United States senators, Joseph Lane and Delazon Smith, and Lafayette Grover, our representative in Congress, were in Washington, D. C. trying to show they had a right to seats, but inasmuch as they represented the state of Oregon, and Oregon was still a territory, they were not able to make much headway.

Stephen A. Douglas, chairman of the committee on territories, had reported favorably on the admission of Oregon on April 5, 1858. On May 18 the United States Senate passed the bill admitting Oregon, by a vote of 35 to 17. The bill was reported to the House, but there it met a snag. The pro-slavery feeling was so strong and the border troubles in Kansas were so much in the public eye that the house preferred debating upon the admission to concurring with the senate bill admitting Oregon. One of the chief arguments of those opposing the admission of Oregon as a state was that the recent census of Oregon showed a population of only 42,677, while it was necessary for a state to have a population of 93,000 to have a representative in Congress.

Another objection was that if Oregon was admitted as a state the federal government would have to assume the war debt resulting from the Indian War of 1855 and 1856. Kansas had rejected the slave constitution, and so efforts were made to prohibit her admission because she did not have a population of 93,000, and the opponents of statehood in Oregon said Kansas and Oregon were on the same footing.

The vote admitting Oregon was taken February 12, 1859. Two days later the President approved the bill and Oregon became a state. On the same day Joseph Lane and Delazon Smith were sworn in as United States Senators from the state of Oregon. On the following day Lafayette Grover took the oath of office and became Oregon's first congressman.

"You can get a better idea of my father," said Miss Whiteaker, "by reading this diary, which he kept for many years". Governor Whiteaker's diary is a graphic picture of the political conditions while Oregon was still a territory. Here is a brief quotation from it:

"I was nominated and elected on the first Monday in December, 1857, took my seat in the state senate and served 60 days. In the spring of 1858, at the convention held by the Democratic Party, my name was placed on the ticket for governor of the state. No hint of the purpose of the convention had been given to me, and I didn't know of the action to be taken until it was announced to me. I was sorry that I was nominated, but I took the field and was elected. Nothing of particular note occurred during my administration.

"In 1861 a revolution broke out and all of the officers of the Oregon state government except myself and Judge P. P. Prim changed their politics to Lincoln. We did not do so and in consequence the abuse of the press and the people was very bitter. In the spring of 1862 another election took place, in which there was a fusion of Republicans, Abolitionists and faithless Democrats under the name of the Union Party. They nominated A. C. Gibbs, a renegade Democrat. I have seen much of the Abolition Party and have lived among its members. I have heard its members lecture, talk, and argue their favorite dogmas. I have had abundant opportunity, during the last 25 years, to inform myself as to what their favorite policy really was and is and what they hope to accomplish. I have become satisfied that all they desire is to have power, and they will make a clean breast of the whole institution of Negro slavery without in the least bettering the condition of the slave. Abolitionism is an exotic brought from Great Britain and transplanted into the New England states, where it has been nurtured and cultivated by ministers of the gospel and other public speakers until it has possessed the sentiments of a large majority of the Eastern states."

The sidelights thrown on the lives and motives of many of Oregon's leading statesmen of this day in this old diary are intensely interesting.

Governor Whiteaker was a member of the legislature in 1866, 1868, and 1870. In 1876 he was in the state senate. In 1879 he ran against Reverend H. K. Hines, the Republican nominee, for Congress and defeated him. So urgent were the Democrats in Congress to have his help that he went to Washington on a special train.

Oregon Journal
July 16 & 17, 1922

HANK VAUGHN

Eastern Oregon's Legendary Bad Man

(Hank Vaughn was a well-known figure in the old days in eastern Oregon, and stories about him often appeared in Fred Lockley 's published conversations. What follows is a small collection of Hank Vaughn stories.)

Richard Cox:
"A friend of mine named Hollis, from Virginia, was one of the early-day merchants of what was then known as Centerville, but is now known as Athena, in Umatilla County, Oregon. His partner's name was Charlie Cleve. One day Hank Vaughn drove into town with a brand new buggy, to which was hitched a spirited team. Seeing Cleve on the sidewalk in front of the store, Hank cramped his buggy and invited him to take a ride. As they drove up Main Street, Hank said, 'Do you think you can hang on, Charlie, if I let 'em out a little?'

"Cleve said, 'Sure. I can hang on.'

"Hank unbuckled the reins, threw them over

the horses' backs, gave each of the horses a slash with the buggy whip, and the frantic horses started down the street on a dead run. Someone tried to head them off, and they swerved and struck a rail fence. The body of the buggy was detached. It flew over the fence and lit in the field right side up with Cleve still sitting in the seat, hanging on for dear life.

"Hank turned a double somersault, and when he had quit rolling, he got up, saw Cleve sitting in the seat, and said, 'Well, you sure can hang on, can't you.'"

Oregon Journal
January 12, 1928

Adam Croasman of Vancouver, Washington:

"During the time I was city marshall (of The Dalles, Oregon, 1881-82) I got word that a cowboy from east of the mountains had come to paint the town red. I saw him coming down the street as hard as his horse could run. I stepped out into the middle of the street and held up my hands for him to stop. He pulled his horse on his haunches to see what I wanted. I said 'We have a racetrack out at the edge of town. If you want to do any racing, go out there. We don't permit it in town.'

"He said, 'My name is Hank Vaughn.'

"I said, 'All right, Hank, you can go out to the racetrack and do your racing, or go to the livery stable and put your horse up.'

"He went to the livery stable and put his horse up. About an hour later I dropped into George Allen's saloon. He said, 'Have you got your gun on you, Adam?'

"I said, 'You know I never carry a gun.'

"He said, 'You better get one. Hank Vaughn is looking for you.'

"When I went to Tim Baldwin's saloon, Tim

said, 'Have you got your gun, Adam? If you have-
n't take mine. Hank Vaughn is looking for you.'

"I said, 'Keep your gun, Tim, and tell Hank
Vaughn when you see him that he can find me on
the street any time he wants.'

"A few minutes later I dropped into another
saloon and, standing in front of the bar, I watched
in the mirror at the back of the bar to see
who came in at the door. I saw Hank come in.
Everybody in the saloon stopped talking. I didn't
turn around, but I watched in the mirror every
move he made. The minute he pulled his gun I was

**"When he was lit up he had an in-
satiable desire to paint the town red, so he
was always riding into saloons and shooting
the lights out."**

---

going to knock him out. He stepped up to me and
tapped me on the shoulder. I turned around and he
said, 'I want to shake hands with you.'

"I put out my hand and said, 'It won't cost
you anything to shake hands with me, Hank.'

"He shook hands and said, 'You are the
whitest police officer I ever met in my life.'

"Turning to the men at the tables and to the
others standing around, he said, 'Come on up,
everybody. The drinks are on me.' When he had
paid for the drinks, he said, 'Come on outside. I
want to speak to you.' When we got outside he
said, 'Where is the best gents' furnishings store
in town?' I took him into a clothing store and he
plunked down a $20 gold piece. 'I want to buy the
best hat you've got in your store for the city
marshal here.' The proprietor bought out a high
silk hat, for which Hank paid $15. Then Hank
asked me to take him to the best jewelry store in

town. He said to the proprietor, I want you to give Adam Croasman here the best cane you have in stock.' He picked out an ebony cane with a gold head, for which he paid $25, and handed it to me. He said, 'I like you. I like your nerve. I like your grit. I like your style. I'll never give you any trouble.'

"Later, at Prineville, Hank got into trouble with a man and shot the man's hand off. In those days Wasco County embraced that district, so that trial was held at The Dalles. When Hank came down I went to him and said, 'Hank, a lot of your friends have come to The Dalles, and also some of your enemies. Pass the word around that I won't have any gun play or any trouble.'

"He said, 'All right, Adam. I once gave you my word that I would make you no trouble, and that goes.'

"The mayor came to me and said, 'There are some men at the Cosmopolis Hotel who want to see you.'

"I knocked on their door and I heard them pull a chest of drawers and some chairs from in front of the door, unlock the door, and open it a crack. I stepped in and said, 'I am the city marshal. What do you want?'

"They said, 'We are the witnesses against Hank Vaughn, and we want protection.'

"I pointed to the rifles leaning against the wall and to their six-shooters on the table and said, 'Did you figure you were going to fight an army? It don't look to me as if you needed any protection. Hank Vaughn isn't carrying any gun, and I won't allow you to carry guns, either. You'll have to turn them over to me till the trial is over.'

"Hank was acquitted and no trouble occurred."

Oregon Journal
March 17, 1926

Sidney Grant Dorris:

"Another man I knew at Prineville (in 1884) was Hank Vaughn. He hailed from Missouri, got in a mixup when he was a young fellow through stealing some horses, shot the sheriff and served time in the pen, after which he settled in Umatilla County. When he was lit up he had an insatiable desire to paint the town red, so he was always riding into saloons and shooting the lights out. He was always good for a stake, and if he didn't have the money he would go out and borrow it to give it to you, but he rarely returned money he borrowed, and it was a dangerous thing reminding him of it. He and Charlie Long shot each other up and both of them were in bed for months. Charlie was finally killed by having his head split open with an ax by a young nestor, and Hank was also killed."

Oregon Journal
September 15, 1929

John Henry Durham:

"In 1889 I was appointed to the police force (in Pendleton, Oregon). One of the first men who came to congratulate me was Hank Vaughn. He said, 'John, I like you. As long as you are on the force, I won't make any trouble for you. If you ever need help, call on me.'

"One day Deputy Sheriff Phin McBrine said to me, 'I am looking for Hank Vaughn. I want you to help arrest him.'

"I said, 'Go on back to the courthouse. I will get Hank to come up there with me. If we try to arrest him there will be a lot of shooting and someone is liable to get hurt.'

"As we were talking Hank came riding along Main Street as fast as his horse could go. At

225

Bluff Street the horse tried to turn, but, being smooth-shod, its feet flew from under it, and it crashed hard. The fall broke Hank's skull. He had a silver plate fastened to his skull already, but this time his skull was too badly fractured to be patched up, so he died from the fall."

Oregon Journal
September 3, 1925

JOAQUIN MILLER
Poet of the Sierras

Some years ago I spent a most enjoyable
evening with Joaquin Miller and he told me of the
days when he was a barefooted lad, in the winter
of 1852, living near the Looney place, not far
from Santiam City, in Marion County. The following spring the family moved to Lane County, taking up a place near Coburg, where George Melvin
Miller of Eugene, Joaquin's youngest brother was
born in the spring of 1853. When I visited George
Melvin Miller a day or so ago in Eugene I asked
him to tell me of his brother's early life.

"Joaquin was born in an emigrant wagon near
the state line of Indiana and Ohio," he said.
"Mother named him Cincinnatus Hiner Miller. She
gave him his middle name out of respect for Dr.
Hiner, who attended her when Joaquin was born.

"Father, whose name was Hulings Miller, was
a school teacher. Before they came to Oregon my
parents moved about from place to place as my
father secured positions as teacher in different
school districts. Father was very skillful
in making pens from goosequills. While he was

227

teaching in Randolph County, Indiana, one of his
pupils was Joe Lane, who later became Oregon's
first territorial governor. In those days school
was always dismissed during sugar making time, as
the pupils had to help gather the sap and boil it
down to sugar. Money was scarce and my father wa
occasionally paid in maple sugar or coonskins.

"Father bought a place on the Miami Reservation. The neighbors gathered from miles around
to help him build his cabin. It was a crude af-

"In a fight with the Indians he was
shot through the neck with an arrow. A
squaw nursed him back to health. He lived
with the Indians for a year or so. They
called him 'The Fool', for the wound in his
neck and head affected his memory."

fair, with a puncheon floor, oiled paper for
window panes and roof of split shakes held down
with weight poles. Of evenings my mother and the
children would pick wool, comb it and card it
into rolls and my mother would spin it into
cloth.

"While they were at work with the wool my
father would read to them. He read and reread
Fremont's account of his explorations of the
west. The western fever got into the blood of all
of the family. He also read Senator Linn's
speeches in Congress about Oregon. He borrowed
the volumes of Fremont's travels from Major Mc-
Culloch, the Indian agent, later secretary of the
treasury in the cabinets of Lincoln and Arthur.
Reading aloud, spelling bees, house raisings,
corn huskings, muster days with their inevitable

'corn liquor' and fist fights, were the principal amusements of the people of that day.

"Our family started for Oregon on March 17, 1852, and were seven months and five days on the road. They reached St. Joseph, Missouri, on May 10, and five days later started for Oregon. They had two wagons and eight yoke of oxen, with a team of horses and a light vehicle. The horses and carriage they sold at Salt Lake City.

"My first recollection of my brother Joaquin is of a restless lad, a lover of the outdoors, a fine shot with a pistol and rifle and a good horseman. My brothers, John, Hiner, and Jim, went to school at West Point. They lived in a cabin near the schoolhouse, coming home over Saturday and Sunday.

Hiner and Bill Willoughby one afternoon climbed up on the point of rocks for which West Point is named and began rolling rocks down. One of the rocks hit one of Cady's cows and broke her hind leg. Bill Willoughby was 15 and Hiner 13. They were afraid to go home and face the music, so they ran away to California. Father heard they were on their way south, so he struck out on horseback and overtook Hiner near Jacksonville and brought him back. Hiner soon struck out again, though, and joined a party of miners. He was given one twenty-seventh of the cleanup for doing the cooking. He got 31 ounces of gold dust as his share. Whenever he came home he dressed like a dandy and was free with his money.

"In a fight with the Indians he was shot through the neck with an arrow. A squaw nursed him back to health. He lived with the Indians for a year or so. They called him 'The Fool', for the wound in his neck and head affected his memory. Eventually he came back to Eugene, attended Columbia College and was in the first class graduated.

"Hiner joined Walker, the filibuster, in Nicaragua in 1855 and fought with him. He went to

Idaho and made a lot of money. Returning to Eugene, he bought a newspaper. It was suppressed by the government, as Joaquin took the side of the South.

While he was running this paper he saw some poems of Minnie Myrtle of Port Orford in a paper published at San Francisco, called the Golden Era. He corresponded with her, rode horseback to Port Orford and, though they had never seen each other, they were married the next day. Returning on horseback, they stayed in Eugene till their first child, Maud, was born. When she was a month old they started on horseback for Canyon City, carrying Maud in a basket swung from her mother's saddle. They drove a band of cattle to the John Day and Canyon City mines. Soon Joaquin was appointed county judge of Grant County. Two sons were born to them while they lived at Canyon city. Maud went to school in Canada and married an actor named McCormack.

"Joaquin and his wife later separated. He went to England, South America, and the Orient. She went to New York City. Joaquin married Abbie Leland. They had a daughter, Juanita. My mother lived with Joaquin on the heights above Oakland, California, for many years. She died at his home when she was 91 years old.

"My brother Joaquin certainly lived an unconventional and adventurous life. He was a law unto himself--as are most men of genius."

When Minnie Myrtle Miller, the wife of Joaquin Miller, died, she left among her other papers a diary in which she writes of her early married life with Joaquin Miller. She died at the age of 37. In paying tribute to his wife, in a series of sketches he wrote for a Walla Walla paper 40 years ago, Joaquin Miller says:

"Here is one leaf from her journal, or rather, I think, her recollection of the journey, which she left me along with her other papers when she died.

"'One night of that journey I shall not soon forget. There had been some fighting ahead of us and we knew the foe was lurking in ambush. They made a kind of fort of the freight, and while we lay down in the canyon, baby and I, away up on the high sharp butte Joaquin stood sentinel. And I say this, tonight, in his behalf and in his praise, that he did bravely and saved his loved ones from peril that night. There he stood on that dreary summit a target for the foe, and no one but me to take note of his valor--stood till morning grew radiant, stood till the night was passed. There was no world looking on to praise his courage and echo it over the land; only the frozen stars in mystic groups far away, and the slender moon like a sword drawn to hold him at bay'.

"Reaching the mines in safety, I, as de-tailed in a previous sketch, practiced law, mined, fought Indians and, indeed, was the busi-est of men. I planted the first orchard in all that land, pushed ahead as hard as I could, and tried to be punctual and steady and thoughtful. Yet I was still but a lad in years. I was elected judge of the county and had begun to write the 'Songs of the Sierras'. My life was a sober and severe one. For without learning, I was trying to administer the law. Without knowing how to read or spell, I was trying to write a book. I was walking a new road of life now. All was strange. What availed my knowledge of woodcraft in the court of law? The mystery of making fire by the friction between two sticks of wood, the secret of finding water in the desert by the flight of a bird, the cunning of foretelling the force of the coming winter or the depth of the snow, all these and the like were of no use now.

"If the shrewd and sharp lawyers who bullied and beat me had come into my elements, I had

231

beaten them. But I had chosen to enter theirs and
must be equal to the undertaking. And so it was I
worked and studied as never man worked and studied before. Often I never left my office till the
gray dawn, after a day of toil and a night of
study. My health gave way, and I was indeed old
and thoughtful.

"Well, all this, you can see, did not suit
the merry-hearted and spoiled child of the mines
at all. Then she was not so ambitious as I was;
then she had not such a strange wild life behind
to haunt her. She became the spoiled child here
that she had been at her father's and naturally
grew impatient at my persistent toil and study.
But she was good all the time; good and honest
and true in all things and in all ways; understand that distinctly. And let me say here, once
for all, that no man or woman can put a finger on
any stain in the woman's whole record of life, so
far as truth and purity go. But she was not happy
here. Impatient of the dull monotony of the exhausted mining camp and longing for the sea and
the old home that almost overhung the sounding
waters, she took her two children and returned to
her mother, while I sold the little home we had
built and kept together, the new orchard and the
lanes of roses we had planted together, and remained there in the camp, promising to follow
her, yet full of ambition now to be elected to a
place on the supreme bench of the state, and I
remained and worked on to that end ceaselessly.

"She had been absent from me quite a year
when the convention was called and I went to
Portland, seeking the nomination for the place I
desired. But the poor, impatient lady, impulsive
always and angry that I should have kept so long
away, had forwarded papers from her home, hundreds of miles removed, to a lawyer here, praying
for a divorce. This so put me to shame that I
abandoned my place and in a rage and disappointment formed a conclusion with her lawyer to give

her a pretense of that which she professed to desire. Yet I knew quite well that this was only a romantic and foolish freak that meant nothing. How often she has written me that she did this only in order to get me to come home to her, and that she did not dream she could be divorced unless I came to her when the action was brought. Nor could she, in fact. But a court was in session, and her lawyer, who looked to me only for his fee, entered the case, and in about the time it takes to write it the sham decree was announced to the world, while I was sailing away for other lands. Of course, the whole pitiful proceeding was as nothing; but her lawyer, now dead, got his fee from me, and never betrayed the treachery to her. And it was perhaps quite ten years before she by chance met someone who told her the truth."

I have often wondered if Joaquin Miller was not thinking of his broken-hearted wife and their three children when he penned the following lines:

THE MOTHERS OF MEN

The bravest battle that ever was fought!
Shall I tell you where and when?
On the map of the world you will find it not--
'Twas fought by the mothers of men.

Nay, not with cannon or battle shot,
With sword or nobler pen!
Nay, not with eloquent words or thought,
From mouths of wonderful men!

But deep in the walled-up woman's heart--
Of woman that would not yield,
But bravely, silently, bore her part--
Lo, there is that battle field!

No marshaling troop, no bivouac song,
    No banner to gleam or wave;
But oh! these battles they last so long--
    From babyhood to the grave.

Yet faithful still as a bridge of stars,
    She fights in her walled-up town--
Fights on and on in the endless wars,
    Then silent, unseen, goes down.

Oh, spotless woman in a world of shame;
    With splendid and silent scorn,
Go back to God as white as you came--
    The kingliest warrior born!

"I had not been greatly fortunate at best. A few thousand dollars I had thrown up as a wall between myself and work; but I had grown so impatient of this moderate position in life, and I so wanted to get a great fortune and return to the West that I deliberately staked all in Wall Street and, of course, lost all.

"I, beaten and discouraged and broken in health, had retreated to a garret and was then again preparing to use my pen, when one stormy night a strange woman crept upstairs and told me in a wild whisper that my wife, 'Minnie Myrtle', was in the city and must see me. And how helpless I was to help her, or anyone, now! I had seen her but once for nearly a dozen years. And such years! Let me not recite any of the horrors they hold, in this connection; and yet I heard from her all the time, and while she wrote against me and lectured about me and did all that made my life so miserable, she did not really mean my ruin; but, thinking me strong and prosperous and happy, she exhausted her wit and sarcasm on me and laughed that she might not weep. But in time she drove me nearly mad, and I left the country and proposed never to return. My publishers, Roberts Brothers, at Boston, had sent her $50 a month as regularly as the months came, all of the time. She was receiving that sum and perhaps as much more directly from myself, as I could spare it, all the time I was in Europe; and she received these sums for years after her marriage. But the poor, spoiled child of Port Orford never quite got over her childish love for wasteful follies and dress and show and travel, and so was forever pinching and in debt.

"And now, having hastily passed over all those terrible years, we come to the closing chapter of this singular life. I followed the good woman who came to me that stormy night, in silence, till we came at last to a little back room in the top of a house, with a bed in the center and a doubtful fire struggling in the grate. The good woman turned away and left us in the room together. The place was almost dark. She did not give me her hand, but stood before me with one hand holding on the bedpost, a long time silent.

"'I have come to you at last,' she said, after a while.

"'You have come to drive me from the country again.'

"'I have come to you to die!' she said. And as she turned so that the light was on her face, I saw that it was so. And then we sat down and had a long talk. It was our last talk. I was not very kind. God knows, I am sorry now. She wanted most of all to see her little girl, whom I had taken from her and placed in a convent school in Canada three years before, and it seemed to break her heart when I refused to send for her to come. By and by, however, when I promised her that she should surely see her before she died, she became reconciled. She talked with calm unconcern about her coming death, reminded me of my promise, and told me she had brought me all her pa-

235

pers; some that we had written together before I had learned to spell. There was a valor, a sweetness, too, and a dignity, a large charity, in all she said and did now, in the twilight of life, that won all hearts to her entirety. My secrets she kept till the grave closed over her, and she never complained of anything or anyone, but was patient, resigned and perfectly fearless and tranquil to the end. But the end was not so near, after all. When I went back to see her one day she had gone and left no word where she could be found. Then I began to fear and doubt her promise. The winter wore away and April came. Then they came to tell me, from her, that she was dying, and I must keep my promise. And so I arranged for her child to come and I went every day to assure her that she was coming and to take her some flowers and whatever kind messages and encouragement I could.

"Wearily the days went by, till away up in May, the month in which she was born. Then the child came, and the good people, the gentle, loving people who kept with her and cared for and loved and petted her in these last days, said it was like religion to see them together, and that the dying woman in her last days was very, very happy. And so Minnie Myrtle died last May, here in New York. When I went to look on her dead face, a strange fancy of hers--she had set all about the foot of the bed, where she could see them, all the flowers I had sent her, the withered ones and all. There was quite half a trunkful of papers which she had brought and entrusted to me, some of them suggesting wonderful things, great thoughts and good and new; for much that she wrote--and maybe this is not just praise--was better than any writing of mine. But she lacked care and toil and sustained thought. I bought a little bit of ground in Evergreen Cemetery and there the hand that writes this laid the dear, tired lady to rest, forgiving and begging

God to be forgiven."

(Tribulations of the wife of a man of genius whose fame is nation-wide and wider, are set forth in an old document which comes in Mr.

"He started a paper at Eugene, but feeling was very acute during the Civil War and the government suppressed his paper because he sympathized with the South, on the principle that the South was getting the worst of it and was the underdog."

Lockley's way and is here reproduced.)

While at Salem recently I dropped in for a visit with Miss Cornelia Marvin, Oregon's State librarian. She is often referred to as Oregon's most useful citizen. Whether or not this is so I am not prepared to say, but I do know that if there are any citizens of Oregon who are more useful, busier, or more enthusiastic they will have to go some. Knowing my interest in anything pertaining to Oregon's literary characters, she gave me an article written at Salem, November 5, 1871, and published in the press of the state that gives an interesting sidelight on the career of Minnie Myrtle Miller, one of Oregon's gifted singers. The article, as published, was entitled 'Mrs. Joaquin Miller's address to the People of Oregon', and reads as follows:

As Joaquin is now expected at Portland, I deem it my duty to say a few words in his behalf to the people of Oregon. I have received many letters from different sources requesting me to disclose as much of his conduct toward his children as I will. Although I feel that these things concern no one on the face of the earth but my children and me, still he belongs to the world now, and I have remained silent until remarks have been carried so far as to make my children subjects of idle gossip, and I deem it right to now ask a truce to charges and accusations, and request of you to behold the poet and receive him in a manner that will give due tribute to his genius and success.

Mr. Miller has earned a fame, and an appreciation of his efforts should be awarded him. He is a man of literary culture and research; he has read constantly, industriously, and had command of the very best literature, ancient and modern. It has been his sole ambition for years to go to Europe and acquire a literary fame. He felt, and justly, that he was gifted, and, his mind, being of fine, poetic nature, and his brain very delicately organized, the coarse and practical duties of providing for a family, and the annoyance of children conflicted with his dreams and literary whims. So, when he wrote me that he would be absent in Europe five or six years, and in the meantime I need not expect to hear from him often, as he should be very busy, I asked for and obtained a divorce in the courts of Lane County, and your singer was loosened and free, and no longer chained to the annoying cares of a family. He could give his whole attention to his poems. I myself sympathize with him in his desire to have time and money to 'tamper with the Muses' and cultivate his taste and talent for literature, and I feel that all poets and authors will sympathize with him.

I did not intend that misfortunes should be publicly known. Illness overtook me in Portland,

and, by irregularities of the mails and accidents, we were cut off for some time from communication with our friends. My younger brother was with me, and I did not ask for assistance; but by accident my friends found me. I must ever remain grateful to them for timely and generous assistance; but they can bear me witness that I made no public complaint, and the charges made against Mr. Miller were not made with my knowledge. I was as much surprised to see them as anyone. If, in five years of labor and complete isolation from my relatives and the world, I worked with him, and not even my nearest neighbor or dearest friend heard one complaint or murmur from my lips; if, through that long winter in Portland, I sewed humbly day after day and night after night as long as I was able; passed the offices and residences of our mutual friends, who were leading and wealthy people and chose rather to let my babes come upon the verge of starvation than to blemish his reputation by letting my circumstances be known, it is not likely that after the day of hope came, and all was over, I should publicly make known what I had tried hard to conceal.

As I said before, Mr. Miller felt that he had gifts of mind, and if his system of economy was rigid and hard to endure, it was, at least, a success; and if he needed all his money to carry out his plans, I am satisfied that he thus used it. The bitter experience of the past cannot come again. My babes lived through all, and I am more than satisfied. I am grateful and all is well. The absurd statement of the Eugene Journal that I had indignantly returned money that Mr. Miller had sent me, is incorrect; and its informers are as economical of truth as they are of affection for their own flesh and blood. It would be a sad time to show indignation toward a father when his babes were suffering for the necessaries of life. Joaquin Miller does not claim that he ever sent a

239

dollar to his children, or provided anything for them in any way from the time of his leaving Oregon until about two months ago when he sent me $25. He has sent $50 to Mrs. B. Cook for my little girl, and $25 to my mother, who has the care of my younger children. He will doubtless make explanations which will be satisfactory to those interested when he returns. It is true I had a home with my widowed mother, but the place was dreary and secluded, and there was not a church or school house within 50 miles of my mother's home. So I did not deem it a proper place to educate my children, and I came away, bringing them with me, which was contrary to the decree of the court, which gave the care of the two elder children to the care of my mother. As I brought them away, he was released by law from caring for them, and I have no reason to complain, nor can anyone have, justly. Two hundred dollars a year alimony was allowed, but as it was not secured you will readily see that Mr. Miller was entirely released from any obligation. The marital relations between Mr. Miller and myself are dissolved, but that does not prevent our holding our precious babes in mutual love and protection; and, although there are many false sentiments in society in regard to these things, I beg the privilege of exercising my own judgment in regard to my duty toward the father of my children and my children. As we are both mortal, it would be affectation in me were I to profess to take upon myself all the blame, but I ask to bear my full share.

The many who feel an interest in him are of more consequence than the few who know and love me, and henceforth I would have you deal only with him as a poet and author. Pronounce your judgment upon his books. Know him by his epic heroes. No mortal man can go beyond himself in any conception. When he attempts to he only strikes against the border of his imagination and rebounds further back, and when man attempts to image a god he takes a step back and puts upon the shoulders of his god wings which belong to a lower order of creation. Good sometimes comes from evil. The most deadly pistil exhales a sorrowful perfume and our separation and sorrows produced the poems of 'Myrrh' and 'Even So'. If I have, after all, recovered my health and sometimes smile as others do, I feel that I have some kind of an apology. If I am not today the shadowy, faded woman that might be expected, I beg pardon, and if, as a facetious editor writes, I must "go down the stream of life alongside of Lady Byron, Mrs. Bulwer, and the obstreperous wife of the author of 'Boz'", let that be my punishment.

Minnie Myrtle's real name was Theresa Dyer. She chose the name Minnie Myrtle as her pen name because she lived in Coos County, where the hills are covered with the graceful and beautiful myrtle tree. She died, at the age of 37, broken-hearted. Her poems have never been collected in book form, but are to be found scattered through the colums of the weekly papers of Oregon of 50 or more years ago. Here is a bit of her verse that has in it the longing for rest and peace:

"I am conscript--hurried to battle
With Fate--yet I fain would be
Vanquished and silenced forever
And driven back to my sea.

Oh! To leave the strife and the turmoil,
Leave all undone and skim
With the clouds that flee to the hilltops,
And rest forever with Him."

A few nights ago at Albany I met F. M. French on the street and asked him where I could find J. H. Miller, brother of Joaquin Miller, the poet.

"I know him well by sight," said Mr. French. "He is tall, slender, and has long hair and a long beard, but I don't know where he lives. He used to live in a little shack down by the river bank, back of the foundry. We will hunt up one of the night watchmen, who will undoubtedly be able to tell you."

A moment or so later Mr. French introduced me to J. Q. Rodgers, one of the night watchmen. "Sure. I'll help you locate Long-Haired Miller," said Mr. Rodgers.

We went down toward the bank of the Willamette, up a dark alley, and after rapping on several doors, finally found someone who directed us to where Mr. Miller lives. It was half past eight o'clock when we climbed the stairway to his room, and the house was dark. Mr. Rodgers knocked on the door. A moment later someone asked, "Who is there and what do you want?"

Mr. Rodgers answered, "Open your door. Fred Lockley of the Journal has come to interview you."

I was somewhat abashed by Mr. Rodgers' introduction, but it was effective, for a moment later Mr. Miller came to the door and invited me in. Lighting a small lamp, he put it by the side of the bed, and said, "If you will excuse me, I'll go back to bed," and he pulled the gunny-sacks which served as blankets back into place.

"I lost all my bedclothes and other possessions when the place I was in burned up not long ago," said Mr. Miller. "Lots of people have been after me for an interview, but I have turned them all down. I don't know why I am going to make an

242

exception in your case, but I am. But I want you to be sure to quote me correctly and not get the thing all mixed up as a reporter did who interviewed me some years ago.

"My name is James Henry Blair Miller. I was born near Liberty, in Union County, Indiana, November 9, 1840. I know that date, because when my parents came across the plains in 1852 my mother tore the family records out of the old family Bible and brought them along and I saw them after I was grown. Through some oversight the birth of my brother Cincinnatus Hiner, who later took the name of Joaquin, was not set down, but Mother said he was about 20 months older than I....

"I went to the mines at Orofino in 1861. I was 21 years old at the time, strong as a horse, and lithe as a wildcat. My brother Hiner located me on a good mine, where I averaged $16 a day. Mining was too slow for Hiner, so he started to riding the express with Mossman.

"If you know anything about the history of the west, you know that the winter of 1861-62 was one of the coldest and most severe we have ever experienced. I went to Walla Walla to winter. The town was crowded to the doors, every house being occupied. I lived in a tent all winter. During the winter I took the measles. Before that I was wonderfully rugged and very adventurous. The measles broke my health and broke my spirit, and I have never been so good since.

"The next spring I went back to the mines, but I wasn't strong enough to shovel in the tail race, so I went to catching fish and selling them to the miners...

"You will find all sorts of myths, traditions and lies told about my brother, Cincinnatus Hiner Miller," he said. "There is no question that he was a good poet. Personally, I don't care for poetry, but if anyone likes poetry, I guess my brother's poetry would suit him, particularly his poem on 'Mothers of Men', and that one about

Columbus where it says 'Sail on! Sail on!' I always figured Joaquin, as he called himself, was inconsiderate of the rights of others, inordinately vain, and too fond of praise. He had plenty of moral and physical courage and he was a law unto himself. He never did a thing or refrained from doing it because it was the custom or because other people thought it was right or wrong. He did his own deciding.

"You will hear all sorts of versions of why my brother Hiner left home. Some people say he rolled rocks down a cliff, broke a cow's leg and was afraid to go home and face the music. That's all rot. A family named Willoughby lived near our place. Will Willoughby and Hiner were chums. Will's father had gone to California to the gold mines. Will didn't get along with his stepmother. He thought she was harsh and unreasonable. We were going to school at the Vaughn schoolhouse, near West Point. One day Will said to my brother Hiner, 'I am going to run away and go to California.'

"Hiner said, 'Do you want a partner?'

"Will said, 'Sure. I'd like a partner, but I don't know anybody who would leave a good home and go with me.'

"Hiner said, 'I'll go.'

"The next morning my mother found a note from Hiner, saying, 'I have gone to California with Will Willoughby.'

"Will's father happened to come back from California just about then, so he and my father struck out on the trail of the runaway boys. They followed them as far as Jacksonville and there gave up the quest, for the boys had gone on across the Siskiyous into California.

"What Hiner did in California is too long a story to go into. He lived with the Indians for some time, and his first child was born there. Her name was Shasta. He named her for Mount Shasta. I don't know what tribe her mother belonged to, whether she was a Klamath, a Pit River or a Modoc, but that's neither here nor there. Hiner came back from California and went to the college at Eugene, where he was graduated and was the valedictorian. He started a paper at Eugene, but feeling was very acute during the Civil War and the government suppressed his paper because he sympathized with the cause of the South, on the principle that the South was getting the worst of it and was the underdog.

"While Hiner was running the paper at Eugene he saw some poetry printed in the Albany Democrat and the Golden Era signed 'Minnie Myrtle'. The writer was Theresa Dyer and she lived at Port Orford.   Her sister Emma married Charles Hilbron. I met them later at Canyon City and still later they moved to The Dalles. My brother and Minnie Myrtle corresponded for a while, then he went on horseback to Port Orford, made impetuous love to her, and a day or two later they were married and started on horseback for Eugene. Minnie Myrtle Miller--for, after her marriage, she wrote under that name--was one of the sweetest, truest women I have ever met. She had a brilliant intellect and wrote excellent poetry. My brother never could stand anyone to outshine him, whether in shooting, writing poetry, telling stories or anything else, and so, for his sake, she submerged her own genius and revolved around him.

"When the government shut up Hiner's paper they went to Canyon City. A lot of fancy writers have embroidered this trip until the truth is so buried you couldn't recognize it. They say Joaquin and his wife stood off the Indians and they tell of all sorts of adventures they had. None of this is true. I was along, so I ought to know. They had a little baby girl named Maud. Minnie Myrtle--for we always called her by her pen name--fastened a basket on the horn of her saddle

245

and fastened little Maud in the basket. Minnie
had a gentle saddle pony, so she had no trouble
at all. I had my outfit of pack horses along and
we camped together on the trip from Eugene to
Canyon City. We crossed the McKenzie not far from
what is now called McKenzie Bridge and went over
McKenzie Pass by the road on which now is located
the little town of Sisters. Minnie did the cooking. On my pack horses I had Hiner's library of
law books, for he was going over to Canyon City
to practice law. This was in 1864, and, while we
saw where the Indians had burned houses and had
been on the rampage, none of the Indians bothered
us.

"The sure way to find out what a person is
is to camp with him, and, measured by this standard, Minnie Myrtle, Joaquin's wife, was the best
campmate, and the most agreeable and the bravest
little woman I ever met. Their first child, Maud,
was followed by a son whom my brother named
Brick, for Brick Pomeroy, a spectacular newspaper
writer and author of that period, though little
noted by this generation. He called their next
child Hal. Minnie Myrtle died in her twenties in
San Francisco, and if you ask me what she died
of, I'll tell you it was from worry, humiliation
and a broken heart.

"Some years before his death my brother
Joaquin wrote to me to come to Florence, where my
brother George Melvin was then living. That's
near the mouth of the Siuslaw, in Lane County. We
three went there and had a reunion. That was the
first time we had met in 30 years. While we were
there they had a flower festival--I think they
called it a Rhododendron Jubilee, or some such
name. My brother Joaquin was chosen to crown the
queen of the festival. My son Melvin was working
for his uncle George Melvin, and later he married
the girl that his uncle Joaquin had crowned queen
of the festival.

"When Hiner was county judge at Canyon City he wrote a good deal of poetry, some of which was published in the Blue Mountain Eagle. He gathered up some of his poems and sent them to George H. Himes, who owned an interest in a printing office in Portland. He published this little book of poems under the title 'Specimens'. Later he published another little book called 'Joaquin, Et Al', but neither of these books made much of an impression, except on Joaquin, for he believed in them thoroughly, and when he went to London and republished them, they went over big and made his reputation. Then, after the people over there hailed him as a poet, the people here decided maybe he was one, after all."

"There's a lot of good and bad mixed up in all of us, and while my brother Joaquin had many traits that I personally did not approve, he had many others that were admirable, and I believe his poetry will live, for even I, who knew Joaquin so thoroughly, think some of his poetry is pretty good.

Miles Cannon of Boise, formerly a state official of Idaho, is now a federal official. As a by-product of his travels he writes most interesting and readable articles about the early life of Idaho. His book, "Wa-il-at-pu", which describes the rise and fall of the Whitman Mission, is a real contribution to the history of the west. Mr. Cannon was a recent visitor to Portland, being here on official business. In a recent issue of the Idaho Statesman of Boise, he gives some interesting facts about the early life of Joaquin Miller, the Poet of the Sierras. He says:

On the evening of April 1, 1868, Samuel Lockhart was seated in front of the state office at Silver City, Idaho, when Marion Moore, accompanied by three others, approached. Within the space of a very few minutes, an altercation sprang up between Lockhart and the Moore party, followed by a fusillade of gunshots, which brought to the scene a multitude of excited citizens. Moore received a bullet in the left breast and, running about 50 yards, fell in a dying condition. Lockhart was wounded in the left arm, but believing the injury would soon heal, neglected to have it properly treated, until it was found necessary to have the arm amputated. The operation was followed by blood poisoning, and death came to his relief on the 13th day of the following July.

The trouble seemed to have arisen over a dispute between the Ida Elmore and the Golden Chariot mining companies as to the boundaries of their properties. Finding themselves unable to affect an amicable settlement, all concerned resorted to force. During the month of March, 1868, both properties were strongly fortified and on the morning of March 25 the Golden Chariot force (a San Francisco organization) sallied forth and stormed the works of the Elmore. Desperate fighting continued throughout the day and at intervals during the night, but the following day, owing to the exhausted condition of the combatants, the engagement became less furious. Casualties as reported were, two killed and several wounded and missing. On the 28th Governor Ballard issued a proclamation ordering the belligerents to disperse and a squad of United States cavalry from Fort Boise was sent along to see that the proclamation was duly respected. On the 29th the troops appeared on the scene and as a result the warring miners were able to compromise their differences without further affusion of blood.

The untimely death of Lockhart, who was one of the belligerents, entitles him to a more prominent place in the annals of the pioneers than the Silver City affray naturally would accord him. Back in the early '50s, Sam and his twin brother, Harry, were members of a colony of some ten or 12 families who settled on Pit River some distance above its junction with McCloud River, Shasta County, California. The town of Shasta, situated about seven miles northwest of the present town of Redding, was then the county seat.

In January, 1857, the Pit River or Digger tribe of Indians fell upon the colony and massacred every member with the exception of Sam Lockhart, who was temporarily absent down the river at the time. His twin brother, Harry, was among the slain, which so angered Sam that he swore undying vengeance against the whole tribe that had participated in the slaughter. Though often warned and several times arrested by the federal authorities, he persisted, as soon as released, to make Digger hunting his principal occupation.

During the winter of 1859-60, he planned a raid on a small band of these Indians living on McCloud River, and had succeeded in picking off a few warriors, when he discovered a log cabin situated in a wooded recess of a small tributary. Careful investigation revealed, to his amazement, the presence of a white man living with a Digger squaw. Lockhart, actuated by the presumption that they had been implicated in the massacre, was in the act of shooting both the white man and his squaw, when the former pleaded his innocence of any connection with the crime and pitifully begged for the life of himself and consort. Lockhart, upon reflection, concluded to take his suspect before Judge Rosborough of Yreka for examination and advice. He thereupon tied the captive on the back of an Indian pony and escorted him before the magistrate. The judge at once instituted a searching investigation lasting two nights and a day, during which time Lockhart stood guard over the prisoner and assur(ed) him that if he attempted to escape his hide wouldn't hold shucks. The judge was unable to attach any blame to the man, who it was ascertained, was none other than Hiner Miller, who latterly became more or less distinguished as Joaquin Miller, the Poet of the Sierras. The judge, with much difficulty, persuaded Lockhart not to shoot the captive, who, upon regaining his freedom, made a hurried exit from the country.

Miller, according to the Shasta traditions, lived at that place and vicinity during the years 1856 to 1859, inclusive, and after his precipitous departure his squaw made that her home for many years. He joined the Pit River band in 1856 and for two years lived in the log cabin at the foot of the Shasta Mountains, where in 1857 his half-breed daughter was born.

It was in the midst of this sort of wild life that Miller first tried his hand at poetry. It was here likewise that he took the name "Joaquin", evidently adopted from Joaquin Murietta, a noted Spanish outlaw who lived in the upper San Joaquin Valley before the American occupation.

After leaving Shasta, Miller read law a few weeks in Oregon and was admitted to the bar by Judge Williams, formerly a member of President Grant's cabinet. He then made his appearance in northern Idaho where, unable to do anything at the law, he rode the pony express between Walla Walla and Orofino. After the mining excitement abated somewhat he drifted out of the state with the receding tide.

Lockhart followed the Diggers until he had killed every one implicated in the massacre on Pit River--estimated at 25. He then left California and took up his abode at Silver City, only to meet with death under conditions most distressing as well as unfortunate.

George Melvin Miller:

"My father was a school teacher, though he never taught school in Oregon. Father was a very silent man. Although reared in a Quaker family, he was a strict Methodist, and was very religious. We never ate a meal without his asking the Divine blessing upon it. If farm work interfered with family worship, the farm work had to take second place. He was a man of very even temper. I doubt if he ever swore in his life. He didn't know one card from another. He never drank nor smoked. My brother Joaquin did not follow very closely in Father's footsteps. Father said Joaquin had plenty of reverence, but very little piety.

"We lived plainly, but always had plenty of wholesome food. Mother made wheat hominy and served it with honey. She often boiled whole wheat, which we ate for breakfast, served with rich cream. Matches in those days were an expensive luxury, so we kept the fire going all night by covering the coals with ashes. One time I forgot to rake ashes over the coals and the fire went out. Next morning I had to go half a mile to the nearest neighbor and borrow some live coals.

"When I was 19 years old I taught school. While teaching school I studied law. I was admitted to the bar in 1880.

"My brother Joaquin was 12 years older than I. He was born in 1842. When he was 16 he and a neighboring boy named Bill Willoughby were up on the Bluffs at West Point near Coburg one afternoon and began rolling rocks over the face of the bluff to see them jump. Just as one of the larger rocks they had dislodged went over the edge, a neighbor's cow, startled by the racket made by the previous rock, stepped out of the brush and started across the hillside. The cow saw the rock coming, and instead of getting out of the way, looked up stupidly to see what was going to happen. It happened all right, and the cow went down with a broken leg. Joaquin and Bill Willoughby didn't want to face their parents nor the owner of the cow, so they went to southern Oregon. Joaquin got a job cooking for some miners at a placer camp. From there he drifted to northern California. He turned his hand at whatever job was handiest.

"Finally, believing that the indignation of the owner of the injured cow had subsided, he came back to the farm. A little later he went to Eugene and attended Columbia College. He was the valedictorian for the last class that graduated from that institution. He was about 19 at the time.

"After graduating he decided to go back to the mines near Jacksonville. He was there for a little while, and from there went to the Scott's Bar country and the placer districts near Shasta. He cooked, mined, and herded cattle, and for a while lived with the Indians. I remember when he came home he was dressed in a beautiful suit of tanned buckskin.

"He didn't stay home long. There was a lot of talk about the richness of the mines up in the Idaho territory, so he went up there. He went into the express business. He and a man named Mossman were partners in a pony express line which operated under the title of Mossman and Miller's express. They took out gold dust and brought in letters and papers. He made good money. When he came home from eastern Oregon and Idaho he had over $10,000 in gold dust.

"Joaquin was always quite a hand to write. While at the mines he wrote articles for the Golden Era of San Francisco. In almost every number of this publication poems appeared signed 'Minnie Myrtle'. Joaquin was always fond of poetry, so he began corresponding with the author of these verses. 'Minnie Myrtle' turned out to be the pen name of Theresa Dyer. She lived at Port Orford. This correspondence led to their being engaged. Joaquin was always more or less impetuous. He wrote her he would be over on a certain day, and for her to be ready to marry him. They had never seen each other, but the romance of the thing appealed to her. When Joaquin got there she was ready for the ceremony. They were at once married and the next day started away on horseback on their wedding journey.

"I was very fond of Joaquin's wife. She was not only mentally alert and vivacious, but exceedingly handsome. She was really a very fine woman. They had three children--a daughter, Maud, and two sons, George B. and Harry. The two boys died when they were children. Maud married a theatrical man named McCormack. She died when she was 28, leaving one child, who, I believe, is living at San Jose.

"I always called Joaquin 'Hiner'. In fact, most of his friends did. A few of them called him Cincinnatus, which was his first name, but Mother always called him Nat. After his marriage he became editor of the Eugene City Review, now the Eugene Daily Guard. He and Tony Noltner ran the paper. Tony was an old-line Democrat. During the Civil War the paper took the side of the South and was suppressed by the government authorities for sedition. I asked Joaquin why he wanted to side with the rebels. He said he always believed in helping the underdog.

"After the government had suppressed their paper, Joaquin moved to Canyon City. If you will look up the old Canyon City Journal, which was issued in the fall of 1868, you will find many of Joaquin's poems. This paper was called 'The City Journal, a paper for the miner, farmer, mechanic, and professional man'. In those days my brother signed his poetry C. H. Miller, instead of Joaquin Miller. In that same issue you will find the following advertisement. 'C. H. Miller, Attorney, Etc. Will practice in all courts except the County Court. Office in old Court House, Canyon City.

Canal boat driver, welldigger, prospector and miner, Indian fighter and Civil War veteran. That, in brief, is the record of Joseph D. Myers of Eugene, who was born 86 years ago in Switzerland. When I visited him recently, in company with George Melvin Miller, brother of Joaquin Miller, he said:

"I saw service with Hiner Miller, for that was the name Joaquin Miller went by 60 years ago. In March, 1864, Lieutenant J. A. Waymire, with a detail of 20 troopers, of whom I was one, was sent to Canyon City to clear the country of marauding Indians, who were making things strenuous for the settlers. An Indian slipped into Canyon City, where there was a corral full of horses, let down the bars and stampeded the horses. This was the last straw, so the citizens of Canyon City raised a company of 30 men and, with Hiner Miller as captain, started out to recapture the horses.

"Hiner Miller, with his party, started on the trail of the Indians, and Lieutenant Waymire, with his 20 troopers, joined him near where the town of Burns was later located. We followed the Indian trail through the center of the valley. Miller, with his party, took one side of the valley and we took the other, to be able to keep them from escaping. One of our men suddenly spied, at a considerable distance, a lot of the Indians jumping up and down and making all sorts of queer movements. We kept out of sight and crept up on them and when we got close enough to

rush them we discovered that instead of a party
of Indians we had surrounded a bunch of sandhill
cranes, which had been jumping up and down and
acting in the ridiculous way that sandhill cranes
do.

"As we came back one of our men was wounded
from a shot from the brush, and a little later we
ran onto a party of between 40 and 50 Indians. At
first we were afraid the Indians would escape,
but pretty soon we began wondering if we ourselves could escape. We would charge right into
them, emptying our pistols, then fall back and
reload our pistols and guns and again charge
them; but they didn't give way. The Indians would
charge us, lying clear over on the sides of their
horses so they were out of sight, and the only
way we could kill an Indian was to shoot his
horse badly enough to down it, and then, when the
Indian got up to run, take a shot at the Indian.

"Miller and his men heard the firing, so
they hurried up and joined us. Our combined party
headed for the foothills. This was the first of
April, 1864. That night we had a heavy snowstorm.
The next day we reached the foot of Steen's
Mountain, where we camped. We sent out scouts,
who located the Indians. We worked our way back
toward Canyon City. We saw that the Indians were
trying to close the gap in the hills, so we
watched closely to keep from getting ambushed.

"One of the squads that we sent out--Ser-
geant Casteel with four of our men and one of
Miller's men--was ambushed by the Indians. Hiner
Miller's mule was shot through a leg.

"The Indians gradually closed around us,
leaving only a little gap for us to get away.
Near this gap was a small hill. Lieutenant Waymire told me to take four men and, with all
speed, to take the hill, to prevent the Indians
from getting there, as they would be hard to
dislodge from the hilltop, and if they were there
they would command the gap through which we had

to make our way. With four men I started for the top of the hill as fast as our horses could run. The Indians saw what we were trying to do, so they started from the other side as fast as they could go to get to the hilltop first. We reached the summit of the hill together. We emptied our pistols in the Indians' faces; so they turned around and beat it down the hill again.

"The Indians had very much better guns than ours. We had old-fashioned Yager guns, which would not shoot as far as the guns used by the Indians. We shot at the Indians till we had only 15 rounds of ammunition each. That is, some of us had more and some had less, but when it was divided up, it gave us 15 rounds apiece. Part of our men were with Hiner Miller. Lieutenant Waymire and the rest of us started for camp. Miller and his men got to camp at two a.m., but Sergeant Casteel and his men were still missing. Lieutenant Waymire, leaving me in charge of the camp, started out with the rest of the men to hunt him up. They found where the Indians had ambushed our men, who had put up a hard fight. Sergeant Casteel was the last of the detail of six men to be killed. They found his body not far from Sheep Rock, on Crooked River, near where the town of Redmond was later built. In talking with some of the Indians later they told us Sergeant Casteel had been very hard to kill. It took a good many shots to finish him. He had killed six or seven Indians before they finally killed him."

Judge C. C. Goodwin:

"Joaquin Miller had a head of gold, breast and arms of silver, but all the rest 'potter's clay'. A half-savage chained to a star. His soul took in every glory of nature; the hills, the forest, the overhanging dome of the sky, the stars above, the boom of the deep-sea surges bringing, in an unknown tongue, messages from far-off lands--all these were delights to him. The songs of the birds always met a response from him, but an Indian wickiup suited him as well as a palace, and when in the deep night the scream of a complaining cougar came to his ears he smiled and said low to himself, 'We are in accord'.

"A little more, and he would have been out and out a naked savage; a little more the other way and the angels in heaven would have bent their ears toward the earth to listen to his melodies. Of the earth he was exceedingly earthy, but all the time the incandescent lights of his soul were shining through the coarse material and illuminating it.

"His courage, moral and physical, was superb. He could look any danger in the face and smile, and when the foremost men and women of the land knocked at his rude door he received them with a grace as free from affectation as from apology. While he never felt above the most lowly, he never met a man whom he deemed his superior. He had a native, savage pride which an earthquake could not have shaken.

"In his youth he accepted the sensual side of life, but at night, from his bed on the ground, he had a wireless telegraphy which brought him messages from the stars. He transcribed some of these, and their divinity cannot be questioned. Had his surroundings been more refined, and had he learned a little more discipline in his youth, who knows what he might not have achieved?

"He lived his own way, asking no odds of anyone, and without fear passed on."

Disappointed at not being elected to the Oregon supreme bench and embittered by lack of appreciation of his fellow Oregonians for his two thin books of verse, "Specimens", and "Joaquin Et Al", Judge Miller sailed for England where he made an almost instantaneous success. Returning to this country, he wrote a letter from the Astor House, New York City, on September 22, 1871, that reads as follows:

"As I left England suddenly, barely saying goodbye to a number of friends at hand, I have ever since felt like making some expression of my gratitude to that country for its noble treatment of me and my crude 'Songs of the Sierras', and as the American press has, as a rule, treated me with similar generosity, and as I am about to return for a time to the Sierras and my home on the Willamette, I take the occasion to briefly thank both countries together.

"First, let me speak of England, for was she not first to speak of me? Looking back a few months to a venture that now seems to me like a dream, I am bound to say that the conduct of that country in holding up my hands when they were not strong, when, in fact, I had neither money, name, nor influence, appears to me every day, as I recall it, manly and generous beyond calculation. England, the terms of expression of thanks are threadbare. Permit me to say simply, 'I thank you!' I stood by Niagara the other day and kissed my hand to Canada, and, with the experience of the last six months rushing across my mind, I said, hat in hand, 'England, I thank you!'

"While the American press has been more cautious and qualified in its reviews, I believe, as a rule, it has been honest and well-meaning. England was treating with a stranger who appealed to her generosity, and so she refused to see faults, while she could find any merits to commend. America, however, is anxious and concerned about her literature, and is ready to point out faults, that they may be avoided in the future. At least that is what the author of the severest criticism I have yet seen, writes me, and I am ready to believe him. The public is full of good will. The sale of the book proves that and I have nothing now to complain of. I shall return to the Sierras, and to the pastoral banks of the Willamette, glad and grateful and with lifted face."

Oregon Journal
April 6 & 16, 1920
October 28, 1921
December 15, 1923
December 27, 1924
Others, undated

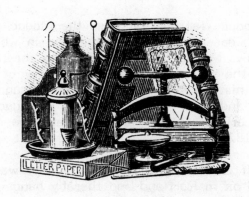

JEFF C. RIDDLE

An Indian View of the Modoc War

(Modoc War history, from the Modoc side of
the case, has been written by a man in whose
veins flows Modoc blood. He sketches for Mr.
Lockley the salient points of his history of that
war. In this installment he tells how misunder-
standing and snap judgment caused a tragedy that
was the origin of that terrible affair, the Modoc
War of 1872.)

Jeff C. Riddle of Klamath County was a recent visitor to Portland and thereby hangs a
tale.

It was 50 years ago that the first skirmish
occurred that led up to the Modoc War and the
killing of General Canby and the other peace
commissioners, resulting in the long and desperate resistance of Captain Jack and his warriors
in the lava beds. Jeff C. Riddle was ten years
old at the time and was present when the Modocs
killed General Canby and his commissioners. Mr.
Riddle's father was an interpreter, and his
mother, Wi-ne-ma Toby Riddle, a member of the
Modoc tribe, brought the warning to the commis-

sioners of the plans of the Modocs to kill General Canby and his fellow commissioners.

"I was born in Yreka, California, November 30, 1863," said Mr. Riddle. "My father, Frank Riddle, was born in Kentucky, September 6, 1832. He came to California when he was 18 and worked as a prospector, miner, and packer, and at freighting, stockraising, hunting, and trapping. My

---

"If you will read the history of our troubles with the Indians, you will find that the trouble has usually started through the unjust action of bad whites, who, after getting into trouble, appealed to the government to help them out of it."

---

father and mother were married in 1862. My mother is a full-blooded Modoc Indian and is a cousin of Captain Jack, who, with other Modoc warriors, was hanged for killing General Canby. Captain Jack's Indian name was Ke-in-to-poses.

"My father prospected and mined in various mining camps of California from 1850 to 1856, when he settled at Yreka, where he lived until 1862. Shortly after marrying my mother he settled on Bogus Creek, about 20 miles east of Yreka. My father was a typical Kentuckian. He loved to hunt and trap. In 1868 and 1869 we moved to the Upper Gap country on Lost River, where Father ran a line of traps. There was never any shortage of meat in our camp, for Father killed hundreds of bears for their skins and we always had elk or deer meat hanging outside the cabin. Father died February 21, 1906, at Yainax, in Klamath County, at the age of 74. There were four children in our family, all boys. My three brothers, however, died when they were children.

"Living a life in the open, as we did, and

always going where game was most plentiful, I had little or no opportunity to go to school. I never went to school but twice. the first time was in California, where I attended for three weeks. In 1876 I went to school in New York City for the same length of time. The way we happened to be in New York City was that shortly after the close of the Modoc War Colonel A. B. Meacham, with Captain O. C. Applegate, my father, my mother, myself and some Modoc Indians, made a tour of the United States. This was in 1876, the year of the centennial celebration in Philadelphia.

"When I was 19 I married the daughter of Chief Schonchin, whose brother, John, was hanged at Fort Klamath. I have five children--two boys and three girls. I have 23 grandchildren and three great-grandchildren.

"You might say I am an author, though my business is raising stock. I wrote "The Indian History of the Modoc War", because men like Drannan and other irresponsible and sensational writers, who know nothing whatever of the facts, wrote books that purported to tell the story of the Modoc War, and I wanted the public to know the real facts about the contest in which Captain Jack, with 51 warriors, held over 1000 government troops, 78 Warm Springs Indian scouts, and a company of Oregon Volunteers at bay from November 18, 1872, to June 1, 1873. If you will read the history of our troubles with the Indians, you will find that the trouble has usually started through the unjust action of bad whites, who, after getting into trouble, appealed to the government to help them out of it. My only interest in writing my history of the Modoc War was to give both sides, without color or without prejudice, so that the truth might be known, and so that the people, having all of the facts before them, could form their judgment correctly. In 1900, 27 years after the close of the contest, my mother was granted a pension of $25 a month for her services in the Modoc War. She saved the life of A. B. Meacham, and if her warning had been heeded General Canby and the others would not have been killed.

"The Modoc Indians got along peaceably with the white miners and emigrants until about 1853. Some irresponsible white men fired on some Indians of the Pitt River tribe, killing several. The Pitt River Indians waylaid and killed some emigrants near the present site of Alturas, California, in 1853. Some of the emigrants hurried to Yreka and gave the alarm.

"Jim Crosby, with about 60 miners, started out to punish the Pit River Indians. They met several bands of Modoc Indians, with whom they had no trouble. They were unable to find the guilty Pit River Indians. On their return from their trip Crosby and his men camped near a band of Modoc Indians. Crosby visited the Modocs and gave them some bacon and bread. Knowing that the Modocs were friendly, Crosby's men did not put out any sentinels that night. They were attacked by a band of about 20 Pitt River Indians and several of the white men were wounded.

"Crosby, not knowing that the attack was made by the Pit River Indians, ordered his men to clean up the Indians in the Modoc camp nearby. There were 14 men, women, and children in the Modoc camp and they were getting breakfast when Crosby's men came. They did not know of the attack on Crosby's camp during the night and were utterly unsuspicious. Crosby and his men fired at them, killing 11 out of the 14. Three of the Indians got away and, going from village to village, told how they had been attacked by the white men without provocation.

"This was the first Modoc blood spilled by the white men. The Modocs scattered, some going to the mountains and others hiding in the thick tules.

"The Modocs had not been able to get word to one of the Modoc bands called the Hot Creek Modocs. They came out to greet Crosby's men with signs of friendship. The volunteers fired at them, killing men, women and children. The next day Captain Crosby, with his men, reached Yreka with a large number of fresh scalps of Modoc Indians to exhibit as a sign of their prowess. Most of these scalps, however, were the scalps of old squaws or children. Captain Crosby and his men were given a big dinner and a dance and his men told how in two pitched battles with the Indians, in which they were outnumbered, they had defeated them. While this needless slaughter of peaceable Indians happened in 1853, 20 years before the Modoc War, it was really the underlying cause of the war."

(Here is continued Jeff Riddle's story of the Modoc Indian troubles. This installment includes an action in which a band of Modocs perished through trusting a white man who promised peace while planning slaughter.)

"Shortly after the massacre of the Modoc Indians by Crosby's men, the Modoc chiefs called a council of all the Indians in that part of the country. Captain Jack's father was one of the principal chiefs in those days. Most of the head men decided that the only thing to do was to fight for their homes, for it seemed they would be killed anyway, and they might as well try to defend their long-time homes and protect their wives and children.

"During this council Captain Jack was a mere boy, not over 15 years old. You know, of course, that boys are not allowed to speak in council, but, being the son of the head chief, he asked to say a few words and was given permission. He said, 'So far, the Modocs have not killed any white people. Our hands are not yet stained with their blood. The white people killed us by mistake, thinking it was the Modocs, not the Pit River Indians, that had attacked them. If we kill the emigrants and the other white people, it will simply mean that we will be killing innocent people and we ourselves will be killed for acts.'

"Jack's father arose and said, 'My son is but a child, but he has spoken good words. I hope in time to come that he will be a wise chief for our tribe.'

"Some of the Indians refused to agree not to kill any white men. Among these was a chief named Legugyokes. He and some of his young men attacked an emigrant train shortly after this, killing some of the white people. Survivors of this emigrant train carried the word of the attack by the Modoc Indians to Yreka and a company of volunteers was raised to hunt down the Indians, my father being one of these volunteer soldiers who came out to kill the Modocs. After the massacre of these emigrants by the Indians, practically all the Modocs took to the mountains, where they lived for the next two or three years. No emigrants were killed in the Modoc country, though a number were killed from time to time in the Pitt River country.

"In the summer of 1856, during the Rogue River Indian War, Ben Wright, with some of his friends, joined a number of volunteers from Yreka and started out to find and kill the Modoc Indians. They killed the Indians wherever they found them, irrespective of whether they were peaceable or on the warpath.

"Meeting a Modoc Indian who could talk English, Ben Wright asked him to gather the Indians together for a peace talk. The runner was sent form village to village and 45 Modoc Indians, with their squaws, gathered at the Natural Bridge to attend the council.

"Wright and his men returned after five days, as they had promised, dismounting near the Indian camp. Wright came to the Modocs and asked the Indians to camp nearer his men, where he could hold a council more easily. He picked out a campsite for them on the riverbank, while he posted his men just back of the Indian camp. Wright furnished the Indians a beef and some flour. Captain Jack's father was there and said he was glad to be able to make pece with the whites, because he and his people were tired of hiding in the mountains.

"Just at daybreak Wright's men attacked the Modocs. Wright met Captain Jack's father, who was gathering small brush to make a fire for breakfast. Drawing his revolver, he shot Captain Jack's father dead and gave the command to his men to fire. The Indians were unarmed and before they could get their bows the whites charged them. The Indians ran to the river, but Wright had posted his men there and as the Indians swam across the river they were fired at and killed. Not a white man was injured, because the Indians were unarmed when attacked. Only five of all the Indian men escaped, and these five were badly wounded. After the Indians had been butchered, Wright told his men to get the scalps, and so the men, women and children were scalped and the scalps taken to Yreka and shown to the citizens, who gave Wright and his men a big banquet and dance.

"Captain Jack's father was dead, so Captain Jack became chief. The Modocs met in council, went to the scene of the butchery and gathered all of the bodies they could and cremated them. Many of the Indians had been shot while swimming the river and were never recovered. For months the Indians watched the river banks to recover the bodies, which they buried.

"The Modocs took to the hills again, where they hid for several years. Jack, though a young man, went to Yreka, where he met the county judge of Siskiyou County and some of the leading citizens, who had learned the real facts of the unwarranted massacre and who promised Jack that such a thing should not be repeated. They told Jack that if he would keep his people at peace and not retaliate for the massacre of his father and the Indians they would see that the white men did not attack the Indians again. They also promised they would not let the white men disturb the Indians nor take their land.

"In 1859 a good many white people began taking up land where Captain Jack's tribe had their home, near the Natural Bridge, on Lost River. Captain Jack was able to keep his Indians from making any trouble, and on their part the emigrants did not for some time disturb the Indians.

"In 1868 a settler named Abe Ball had trouble with a Modoc Indian over a Modoc squaw. Ball decided to let the government settle his trouble for him, so he wrote to Captain Knapp, the agent at the Klamath agency, saying the Modocs were secretly planning trouble for the white settlers. Captain Knapp wrote to Washington, D. C., and in answer to his letter the Indian commissioner at Washington appointed a peace commission to investigate the trouble. A. B. Meacham of Salem, Oregon, was appointed peace commissioner. Colonel Meacham, in company with I. D. Applegate, John Meacham, George Nurse, Gus Horn, and a company of cavalry, was ordered in November, 1869, to go to the home of the Modocs and hold a conference with them. My father and mother were the interpreters. I was present. At this council the Modocs were ordered to leave their homes and go to the Klamath Agency. Captain Jack agreed to do this, providing the white men would protect them from the Klamath Indians, who outnumbered the Modocs and were unfriendly to them. The Indians were told to get ready to leave the next day, which they did, accompanied by an escort of soldiers."

Oregon Journal
February 5 & 6,
1923

BARNEY PRINE
Founder of Prineville

Prineville, Oregon, is named for Barney Prine. When I met him first, 30 years ago, he still retained much of the strength for which he had been famous. He was tall, broad shouldered, spare built and had muscles like steel wires. He was city marshal of Weston, Oregon, in early days. I have lost track of Barney Prine. I suppose he is dead, for the last time I saw him, some years ago, he was quite feeble. On one of my visits to him while he was staying in Pendleton, he said:

"They call me Barney Prine, but I was christened Francis B. Prine. I was born about 12 miles from Kansas City on January 1, 1841. My father, Frank Prine, was born in the south and was a preacher in the Methodist Church, South. My mother, Elsie Daley Prine, was born in Kentucky.

"I was 12 years old when we started across the plains for Oregon in 1853. I drove one of the wagons, to which was hitched two yoke of steers and a yoke of cows. I was only 12 years old, but I was a husky young chap and I stood guard regu-

269

larly with the men. We settled in the forks of the Santiam, about six miles from Scio. In those days all the settlers in the forks of the Santiam were southerners and, of course, Democrats.

"Before long we began feeling a little crowded in the forks of the Santiam, and I decided to go east of the mountains, where I would have more room. Kit Carson was in what is now Crook County, along in 1843. Major Stein built a military wagon road from The Dalles to Fort Harney, crossing through Crook County, during the Civil War. The first man to make a permanent settlement in Crook County was Marion Scott, who located on Trout Creek in 1863. They camped during the summer of 1863 on Hay Creek. In 1867 Howard Maupin came up from near Eugene and settled on Trout Creek. The following year Henry Coleman came up from Lane County and engaged in the cattle business. During the next year or two John Luckey, Anthony Webdell, E. G. Conant and John Toms settled in the Ochoco Valley.

"I went up to the Ochoco country in 1868 and took up a place on which the town of Prineville, which is named for me, is located. I was 27 years old when I went up there. That same year Wayne Claypoole, Bill Smith, Ewen Johnson, and Lou Dougherty settled near the mouth of Mill Creek, while Elisha Barnes, Tom James, and Abraham Zell took up places on Ochoco Creek. William Heisler ran the first store in the Ochoco Valley and I ran the first saloon. Heisler started his store in 1871. Monroe Hodges, who had a place near Corvallis, came up there in 1871 and built a hotel in what is now Prineville. Two years later they started a post office called Prineville, and Daniel E. Thomas was appointed first postmaster.

"When I went up there I started a blacksmith shop and a small store. Two years later I started a saloon. Any of the old-timers will tell you about my string of race horses. When I was a boy

I made considerable money as a foot racer. If you will look up the Albany papers published in 1859 you will see how I cleaned up all the local talent there in a foot race. I ran a mile race once in which 18 started and only three finished, and I was ten paces ahead of the other two. A gambler offered to cover any money the crowd would put up

---

"Things were a little rough in Prineville in the early days. Property wasn't very safe, particularly horses, so we had to lynch a few of the horse thieves, and then things quieted down."

---

that I could beat all comers and give them a ten yard start on a mile race.

"When I started my store and blacksmith shop at Prineville, I hauled my goods from The Dalles. Things were a little rough in Prineville in early days. Property wasn't very safe, particularly horses, so we had to lynch a few of the horse thieves, and then things quieted down. W. H. Harrison and a man named Langdon were killed by the vigilantes. They shot Langdon and hung Harrison from the bridge over Crooked River. Later, Al Swartz was killed, and that same night Sidney Huston and Charlie Luster were hung. There were quite a few other killings, but most of the others were grudge killings.

"I went to school for a while in the forks of the Santiam, near Scio. My school teacher told me that we could make big money by putting out counterfeit money. I wouldn't go in with him and he told me not to mention what he had told me. I met him in Florence in 1862. He left town that day. Later I met him in Boise, where he had set up as a gentleman. I recognized him and he was

271

arrested. During his trial it was proved he was not only a counterfeiter, but he had also been .. a road agent, so they sent him to the pen for ten years.

"I was only 21 when I was in Florence, and I guess I was a little wild. My partner and I happened to strike a rich claim. You can know it was rich when I tell you I spent as high as $1000 a day gambling and treating anybody and everybody that wanted a drink, with drinks a dollar a throw. I was always a great hand to be sociable. I never was what you would call really drunk, but once. When I was five years old my brother-in-law sent me to get a gallon of whiskey. He had me drink all I could to see what I would do. Mother was pretty near scared to death, but he told her that it wasn't my fault--that he had done it just for devilment.

"I moved from Prineville to Weston in the early '70s and was appointed city marshal. Hank Vaughn came down to a dance at Weston once, and, after he had taken a few drinks, he announced that he was going to kill me, but I took Hank's gun away and told him to go home and sober up.

"I used to be pretty much of a plunger when it came to gambling. The fact of the matter is, I was a lucky gambler. When I was a young chap three men combined against me and won all the money I had. I hunted up a card shark and we got those three fellows in a game, and we trimmed them out of over $5000. I never used to drink when I was gambling. You've got to keep a clear head to gamble successfully. The biggest pot I ever won was $6000. We were playing poker and everyone dropped out but another fellow and myself. I kept an ace and a jack and asked for three cards. I got two or more aces in my draw. He had three kings, but my three aces were a little too much for him, so I raked in the pot.

"From Weston I went to Fort Lapwai, where I ran a blacksmith shop for nearly 20 years.

"I have had mighty few fights with men when they were sober. I have had to have a good many fights with men when they were drunk, but I've always figured the best way to handle a drunken man was to wade right in and give him all you've got before he can do any harm to you.

"I got converted at a revival and joined the church, along in the '70s, and a few days later some men came to my place and wanted to play cards. They were fairly lousy with money, and I knew, from watching them play, that I could make a cleanup. I tell you, I had a pretty hard fight with the devil then, and I was certainly sorry they hadn't come before I was converted. It sure was a hard fight, but I won out, and wouldn't touch a card."

Oregon Journal
March 31, 1927

WILLIAM S. LADD

of the

Ladd & Tilton Bank

William S. Ladd, who, with Charles Elliott
Tilton, founded the Ladd & Tilton Bank in Portland, hailed from Sanbornton Bridge, New Hampshire, as did his partner, Mr. Tilton. Mr. Carr,
a resident of Sanbornton Bridge, went to San
Francisco shortly after gold was discovered and
later took a stock of goods amounting to $3500 to
Portland, where he sold it, making a profit of
over $10,000. He returned to New Hampshire in
January, 1851, and when Mr. Ladd learned of his
success he at once decided to go to Portland. At
that time Mr. Ladd was getting $30 a month, wor-
king for a railroad company. He left New York
early in 1851, went to San Francisco, and from
there came to Portland.

Mr. Ladd got his real start toward the fortune that he amassed, when a vessel put into
Portland with trade goods belonging to a Mr.
Gookin. When Mr. Ladd applied to Mr. Gookin for a
job helping him unload the goods, Mr. Gookin
said, "Where are you from?"

Mr. Ladd said, "Sanbornton Bridge, New
Hampshire."

Mr. Gookin said, "Did you know Samuel Tilton?"

"He lived near my father's place."

"Did you know Dr. Ladd?" inquired Mr. Gookin.

"He is my father," said Mr. Ladd.

Mr. Gookin at once engaged Mr. Ladd to help
unload the goods and to sell them, agreeing to
pay him $250 for three months' work. After sel-

"At that time Portland had a population
of 2917, which included the Chinese residents. There were 1163 white males over 21
years of age."

---

ling out Mr. Gookin's goods, Mr. Ladd started a
store of his own.

In 1853 he built the first brick building in
Portland--a one-story structure at 105 Front
Street just opposite the ferry landing. In 1857 a
second story was added to this building, and
here, on June 1, 1859, William S. Ladd and
Charles E. Tilton started the Ladd & Tilton Bank,
the capital stock being $50,000. At that time
Portland had a population of 2917, which included
the Chinese residents. There were 1163 white
males over 21 years of age.

Shortly after this bank had been started
gold was discovered in Idaho and eastern Oregon,
and during the Civil War the principal shipments
from Portland were of gold dust. On April 13,
1862, the Brother Jonathan left Portland for San
Francisco with 1547 boxes of apples, $21,657 in
specie and a miscellaneous shipment of eggs,
lard, hides, wool, beans, and flour. On June 25
the steamer Sierra Nevada left Portland for San
Francisco with a shipment of gold dust valued at

$228,000, 6896 pounds of wool and a quantity of fur. On September 25, the Brother Jonathan left For San Francisco with a shipment of $210,000 in gold dust sent by Wells-Fargo & Co. and also shipments from the bank and various merchants amounting in all to $315,780. During the war the usual rate of interest was one and a half to three percent per month on short loans and ten to 20 percent on long-time loans.

By January 1, 1860, the balance sheet of their bank showed deposits of $49,1891.62. In 1861, Stephen Mead became a partner and the capital stock was increased to $150,000. Within a few years the bank transferred its activities from the second story to the ground floor. Shortly after the close of the Civil War the bank increased its capital stock to $400,000. In 1868 Mr. Ladd let the contract for the erection of a new building, at the corner of 1st and Stark Streets, into which they moved in the fall of 1868.

In 1880 Charles E. Tilton and Stephen Mead retired, William M. Ladd becoming a partner of his father, William S. Ladd. At this time the deposits were slightly more than $1,000,000. The capital and surplus, which amounted to more than $1,000,000 were distributed.

On May 8, 1908, the Ladd & Tilton Bank was incorporated with a capital of $1,000,000, with surplus and undivided profits of $400,000. On January 1, 1911, the bank moved to the new Spalding Building, at 3rd and Washington Streets. William M. Ladd retired from the presidency of the bank in January, 1919, at which time the deposits amounted to over $21,000,000.

Oregon Journal
October 23, 1928
December 14, 1932

JESSE APPLEGATE

Leader of the Cow Column

On April 11, 1843, Jesse Applegate, who at that time lived in St. Clair County, Missouri, wrote to his brother Lisbon the following letter:

"I will start with my family to the Oregon Territory this spring. Lindsay and perhaps Charles go with me. This resolution has been conceived and matured in a very short time, but it is probably destiny, to which account I place it, having neither time nor good reasons to offer in defense of so wild an undertaking. We are all well, and I only snatch this opportunity to write you for the purpose of ascertaining if the same species of madness exists on your side of the Missouri.

"If you are going to Oregon, by all means go this spring, for if Linn's bill passes, next year every man and every man's neighbors and friends will move in that direction. Write immediately and meet us if possible at the rendezvous armed and equipt as the journey requires.

"Your affectionate brother, Jesse Applegate."

The emigrants met at Independence, Missouri. On May 20 a meeting was held at Fitzhugh's Mill, 12 miles west of Independence, to elect officers for the trip across the plains. Jesse Applegate and his brothers Lindsay and Charles, with Daniel Waldo and some others, came from St. Clair County, Missouri. Peter H. Burnett brought a company of his friends and neighbors from the Platte Purchase, in Missouri. Peter H. Burnett, who was later destined to be the first American governor of California, was elected captain of the wagon train. There were about 120 wagons, most of which were drawn by four to six yoke of oxen.

At the crossing of the Big Blue the wagon train was divided. Those who were taking loose stock to Oregon joined what was known as the "cow column", which came on more slowly. This column was piloted by Jesse Applegate. Including the oxen used as motive power, there were about 5000 animals in the cow column. The 60 wagons in this cow column were divided into 15 platoons of four wagons each, the platoon in the lead retaining the lead one day and then taking its place in the rear. Dr. Marcus Whitman joined the cow column on the Platte and traveled with it as far as Fort Hall.

Jesse Applegate brought with him about 100 head of stock. He also brought an abundant store of provisions, such as flour, bacon, dried fruits and vegetables; also tools, household goods, wearing apparel, schoolbooks and his library, consisting of historical works as well as a Bible, Shakespeare and Worcester's Dictionary.

At Fort Walla Walla, now called Wallula, log rafts were made for the trip down the Columbia. One of these rafts met with a mishap, resulting in the drowning of three people, one of whom was Edward Bates Applegate, 11 years old, oldest son of Jesse Applegate.

The Applegates settled in Polk County, where

Jesse Applegate built a grist mill and helped survey the donation land claims of his neighbors. In 1844 the provisional government appointed him surveyor general. Jesse Applegate was elected a member of the provisional legislature in 1845. He revised the organic laws in 1843 and at the subsequent election his revision of the laws was adopted.

In 1849 Jesse Applegate moved from Polk County to Yoncalla, in Southern Oregon. He was elected a member of the state constitutional convention that met in Salem in 1857.

Captain Levi Scott, who came from Burlington, Iowa, in 1844, knowing what a hard trip the emigrants had by the Old Oregon Trail, decided to find an easier way, so he got in touch with Jesse and Lindsay Applegate and some others to see if they couldn't survey an easier route. (In 1846 they) surveyed what was known as the Southern Route...by way of the Rogue River Valley.

Right here is a good place to interject a note of explanation about this new route. Captain Levi Scott, Jesse Applegate, Lindsay Applegate, Moses Harris, John Scott, Henry Bogus, John Owens, Robert Smith, Samuel Goodhue, John Jones, Bennett Osborne, William Sportsman, Benjamin Burch, David Goff, and William Parker--none of whom had any ax to grind--volunteered to try to survey a more practicable route from Fort Hall to the Willamette Valley.

William G. Parker came across the plains in 1843. His sister was the wife of Jesse Applegate. Robert Smith, who was a Virginian, also came to Oregon in 1843. He had married a daughter of Charles Applegate, and his brother-in-law, Stephen F. Chadwick, later became governor of Oregon. David Goff crossed the plains in 1844. Colonel J. W. Nesmith married a daughter of David Goff. Benjamin F. Burch came to Oregon in 1845. I interviewed him more than 35 years ago at his home in Polk County and he told me of his experiences on this trip. John Owens came from Missouri across the plains in 1843. Samuel Goodhue came to Oregon in 1844. He later lived in Salem. Moses Harris, usually known as "the Black Squire", was an associate of Joe Meek. He had been a trapper and mountain man and was thoroughly familiar with the Indians and spoke the Shoshone language. He settled in the Willamette Valley in 1844.

These 15 public-spirited Oregonians traveled through the Willamette Valley and thence through the Rogue River Valley. They crossed the Cascades just north of what is now the southern boundary of Oregon. They made their way along the northern shore of the Klamath Lakes. They crossed Lost River by what is known as the "stone bridge". Part of the company of explorers went on to Bear River, while Jesse Applegate, Squire Harris, David Goff, John Owens and Henry Bogus made their way to Fort Hall. Henry Bogus left the party to overtake a son of Captain Grant. He failed to join Captain Grant's son and has never been heard of since. It is supposed that he was killed by the Indians.

Lansford W. Hastings, who had come to Oregon in 1842, met the emigrants at Fort Hall to try to persuade them to go to California. Many of the emigrants who had started out for the Willamette Valley decided to go by the Southern Route, which had just been surveyed by the Polk County pioneers. David Goff and Levi Scott remained with the emigrants to serve as guides, while Jesse Applegate and the other members of the surveying party went ahead to improve the road. The Applegates asked for volunteers from among the emigrants to help work on the road, and Thomas Powers, Alfred Stewart, Charles Putnam, who later married a daughter of Jesse Applegate, J. M. Wair and William Kirquendall, with a number of others, including Messrs. Burgess, Shaw, and Carnahan, shouldered their axes and went ahead to improve the road.

They dug Antelope Spring larger. They also enlarged Rabbit Hole Spring, and they cut a passable road on the eastern slope of the Cascades as well as improving the road in the Rogue River Valley and the Umpqua Canyon. The Polk County surveyors had been absent from home for four months, so they went on home, leaving explicit instructions to the emigrants to hurry forward so they would not be delayed by the fall rains.

After the guides left, the wagon train was divided, one section being led by Harrison Linville, and the other by Medders Vanderpool. The Indians tried to prevent the settlers from passing through the country. In a skirmish with the Indians, Jesse Boone, a great-grandson of Daniel Boone of Kentucky, killed one of the Indians. Four of the emigrants were wounded with arrows. Daniel Tanner of Iowa died of his wounds, as did a man named Sallee. Whately and Lippincott, who were wounded, recovered.

The emigrants found rough going between the Thousand Springs and the Rogue River Valley. In place of hastening on, they decided to recruit their cattle and linger awhile in the Rogue River Valley. This resulted in untold hardships when they attempted to make their way northward through Cow Creek Canyon. Many of the cattle were lost, the wagons abandoned, and a number of the emigrants died as a result of the hardship.

Not long ago I climbed the hillside back of Jesse Applegate's old home in the Yoncalla Valley and in the private burying ground of the Applegate family I read the following inscription on a plain slab of native sandstone:
"Jesse Applegate, Born July 5, 1811; Died April 22, 1888. Cynthia Applegate, Born August 5,

1813; Died June 1, 1881."

This slab marks the final resting place of one of Oregon's most useful and influential citizens.

Jesse Applegate was a man who would have made his mark in the halls of Congress. He was a natural leader. He was a man who loved justice and who could not be bribed or bluffed into doing a mean or ignoble act. As time goes on he will be recognized as the one to whom in highest degree the success of Oregon's provisional government was due.

Jesse Applegate's father, Daniel Applegate, came of English stock and served in the revolutionary army. At the close of that war he migrated to Kentucky, where he met and married Rachel Lindsay. After 40 years' residence in Kentucky he decided that Kentucky was becoming too crowded, so he went to Missouri. This was in 1823, when Jesse Applegate was 12 years old. A year later Jesse Applegate, though but 13 years of age, was employed to teach school.

During the next eight years he worked at St. Louis. In 1825 he met Captain Clark, who, with Captain Lewis, had made the memorable journey of discovery and exploration in 1804 and 1805 to the richness of the Oregon Country, and of the great pired Jesse Applegate with a desire to see the Oregon Country. Jesse secured work as a clerk in the surveyor general's office at St. Louis.

When he was 17, Jesse became intimately acquainted with the postmaster at St. Louis, Wilson Price Hunt. He spent a good deal of his spare time with Mr. Hunt, who delighted to tell about John Jacob Astor, for whom he had worked, and of his trip to Oregon in 1811. Mr. Hunt told him about the establishing of Astoria, of trading with the Indians, about the beauty, fertility and richness of the Oregon County, and of the great opportunities for trading and commerce in this almost unknown country on the shores of the Pacific. In addition to being postmaster, Hunt ran a fur warehouse in the basement of the post office. Here Jesse would visit him and Mr. Hunt would tell him about the habits of beaver and of the other animals whose pelts he handled.

Through Hunt, Applegate met William L. Sublette, David Jackson, and Jedediah Smith, to whom the vast stretch of country beyond the Rocky Mountains was not an unknown land, for they were not only traders and trappers, but also explorers, veterans in trading with the Indians and in making their way through untracked wilderness. Smith had explored the country between the Great Salt Lake and southern California. From there he had gone northward through California and the Willamette Valley to the newly established post, Fort Vancouver, on the Columbia River, where he had spent the winter of 1828-29. His account of his trip from San Diego to Fort Vancouver, of the perils and hardships he had experienced, of his meeting with Dr. John McLoughlin and of the beauty and fertility of the Willamette Valley made Jesse Applegate eager to see the land of mystery and charm by the sun-down sea.

Jesse Applegate lived in St. Louis from 1825 to 1831, in which year he was married. He was made a deputy in the office of the surveyor general and assigned to field work in the wilder parts of Missouri. He bought a farm in the Osage Valley, where he spent the 12 years from 1831 to 1843, farming and surveying.

Jesse Applegate was opposed to slavery. He would neither buy, own, nor sell Negroes, so he was forced to depend on hiring Negro slaves from his neighbors. Finally, the ever-increasing slave sentiment in Missouri became intolerable to him, so he decided to sell his place, break the friendships of a lifetime and cross the plains to the Willamette Valley. Other emigrants saw to it that their wagons were loaded with plenty of ba-

con, cornmeal, dried fruit and similar supplies.
Jesse Applegate saw to it that in addition to
foodstuffs his wagon should have an abundant
supply of schoolbooks for his children, biog-
raphies, histories, Shakespeare, the Bible, a
dictionary and other food for the mind, as well
as food for the body.

Jesse Applegate's fitness to lead resulted
in his being chosen as the leader of what was
called the "cow column". In coming down the Columbia River his oldest boy, Edward Bates Applegate, was drowned through the overturning of one
of the rafts. He settled with his family in Polk
County and the following year, 1844, was appointed surveyor general under the provisional government. He was elected from Yamhill County as a
member of the legislature in 1845, and without
question was the most influential member of the
provisional legislature. He was able to revise
the organic laws of 1843, which revision was adopted by the vote of the people. Early pioneers
of Oregon always thought of Jesse Applegate as
the lawmaker and lawgiver of the provisional
government. He was one of the members of the
constitutional convention of 1857.

Applegate's home at Yoncalla was a magnet
that drew men of national reputation. He became a
member of the government commission that settled
the treaty claims of the Puget Sound Agricultural
Company and of the Hudson's Bay Company. He was
no orator, but was a charming conversationalist.
His letters and articles not only have facility
but felicity of expression. He was a clear thin-
ker and a logical reasoner. All over Oregon you
will find old pioneers who have saved his letters, for he ws a voluminous correspondent. The
name Applegate is marked in large letters on the
early history of Oregon.

Oregon Journal
October 12, 1923
June 12, 1932
One other, date
illegible

COLONEL E. D. BAKER

United States Senator from Oregon

Baker County, Oregon, was created on September 22, 1862, and was named for Colonel E. D. Baker, United States Senator from Oregon.

Colonel E. D. Baker and President Abraham Lincoln were warm friends. Lincoln, as a reward for his political services to the Whig Party, was offered the position of governor of Oregon Territory. Lincoln was told that Oregon would soon become a state and that he would undoubtedly be elected a United States Senator from Oregon. His wife had no use for frontier life, and set her foot down firmly when it came to going to "the wilds of Oregon Territory".

Curiously enough, Lincoln's friend, Colonel E. D. Baker, who had gone to California when gold was discovered there, came up to Oregon, and at the extra session of the state legislature in October, 1860, Colonel Nesmith and Colonel Baker were elected senators by a fusion of Republicans and Douglas Democrats. Colonel Nesmith received

27 votes for the long term, and Colonel Baker 26 votes for the short term. Judge M. P. Deady, who ran against Nesmith, received 22 votes, and Judge George H. Williams, who opposed Colonel Baker, received 20 votes.

"Immediately upon the outbreak of the Civil War, Colonel Baker...recruited a regiment, of which he was colonel, and on October 21, 1861, while leading a charge at Ball's Bluff, in Virginia, was killed."

Immediately upon the outbreak of the Civil War, Colonel Baker, who was then serving as a United States Senator from Oregon, recruited a regiment, of which he was colonel, and on October 21, 1861, while leading a charge at Ball's Bluff, in Virginia, was killed.

Colonel Baker was an eloquent speaker, an able lawyer and a courageous and patriotic American. In spite of his patriotism, he was frequently the subject of bitter attacks because of the fact that he was born in England.

Recently I ran across a letter from W. Walters, written in 1844, in which the writer accuses Baker of favoring Great Britain, claiming that Baker supported resolutions offered by Mr. Matheny in 1843, which were published in the Sangamo Journal at Springfield, Illinois. Among these resolutions are the following:

"Resolved that it is not the policy of Illinois to encourage the migration of our citizens beyond the Rocky Mountains unless to protect or advance our national honor.

"Resolved that the United States and territories this side of the Rocky Mountains afford ample field and verge for the industry of our citizens."

In his letter, Walters says to Baker:

"You are not in favor of encouraging the settlement of American citizens in the Oregon Territory, but on the contrary, you discourage the migration thereto of our people and recommend to them to settle in the desert between the frontiers of Missouri and the Rocky Mountains. I ask whether it has ever occurred to you, while advocating the doctrine that we have territory enough on this side of the Rocky Mountains, that England now occupies more territory on the North American continent than does the United States and is daily grasping at more and more.

"With these facts before you, can you doubt that the occupation of Oregon by the United States has become a question of national security? Shall Great Britain circumvent our whole continent? Shall that robber nation monopolize the resources and wealth of Oregon? Shall she continue to murder our people settling there under the existing treaty of joint occupation as she has already murdered betwen four and five hundred American citizens within the Territory of Oregon? Shall she be longer permitted to stir up the savages in that region against the American settlers? Shall she be permitted to extend the laws of Canada over Oregon, appoint justices of the peace and administer a regular government within the territory while we, like cravens, are withheld from extending our laws over our rightful soil, under the miserable pretext that the treaty of joint occupancy will not permit us to do what England has already done?

"When you asserted that 'Oregon had not been occupied by our government and then abandoned,' you must have meant the British government, under which you were born, and not the government of the United States, of which you are now a citizen.

"Are you aware that James K. Polk of Tennessee, in January, 1829, proposed to Congress the extension of the civil and criminal jurisdiction of the courts of the Territory of Michigan over all citizens of the United States in the country west of the Rocky Mountains between the latitudes of 42 degrees and 54 degrees 40 minutes north as far west as the Pacific Ocean, and also an exploration and survey of the northwest coast of America between these latitudes, of its bays, inlets, and harbors, and of the Columbia River and its tributaries?

"You are willing to surrender to Great Britain an amount of territory sufficient to form six states. And the territory thus proposed to be given away by you is claimed by Governor Polk as the property of the United States."

All of which goes to show that the Oregon question and the annexation of Texas were hot spots in the days when the first wagon trains began rolling to Oregon.

Oregon Journal
August 7, 1934

ABIGAIL SCOTT DUNIWAY

"Mother of Equal Suffrage in Oregon"

Recently I made a half-hour talk before the Woman's Club and the Pioneers in the library at Hood River. It has been my good fortune to interview a considerable number of the women who had most to do with organizing the woman's club movement in Pacific Northwest, among them Mrs. Abigail Scott Duniway, Dr. Owens Adair, Dr. Mary A. Thompson, Mrs. A. H. Breyman, Mrs. Lucia Faxon Additon and many others.

For many years the women of the Pacific Northwest had been active in the W.C.T.U., and in equal suffrage associations, but it was not until 1885 that the woman's club movement was started. The first club was organized in 1885 by Mrs. Abbie H. Stuart of Olympia. In 1894 Mrs. Stuart came to Portland to inaugurate the work in this state. The first meeting was held at the home of Mrs. W. W. Spaulding. The next meeting was held in the parlors of the Hotel Portland. At this meeting it was decided to exclude from the activities of the club politics, temperance and religion. At this meeting Mrs. Duniway suggested that there be formed a state federation of women's clubs. Mrs. J. C. Card was elected the first president of the Portland Woman's Club.

Among the most earnest of the early workers in the woman's club movement were: Mrs. Julia H. Bauer, whose daughter, Emilie Frances Bauer, became a distinguished musical critic and writer; Mrs. Elizabeth Lord of The Dalles, author of "Reminiscences of Eastern Oregon" and at one time president of the State Equal Suffrage Association; Mrs. Martha E. Dalton, one of the three

---

"Mrs. Duniway began her fight for equal rights for women when, as a school teacher in Lafayette, Oregon, she was paid only half as much as a man who had passed his teacher's examination with a much lower grade. The difference in pay was explained solely on the ground that he was a man, and she was a woman."

---

women who founded the Oregon State Equal Suffrage Association; Mrs. E. L. Smith of Hood River; Mrs. Sarah A. Evans, who later became president of the state association; Dr. Viola M. Coe, Mrs. Clara Waldo, Myrtle Pease Hatfield and Mrs. Martha Jane Foster.

Inasmuch as Mrs. Abigail Scott Duniway was the first honorary president of the Oregon Federation of Woman's Clubs, I am going to discuss her activities briefly, to show what progress has been made during the last half century.

The parents of Abigail Scott Duniway were born in Kentucky. They were married on October 22, 1830, in Tazewell County, Illinois. Mrs. Duniway was born on October 22, 1834, and was the third child in the family. Mrs. Duniway was still in short dresses when she made her first political speech. She was an ardent Whig, so she called the village children together and in her speech championed the cause of "Tippecanoe and Tyler too".

In those days everybody worked, including Father, so Mrs. Duniway and her brothers and sisters had but little time for play. She worked in the sugar camp, carrying buckets of sap to be boiled down. She picked wool and pared and cored apples for dried apples. On rainy days and during the evenings she and her sisters were kept busy, spinning, spooling, reeling and hanking the wool yarn which her mother dyed and wove, for her mother made not only the blankets for the family but also the cloth.

Reverend Neil Johnson, Mrs. Duniway's uncle, crossed the plains to Oregon in 1851, so the following spring saw the Scott family westward bound for the Willamette Valley. Mrs. Duniway's mother died on June 20, and she was buried by the side of the Oregon Trail. The Scott family spent the winter at Lafayette. In the spring of 1853, Mrs. Duniway secured a position as teacher of the school at Cincinnati, as Eola was then called. Here she met Ben C. Duniway, who had taken up a donation land claim in Clackamas County. They were married and for the next four years lived at Needy, in the Hardscrabble neighborhood, in Clackamas County.

Within two and a half years Mrs. Duniway had two children—Clara and Willis. In addition to caring for her children she took in boarders, did the family washing, and made thousands of pounds of butter.

The Needy neighborhood was well named, for while most wives were allowed to have the butter and egg money as pin money, every cent in that house had to go to pay taxes and buy groceries. When they had been married four years they sold this place and bought a farm in Yamhill County. In spite of the care of her children and her multitudinous duties, Mrs. Duniway worked far into the night and wrote a book entitled "Captain Gray's Company", which was later followed by various other books.

Fortune smiled upon them and they were doing well until Mr. Duniway, to accommodate a neighbor, became a surety on a note and as a consequence they lost their farm. Shortly thereafter her husband met with an accident from a runaway team, which made him a cripple for the rest of his life, so thereafter Mrs. Duniway had to assume the responsibility of the support of the family. She kept boarders at Lafayette, at the same time teaching school. She got up in summer at three o'clock and in winter at four o'clock so as to do the washing, bake the bread, and get the housework done before going to school at nine o'clock. Later she moved to Albany, where she taught school. With a capital of $30 she started a millinery business there and made money.

In 1871 they moved to Portland and on May 5, 1871, she issued the first copy of The New Northwest. She made her first public address in 1871, in introducing Susan B. Anthony. She began speaking for equal suffrage. The ministers refused to allow her to hold meetings in the churches, so she held meetings in theatres and dance halls, and as a consequence the pulpits thundered denunciations at her as a lost and shameless woman. She was the first woman to visit the legislature, which she reported in 1872 for her paper, The New Northwest. When the pastor of her local church refused to allow her to speak at prayer meeting she said, "Let us pray," and for 20 minutes she told the Lord how necessary it was to have equal suffrage.

After 40 years of strenuous work Mrs. Duniway lived to see her life ambition of equal suffrage become a law.

Oregon Journal
March 3, 1928

(Note: The following, also found in the Lockley files, appeared in the Oregon Journal in commemoration of Abigail Scott Duniway's 100th birthday.)

Portland tomorrow will honor the memory of Abigail Scott Duniway, "mother of equal suffrage in Oregon", for Monday (October 22, 1934) will be the 100th anniversary of the birth of the woman who, for 44 years—from 1871 to 1915—devoted herself to advocating equality of rights and opportunities for women. She lived to see Oregon grant the vote to women in 1912, and at the request of Oswald West, then governor, wrote the proclamation stating that equal suffrage had been granted, and had the honor of being the first woman to register as a legal voter in Multnomah County. Mrs. Duniway died in Portland, October 11, 1915, just 11 days before her 81st birthday.

At the grammar school in Eastmoreland which bears her name, a special program will be given tomorrow morning at assembly. Robert E. Duniway, grandson, will present a picture of Mrs. Duniway to the school on behalf of Dr. Clyde A. Duniway, Northfield, Minnesota, a son of the suffrage leader. Leslie M. Scott, a nephew of Mrs. Duniway, will represent the Scott family at the school. Mrs. Duniway was a sister of the late Harvey W. Scott, long editor of The Oregonian.

Other grammar and high schools throughout the city will observe the centennial of Mrs. Duniway's birth with special programs, and Girls' Leagues in the high schools will eulogize the woman whose devotion to the "gospel of liberty", as she called it, won for their mothers and will insure for themselves some day the right to vote, transact business, own property, and take their places in the work-a-day world equally with men.

Book departments of Gill's and the Meier and

Frank Company's store will display Mrs. Duniway's books, which today, 19 years after her death, still are in demand among collectors of the works of Oregon authors and students of Oregon history.

Mrs. Duniway's first book, "Captain Gray's Company," story of the six months' trip she and her parents, brothers and sisters made across the plains from Illinois to Oregon in 1852, when she was 18, was published in Portland in 1859, the year Oregon became a state. Not more than six copies are known to exist today, however, of the work said to be the first novel ever printed and published in Oregon. Her other books were "From the West to the West", again a story of the trek by ox team from the middle west to the far west; "Path Breaking", telling of her suffrage work, and "David and Anna Matson", a romance in verse form.

Mrs. Duniway began her fight for equal rights for women when, as a school teacher in Lafayette, Oregon, she was paid only half as much as a man who had passed his teacher's examination with a much lower grade. The difference in pay was explained solely on the ground that he was a man, and she a woman.

She resolved to expose fully these conditions: that a married woman could legally own no property and that under the law even her bridal trousseau given by her father belonged to her husband; that women were taxed without representation; that the only vocations open to women were teaching, housework, millinery and dressmaking; that, most important of all, women could not vote.

In 1871, Mrs. Duniway moved with her husband and six children to Portland, where she started a weekly newspaper, The New Northwest. Mr. Duniway had been severely injured in a runaway accident, and the wife and mother had to carry on for the whole family. Her five sons helped her publish the paper. It was a startling innovation in those times for a woman to dare to become an editor, and especially of a paper which boldly declared that its mission was to advocate equal rights for women before the law, with the ballot for women as its goal.

The same year, Susan B. Anthony, great women's suffrage leader in the nation, came to Oregon on a lecture tour. She prevailed upon Mrs. Duniway to accompany her through Oregon and Washington, and through her encouragement Mrs. Duniway ventured to speak in public for the cause so dear to her. She found she had as much and more talent for public speaking as for writing, and traveled all over Oregon, Washington, and Idaho by train, stage, steamboat, and on horseback, lecturing for equal rights for women politically, financially, and socially.

Like other pioneer leaders in reform movements, Mrs. Duniway was for many years the object of ridicule and even abuse and slander. But with the success that came in the later years of her life she became known as "Oregon's Grand Old Woman" and "the mother of equal suffrage in Oregon".

Today her name is inscribed in the hall of fame in Washington D. C.; of the Daughters of the American Revolution; a public school and park in Portland are named for her, and the National League of Women Voters lists her on its honor roll.

The Oregon League of Women Voters raised $1000 for a hall of fame endowment fund in 1930, and when Mrs. Duniway's name was submitted to the national league the national organization announced that it was "most desirable" for its honor roll and the committee felt it unnecessary to submit the name to a vote.

Instrumental in this were Mrs. C. B. Simmons, Mrs. Elliott R. Corbett, Mrs. Thomas D.

Honeyman, Mrs. Eldon J. Steele, and Mrs. G. M.
Glines. The same group recently headed a committee of the Oregon League which fostered a resolution honoring Mrs. Duniway on the occasion of
the 100th anniversary of her birth.

Oregon Journal
October 21, 1934

BEN W. OLCOTT

Governor of Oregon

(Herewith is introduced Ben W. Olcott, governor of Oregon, whose personal career Mr. Lockley proposes to trace in this and succeeding articles. It need only be said at this stage that the sketch will illustrate the extraordinary adaptability and versatility which are among the true American's most conspicuous and valuable traits.)

One of the hardest men in the state to secure an interview from is Governor Ben W. Olcott. Ben is one of the most approachable and friendly officials who ever occupied the gubernatorial chair, but when it comes to talking about himself he changes the subject. Ben and I have known each other fairly well for 25 years or more. A day or so ago I dropped off at Salem to get an interview from him. We had traveled from Portland to Salem together a short while before on the Oregon Electric and Ben had told me some most interesting experiences he had while in Alaska, so I thought I would get his permission to make use of them. When I went to see him he invited me to spend the day with him, so I could get an idea of just what the job of governor included and what he does to earn his $13.69 a day salary. I stayed with him from about nine o'clock in the morning till 11:30 that night, and I want to say he comes as near earning his salary as anybody I have met for many a day.

"There are so many board meetings and so many interruptions during the day that I like to come back after supper to clear my desk of work,"

"...I shall ask you to forget that he is governor of Oregon and I will tell you what I know of him as a water rat, printer's devil, shoe clerk, farm hand, surveyor, wool buyer, digger of sewers, bank clerk, prospector and miner, camp cook, expert accountant and auditor, hop-picker, trapper, homesteader, dog team driver and musher..."

Governor Olcott said in explanation of his 14-hour day. I tried to get him to talk about what he has accomplished as secretary of state and as governor, but he said, "See here, Fred. I am going to ask a favor of you. Please don't write anything about my work as secretary of state or as governor. If my work has been good it will speak for itself, and if it hasn't you wouldn't want to praise it. Now this thing of blowing your own horn and telling the public what a wonder you are doesn't appeal to me. To tell you the truth, I am not even fond of being panned, though I often have to do things that, in my opinion, are for the best good of the state, that result in people who have selfish or ulterior motives, panning me good and plenty. Let's cut out the interview and we will have a chance during the day to do lots of visiting and you can write whatever you please, so long as you don't boost me or my work."

Personally, I don't see why I shouldn't praise or blame his actions, for the Supreme Court has decided that he is governor of Oregon for the next several years, so whatever I write cannot be construed as political boosting. In deference to his wishes, however, I shall ask you to forget that he is governor of Oregon and I will tell you what I know of him as a water rat, printer's devil, shoe clerk, farm hand, surveyor, wool buyer, digger of sewers, bank clerk, prospector and miner, camp cook, expert accountant and auditor, hop-picker, trapper, homesteader, dog team driver and musher along the shores of the Bering Sea, Alaska sourdough and aviator, and will kindly overlook the fact that by his quiet, modest, winning personality and his efficiency he has made one of the best secretaries of state Oregon ever had and that he is making a fearless and capable governor.

We were talking of his boyhood at Keithsburg, Illinois. "In those days there was lots of rafting and freighting on the Mississippi River," he said. "We boys were regular water dogs. We were in the river all summer long. Our favorite swimming place was near the Iowa Central bridge. We used to play in the waves made by the passing steamers. The great ambition of any of us 'water rats' living in the river towns was to be able to swim across the river, touch the opposite bank and swim back, without resting. My father owned a little grocery store near the river. Mother couldn't keep me out of the water, so she made me work in my father's grocery store during the summer vacations, to my great disgust.

"When I was a boy my great ambition was to become a pilot or the captain of a river steamboat. We lived not far north of Hannibal, Missouri, the home town of Mark Twain, and his car-

eer as a river pilot made even more of an appeal
to me in those days than his literary accomplishments or his reputation as a humorist. I remember going to Hannibal and hunting up Mark
Twain's home and going out in the back yard to
see the board fence he had the boys whitewash.

"The far horizon has always proved an irresistible lure to me. When I was in high school
four of us decided to see the world, particularly
Oklahoma and Texas, where there were Indians and
cowboys. 'Skinny' Flynn, 'Turkey Egg' Nevius,
Jake Fleming and I struck down the river afoot
till we reached Fort Madison where we took the
blind baggage on the Santa Fe for the southwest.
The brakeman ditched us. We caught a freight and
rode the rods till we were again ditched. We rode
the bumpers and sidedoor Pullmans and finally had
to hit the ties. A farmer saw us and offered
Fleming a job at small wages, but plenty to eat,
so Jake postponed his travels. At Lincoln, Nebraska, Nevius succumbed to the offer of a job in
a hotel. Skinny and I got as far as Wichita,
Kansas, before ever-increasing appetite caused us
to apply for a job in the Jacob Dole & Sons
packing house. We worked there all summer till
our desire to kill Indians was thoroughly satia-
ted by seeing so many hogs and steers killed.
That fall we decided that, after all, Keithsburg
and home looked pretty good to us, so we took a
job punching cattle on a cattle train bound for
the Chicago market."

His friends--and he has a host of them--call
him Ben, but he was christened Benjamin Wilson
Olcott. His mother's maiden name was Wilson,
hence his middle name. His father's name is Hiram
Wallace Olcott.

When Ben was in his teens he landed a job as
printer's devil on the Keithsburg, Illinois,
News. The proprietor was one of the old school.

He carried ads for all the "wet goods emporiums" in town, and took it out in trade. If Ben's middle name were not Wilson it would be "System and Order", and after he had been there a few weeks and had noticed that the proprietor made no attempt to keep any record of the money that came in nor (of) the expenses of the shop. Ben, who had taken bookkeeping in high school, suggested installing a set of books and a cost system. The proprietor goodnaturedly consented, with the remark that he was afraid it would prove too good a check on how much of the paper's income went over the bar. Many of the subscribers were in arrears for the paper, so Ben sent outstatements, writing on the bottom of the statements, "Please remit at your earliest convenience". When the irate subscribers began writing in that they had already paid, and had their returned checks to prove it, the proprietor shook his head and said, "You see, Ben, what comes of these new fangled schemes in keeping track of the money we get in. Too much education is a bad thing. You mean well, but the old way is the easiest, and lots less trouble."

Ben got hold of a copy of Washington Irving's "Astoria", and right then and there decided to come out to Oregon. Wages had been rather uncertain and irregular, so in lieu of wages the owner of the paper gave him a letter to the advertising manager of the Northern Pacific at St. Paul, requesting him to give Ben a pass to Portland, Oregon, and return. The return portion of that pass is still unused.

"...When a young fellow is 20 he feels the lure of the winding road and he wants to know what the country looks like over the next hilltop. I came to Salem and landed a job as bookkeeper and shoe clerk for William Brown & Company. Selling shoes did not particularly gratify my love of adventure, so my roommate, Os West, and I planned to go to southern Oregon and spend the summer prospecting. Something came up that upset Os' plans, so he couldn't go, but I decided to go anyway. I spent the summer in southern Oregon, working for a time on a stock ranch not far from Ashland. When I came back to Salem in the late fall of 1893 the hard times were at their very worst and there were three men for every job. I landed a job on the Putnam ranch at Eola, working for my board. Speaking of Eola makes me think of how astonished I was up in Alaska to see a riverboat whose name was Eola. I hunted up its owner and found he was a Polk County boy who had lived at Eola. The Putnam Ranch at Eola is now owned by Senator I. L. Patterson.

"The next spring I went to work for my old boss, William Brown. He had sold his shoe store and was buying wool and hops. One day a tall, slender farmer came in from Waldo Hills to sell his wool crop. I bought it off him. He was T. T. Geer. From Brown's I went to work in the Ladd & Bush Bank. I was what the boys termed a 'deck-hand'. I was bookkeeper and handy man. I worked under Claude Gatch. Among my fellow clerks were Steve Sanford, Os West, Harry Stapleton, Alec Moir, Fred Beak and Joe Baumgartner.

"I worked there for three years, and then the longing for change and adventure became so strong I decided to go up into British Columbia, where a gold strike was reported in the Fort Steele District. Ham Fletcher, son of Governor Fletcher, Henry Kundret and myself went up to Spokane where we outfitted for the mines. Buying our packhorses and loading on our plunder, we started northward up the Kootenai River. We spent the summer in virgin country, prospecting. There were plenty of deer, bear, bighorn sheep and mountain goats, so we lived on the country. When we tired of game we could catch all the trout we could eat in a few minutes' fishing. For weeks at a time we were out of all touch with civilization. It was a wonderful summer, with one exception, and that was we didn't find anything in the mineral line worth locating. When the snow drove us out we went to Fort Steele to earn a grubstake for next season.

"Prospecting is one occupation where hope springs eternal in the human breast. Fort Steele was putting in a sewer system. I landed a job of sewer digging. I never before nor since saw harder ground. It was a cemented gravel and every time your pick hit the ground the pick handle stung your hands and made your arms tingle. Henry got a job as a compositor on the paper at Fort Steele, so he had it pretty soft. When the sewer was dug we all laid off and I landed a job as lumberjack out in the 'brush', as they call the woods up there.

"While I was in the woods I was offered a job at better pay as chainman on a surveying party to survey the alternate sections of grant land along Elk River for the Crows Nest branch of the Canadian Pacific Railway. We hauled the supplies on toboggans and traveled on snowshoes, for the snow was deep up there in the mountains and along Elk River. We traveled light, living in tepees which we bought from the Indians. Our party was composed of trappers, lumberjacks, and prospectors. We were all outdoor men and worked all winter through all sorts of weather, living largely on deer and bear meat, beans, camp bread and coffee.

"That spring Dewey sank the Spanish fleet in Manila Bay and the war was on. I worked my way down the Kootenai as a deckhand on a steamboat to go to Spokane and enlist. When I got to Spokane enlistments were closed. I couldn't find anyone who wanted to let me have his chance to go, so I struck out into the newly opened Colville Indian agency and spent the summer prospecting along the Canadian border. Jonathan Bourne had a mine up there called the Mountain Lion. The Republic turned out to be rich.

"While I was at Fort Steele I ran across Jim Wardner, discoverer of the Bunker Hill Mine in the Coeur d' Alene country. He was a most interesting chap. He told me all about the discovery of the Bunker Hill and that the mule that was the real discoverer of the hidden mineral wealth of that district had been retired on a pension and he had shipped him down to a farm near Eugene to spend his last days.

"In the summer of 1898 I received a telegram from home telling me of the serious illness of my sister, so I took the next train for Keithsburg, Illinois. She died shortly after I got home.

"Father wanted me to help him in the bank, so I spent the next six years as his cashier. Often of an evening as I sat in front of the home fireplace I would see in the flames the smoke of my campfire curling up through the tops of the fir trees. I would smell the odor of bacon frying or hear the sputter of frying trout. My legs would ache for the feel of snowshoes. When the logs snapped I would hear the crack of my gun and see a bighorn sheep or a deer leap up to fall in a heap. So in 1904 I answered the Call of the North and started for Alaska. At Seattle I bought a ticket for Nome aboard the old treasure ship Roanoke. We went by way of the inside passage and it certainly was a wonderful trip. I spent the summer, fall, and part of the winter at Nome...

"There are two Christmas days that have special significance for me. I was married on Christmas Day, 1912, and it was on Christmas Day, 1904, that I started from Nome, Alaska, by dog team for the Cleary diggings near where the town of Fairbanks was later built. Bert Spencer, who formerly was on the Wells-Fargo run between Portland and San Francisco, and is now in Oklahoma boring for oil, but who at that time was an employee of the N. A. T. & T. Company, and I decided to make the 1000-mile trip so as to be in on the ground floor before all the good claims were taken. We bought two good sledge dogs of Carrie Beaton, who, as you doubtless know, is said to be one of Rex Beach's characters in 'The Spoilers', as well as in his story, 'The Silver Horde'. We bought three other sledge dogs, and with the five and our sledge we went up the beach past Solomon and Topcock, across Norton Sound to the Indian village of Kaltag, where the famous Kaltag portage to the Yukon River is located. We went up the Yukon to Fort Gibbons, near the mouth of the Tanana and thence up the Tanana to Cleary Creek.

"The trip took just 30 days. It was midwinter, so we lost a few days on account of heavy storms, but at that we averaged over 30 miles a day. We were on the way long before daylight. We never stopped for lunch, and we kept up a slow dog trot all day long. We had taken along a good supply of frozen salmon to feed the dogs, so at noon we would eat a good sized slab of this dog feed as we trotted along, which took the place of lunch very acceptably. We stopped overnight if possible in deserted cabins left by woodchoppers or prospectors. Before leaving Nome we had hired an Eskimo woman to make up a sleeping bag apiece out of Siberian reindeer hides, so we kept fairly comfortable in spite of the thermometer's trying to crawl out of the bottom of the glass.

"When we got to Fairbanks we traded our dog team for a good cabin. Fairbanks soon became the largest log cabin city in America. When the glory of Dawson began to wane, the stampede occurred to Nome, and when Nome ceased to grow, the rush started for Fairbanks. Most of the residents of Fairbanks that first year were old sourdoughs from Dawson or Nome. As soon as the season opened, I landed a job as shoveler on a claim on Cleary Creek. The two principal producing creeks in the Fairbanks District at that time were Cleary Creek and Fairbanks Creek. Captain E. T. Barnett, founder of the town of Fairbanks, started a bank and put me in as paying teller. Later I became gold dust teller and buyer. The gold there was very rich, running in value from $19 to $20 an ounce. Another bank came in, so Captain Barnett made me gold dust buyer on the creeks. It was my job to go from claim to claim on the creeks all through that district and buy gold

---

"If those and similar stunts are the ordinary routine of a jellyfish, then we need more jellyfish of that type."

---

dust. Our bank loaned lots of money for the development of the claims. The interest rate was 10% a month. You have to have a pretty good claim to be able to pay 120% a year, but many of the claims were exceedingly rich.

"I went out for Captain Barnett to oversee the cleanups on Swiftwater Bill's claim. His claim was Number 6 above discovery, the richest on the creek. Swiftwater Bill made a fortune and a worldwide reputation in the Klondike. He was the most expert man at cleaning gold I ever saw. He used a system of dry cleaning that would absolutely take all the black sand out of the gold. He did it by a peculiar tipping of the gold pan and a quick twist of his wrist. He told me he had learned the system in the John Day country in eastern Oregon. He taught me his system and I practiced for hours a day for weeks until I became expert at it. I used the system in the bank later and it used to make the old sourdoughs sit up and take notice. Later I was sent out as manager of a branch bank at Chena near Esther Creek where the Berry boys, Clarence and Frank, were operating.

"I came out on the last boat to go up the river in the season of 1906. We went up the Yukon past Dawson and thence by the White Pass and Yukon train to Skagway and on by steamer to Seattle and on to Portland. After returning to Salem, I got a letter from Captain Barnett asking me to come back as manager of his mining interests on the creeks in the Fairbanks District. It was a most attractive offer, but I had taken up other work, so I turned it down. The man who did accept the place was shot and killed two months later in a dispute over a contested claim on Vault Creek, so maybe it's just as well that I turned it down.

Shortly after Ben Olcott returned from Alaska, in the late fall of 1906, Governor George E. Chamberlain appointed him as the state's representative in the case of the Title Guarantee & Trust Company failure, as State Treasurer Steel had deposited approximately $200,000 of the state's school funds with that institution. When the state's claim was satisfied, W. C. Bristol, who represented American Surety Company, asked Olcott to stay on the job, representing him in the settlement. When the Surety Company had adjusted the matter, R. S. Howard, representing the Ladd & Tilton Bank, employed Olcott to help wind up the receivership of the company. When its affairs had been cleaned up, Olcott started in business for himself as public accountant, experting the books of various counties, as well as business firms. In 1910 he took up a homestead near Bend, in Crook County, where he spent the next year. On April 17, 1911, Governor West appointed him secretary of state to fill the unexpired term of Frank W. Benson. He was elected to that position in 1912 and again in 1916, at which election he carried every county in the state except Polk. On the death of Governor Withycombe, March 3, 1919, he became governor.

Now, having got all these statistics and

miscellaneous facts out of my system, and having told them as briefly and as colorlessly as possible, in compliance with my promise to Governor Olcott, I can get myself into high and follow the governor's trail. As a matter of fact, one would have to get into high, give her all the juice she's got, and step on the accelerator, to keep in sight of the governor, particularly during mid-June last year. When a man goes from the state capital to Portland in 40 minutes and then travels from Portland to Albany in 71 minutes, from Albany to Cottage Grove in 56 minutes, on to Roseburg in 45 minutes, thence to Grants Pass in 92 minutes, and is at Ashland 37 minutes later, he is certainly going some. That is exactly what Governor Olcott did last June, for I copied the figures from the official record made by Lieutenant Colonel H. L. Watson, J.M.A., A.S.A., who in a JN 4 No. 45281 flew, with Governor Olcott as a passenger, from Portland to Mather Field in California in 10 hours and 45 minutes actual flying time.

The official log shows the exact altitude at the various points en route. For example, between Ashland and Redding the height at which they flew varied from 6400 feet to 8400 feet. In addition to doing straight cross country flying with Colonel Watson, Governor Olcott decided to get all the thrills there were, so he went up with Lieutenant James S. Krull, who put his machine through its paces and did acrobatics and stunt work, such as looping the loop, nose diving, tail spinning, banking and all the other spectacular stunts performed by an expert aviator.

I would like to see some of the men who think Governor Olcott is a "jellyfish" up in the air with him, or mushing along in an arctic storm, driving a dog team on a 1000-mile hike, eating frozen salmon that had been taken along for dog feed. If those and other similar stunts

are the ordinary routine of a jellyfish, then we
need more jellyfish of that type.

Oregon Journal
February 21, 24,
25, 26, & 27, 1920

HERBERT HOOVER

President of the United States

Herbert Hoover was paid a dollar a year when he worked for the government during the World War. When I knew Bert, when we were neighbors in the Highland addition to Salem, he was paid $30 a month, which is about a dollar a day. When I asked N. C. Maris recently how much he paid Bert Hoover when Bert worked for him at Newberg, he said:

"We paid Bert a dollar a week. He cleaned the stable, milked the cow, fed the pigs, got in the wood and did other chores for his dollar a week. Bert was about 13 at that time. As you know, he was an orphan.

"When he started to work for us my wife said, 'Bert, you should take more pride in your personal appearance. Your fingernails are in mourning. You didn't wash very carefully behind your ears. Your hair is unkempt. I always cut their hair for my boys, so, if you like, I will cut your hair.'

"Bert was deliberate in his speech. He thought it over and said, 'All right. Go ahead.'

"She cut his hair, and Bert put his hand in his pocket and said, 'How much?'

"My wife is something of a tease, so she said, 'Well, I did a pretty good job. I guess a quarter will be about right.'

"An anguished look came over Bert's face and slowly, very slowly, he put his hand into his pocket and slowly brought out the quarter she had paid him on account and handed it to her. My wife laughed and said, 'I was only joking. I am not going to charge you anything for cutting your hair. Keep your money.'

"Bert didn't smile very often. He was a very

"We paid Bert a dollar a week. He cleaned the stable, milked the cow, fed the pigs, got in the wood and did other chores for his dollar a week."

---

serious boy. But he put his quarter back into his pocket with great alacrity and gave her a beaming smile."

"He never volunteered any information. When you asked him a question he thought it over and usually gave you a surprisingly good answer. He wasn't much of a hand to play. Life seemed a serious business to him. He was a bookworm, and he read good, solid books. His uncle, Dr. H. J. Minthorn, was another person whose conversation was yea and nay. He said what he had to say, and said no more. He didn't speak unless he had something to say, which is more than you can say of many people."

Oregon Journal
February 3, 1928

SAM HILL
Road Builder

In 1912 C. S. Jackson, publisher of the
Journal, called me into his office one day to
meet Samuel Hill. Mr. Hill believed that a wonderful highway could be built along the banks of
the Columbia River from The Dalles to Portland
and eventually to the sea. Most sane, sensible,
and conservative men shook their heads and said,
"You mustn't let Sam Hill carry you away with his
enthusiasm. He is a dreamer."

However, Mr. Hill enthused a few public
spirited citizens of Portland, including Simon
Benson, John B. Yeon, Rufus Holman, C. S. Jackson, Julius Meyer and a few others, and that
summer a group of men, with Mr. Hill, made a trip
on foot over the proposed highway. Probably the
project would have been dropped when they saw
something of the difficulties incident to the
construction of a highway through hills of solid
rock and over a mountain of moving rock, had not
Mr. Hill put up his own money to take Samuel C.
Lancaster, an engineer employed by the United
States government in the road department, to Europe, to study the roads in Switzerland. Mr. Hill
gave not only his money but his time and enthusiasm in unlimited measure, and today the Columbia
River Highway is known all over the world. Not
even the world-famed Axenstrasse on Lake Lucerne,
in Switzerland, excels in scenic beauty and in

excellence and durability of construction the Columbia River Highway.

For a good many years I have been making jaunts over the west with Samuel Hill. A day or two ago he was in Portland on his way to Hoquiam, where he made an address to the Washington State Chamber of Commerce. When I asked Mr. Hill to outline briefly what he said at Hoquiam, he responded:

"You know me well enough to know that I believe the best service rendered the public is by those who do not work for money but who work because they believe in the cause and because their patriotism leads them to serve the public. This, I believe, is the spirit that should animate and inspire the members of any local or state chamber of commerce.

"My message to the Washington State Chamber of Commerce was to tell them that the time has come when they should take account of and marshal the assets of their state, to see what they have and to prepare for the future. I tried to impress upon them that we are trustees for the assets of the state and that we should conserve the heritage for those who come after us.

"No effort has been made, so far as I know, to make what might be called an industrial survey of Oregon or Washington. I believe we should not only learn what assets there are but we should plan to utilize and conserve these assets. I suggested to them that a committee of five should be appointed to work out a plan and submit it to the directors of the association and that the directors should be empowered to act if they approved the plan. Because my good friend John J. Donovan has special ability as an analyst and an organizer I suggested that he be made chairman of the committee.

"First of all, there should be a committee to study the soils of the state. I wonder if you realize how important to agriculture such a study would prove. This committee should also study and classify the waterpowers of the state and also look into and suggest a plan for coordinating the transportation of the state. Because, when all is said and done, transportation is a measure of civilization, and without transportation the products of the state cannot be moved to their destination.

"It goes without saying that the highways should feed the railroads and the railroads should be feeders to the waterways. I believe

---

"...I believe the best service rendered the public is by those who do not work for money but who work because they believe in the cause and because their patriotism leads them to serve the public."

---

that all of the assets in the state should be utilized, but to do this intelligently we must know what these assets are. We must feel a personal responsibility in the wise use of these assets.

"Some years ago I investigated conditions in Oregon. Oregon has 96,800 square miles, and is almost one half the size of the German empire prior to the war. One fourth of Germany was waste land, one fourth was given over to reforestation, so that what remained was about the size of the state of Oregon. Germany is not considered a thickly populated country, such as Holland or Belgium, for example, and yet, if Oregon were as densely populated as Germany we would have here a population of 31,500,000.

"It was my good fortune and honor to be chairman of the advisory board of the highways in Washington. Later I was entrusted with a similar

work in Oregon. Did you ever stop to think that
your highways up and down the coast meet at con-
venient points, so that the highway system is
practically a unit as far as California, Oregon
and Washington and British Columbia are concerned?

"Much remains to be done. The efforts and
services of the various state institutions, particularly the agricultural college, the automobile club, and other bodies seeking to serve the
public should be made use of and we should also
secure the hearty cooperation of the different
branches of the state government.

"We all know that the progress of the world
comes through the sacrifice of the few for the
benefit of the many. I believe that men should
seek to serve the public through organized bodies, such as the Chamber of Commerce, and not
have to be solicited to join, for I think it is
an honor to belong to and serve with a group of
men who realize the pleasure to be secured from
service to their fellow men.

"You and I, Fred, know that lots of people
laugh at me and refer to me as a visionary and a
dreamer, and yet, before the edifice can be
raised, the architect must look ahead and see it
in his mind's eye. No longer am I laughed at for
my enthusiasm for good roads. When you and I are
drifting dust, people will realize that I had a
vision of the future, when they visit what is to
be a beautiful and worthwhile museum at Maryhill.
It isn't what we get that counts, but what we
give, and the gift of one's energy, enthusiasm,
and time is often worth more than the mere gift
of money.

"I celebrated my 71st birthday recently, but
I hope that for many years to come I shall retain
my enthusiasm and strength to serve my fellow
men."

They say it is better to wear out than rust out. Sam Hill will never rust out. He is always on the go—he has many interests, and works as hard at doing things for his fellow men as though he were working for his own personal profit. After all is said and done, I imagine a man does get more satisfaction and bigger dividends from service to humanity than in merely accumulating money for himself.

Mr. Hill and I spent the day together. We were seatmates from Spokane to Missoula. He told me of how he happened to become interested in good roads and of the many years of work he has put in on improving the roads in the Pacific Northwest. He told me of his proposed highway of flowers and also of the work he is doing on the Canadian border to commemorate the 100 years' peace between our country and Canada. Interesting as are all these subjects, I am going to postpone the telling of them to a future occasion and tell something about Sam Hill himself.

"One of my early ancestors, whose name, like mine, was Sam Hill, was treasurer for Oliver Cromwell," said Mr. Hill. "When King Charles II came to the throne, in 1660, Sam Hill came to America. In reading his diary I ran across this quaint statement. He did not like to say that if he stayed in England he would lose his head, so he wrote: 'I find the climate of England very unwholesome, so I am going to seek a change of climate.' He came to North Carolina. He had had his fill of fighting, with Cromwell, so he joined the Quaker Church. If you will look up the history of North Carolina, you will find that Sam Hill was arrested for refusing to bear arms or to turn out on muster day.

"My father, Nathan Branson Hill, was born in

North Carolina. I was born on May 13, 1857, on my father's 39th birthday, and, like my father, I was born in North Carolina. My mother, whose maiden name was Eliza Leonard Mendenhall, was also a native of North Carolina. Mother's people hailed originally from Gilford, England. Father attended Haverford College, in Pennsylvania. Haverford is about nine miles from Philadelphia. Father took his doctor's degree there in 1878, and I founded a chair there, in my father's honor. From there, Father went to Jefferson Medical College, at Philadelphia, and later to the Ohio Medical College, at Cincinnati, where he graduated.

"My father became one of the strong men of North Carolina. Quakers are accustomed to persecution, and the more they are persecuted the stronger are their convictions and the more loyal they are to them. My father was a strong believer in the Union, and he was unutterably opposed to slavery, so you can imagine that, living in North Carolina, his views were not always popular.

"In spite of his views, he was a leader in the state. He built the first cotton factory south of the Mason and Dixon Line. He was vice president of the Bank of North Carolina and to improve the conditions of the farmers and to make the country more prosperous he agitated for the construction of better roads and he himself was instrumental in the building of 44 miles of plank roads. My father was the head of the 'underground railroad' in North Carolina. Charles Coffin had charge of the other end of the railroad, at Indianapolis, and Mr. Harris was head of the Canadian end, at Guelph, Ontario, which, by the way, was the home of my father-in-law, James J. Hill.

"So great was my father's reputation for integrity and business sagacity that many wealthy planters made him executor of their wills, knowing he would not allow their own flesh and blood, their sons and daughters by octoroon slaves, to go on the auction block. When a planter's estate was being settled and his slaves sold, Father often bought the sons and daughters of the planter, by his slaves, and shipped them north. On one occasion Father bought three young men who were put up at auction, as he knew they were the

---

"At the time when it meant a prison term to teach Negroes to read or write, Father bought books in the North and brought them South, furnishing them to the Negroes, so they could learn to read and write."

---

sons of a neighboring planter, a friend of Father's. One of these slaves bore a striking resemblance to the planter, had blue eyes and fair hair, and from his appearance no one would believe he had any Negro blood. Father sent these three slaves north. The one man who looked so much like a white man settled in Boston. He became the owner of three ships plying between Boston and New York. At the time when it meant a prison term to teach Negroes to read or write, Father bought books in the North and brought them South, furnishing them to the Negroes, so they could learn to read and write.

"As vice president of the Bank of North Carolina my father was instrumental in loaning money not only in North Carolina, but all through the north and along the frontier. He made a trip to St. Paul and Fort Snelling, to pass upon loans there. When it was evident that there was to be war between the North and the South the directors of the Bank of North Carolina met to decide what they should do about their loans in the North. They had $15,000 on deposit in New York City.

Fort Sumter had been fired upon, and they were afraid they were going to lose the money. Father was known to be in sympathy with the North, so they wanted him to collect the money. Father gave his personal check for the $15,000 and took a draft on the New York bank. He mailed this to his brother in St. Louis, telling him to go to New York City, draw the money in gold, and hold it for him. When we escaped from North Carolina that $15,000 in gold came in very handy. We went to the home of my Aunt Nancy at Carthage, Indiana, where my father's brother turned over the $15,000 in gold to Father. Father gave $5000 each to two of his brothers, and with the other $5000 we went to Minnesota.

"My father was away from home attending to a medical case shortly after the breaking out of the Civil War. My father was so much loved and respected by our neighbors that none of them would have allowed us to suffer any harm, but some men from another community, hearing that my father was a strong Union man, came to our house to kill Father. Naturally, they did not announce their intention, but Jim Brown, one of our Negro servants, who was devoted to my father and mother, heard by the Negro grapevine telegraph they were coming. 'Uncle Jim' was not only devoted to us but he was very courageous and intelligent. We happened to have a lot of schoolbooks in the house that Father had sent North for to give to the Negro slaves. We also had some books which were known as abolition books. Mother invited the men in, and said, 'I regret that my husband is not here to receive you, but if you will come in and wait for him, I will get supper for you.' While the men were waiting in the parlor, Mother gathered every school book and abolition book and burned them in the kitchen stove.

"She sent one of the servants to call Uncle Jim Brown. When the strangers had come she had told Uncle Jim to take Father's saddle horse,

Gray Laurel, out of its box stall, to make room for the saddle horses of our visitors. Gray Laurel was the fleetest mare in that part of the country. My father was fond of fast horses. Father never allowed anyone but himself to ride Gray Laurel. Mother told Uncle Jim to watch his chance and lead Gray Laurel back of the barn, where he could not be seen, and mount her and ride to the crossroads and wait there till her husband came and to say to him, 'Your wife is worried about her mother. She is sick. Will you ride there at once and see if she is all right. She said to Uncle Jim, 'Don't tell my husband that there are some men at the house here waiting for him, for if you do he will come home to protect me, and the men will kill him.'

"Uncle Jim rode to the crossroads and when my father came he gave him the message and Father changed his saddle to Gray Laurel and started off for the home of my mother's mother, while Uncle Jim rode back on the saddle horse my father had been riding. The men waited till after ten o'clock, and then they said they would have to search the house for abolition books. They searched, but did not find succeed in finding any. They waited till nearly midnight for Father and finally rode away.

"Mother had Uncle Jim get out the wagon and in the bottom of it she put a trunk filled with clothing for us children. Uncle Jim put hay over the trunk, and Mother sent one of our servants, with this load of hay, to drive to her mother's. Meanwhile, she put a few necessary articles into a couple of carpetsacks and we started, apparently, for town.

"When we reached my grandmother's house we found Father there, very much upset at having been sent on a wild goose chase, for he found that no one was sick and his services were not required. Mother told Father what had happened, and he agreed that they would have to abandon their home and everything in it and try to make their way north.

"To have started north would have been fatal, for we would have been taken off the train and Father would have been made a prisoner. We went to the station and Father bought tickets for Georgia. In Georgia he bought tickets for Alabama, and from there we went to Tennessee and thence to Kentucky. We were now among strangers, who would not be so suspicious of us. Mother told all of us children to say, 'We are going to visit our Aunt Nancy,' when people asked us where we were going. We didn't know where Aunt Nancy lived, so we were perfectly safe not to give our destination away. We crossed the river at Indianapolis, Indiana. I was only four and a half years old, but I remember very distinctly seeing men wearing narrow caps and dressed in blue uniforms, who were cooking meals in the street. I thought it was very unusual. I also remember seeing their guns stacked, and wondering why they had guns in town. From Indianapolis we went to my Aunt Nancy's at Carthage, Indiana. We stayed there several months.

"Another thing I remember very distinctly is our trip up the river to St. Paul. We went on a boat called the War Eagle. Father had $5000 in gold. He was afraid that if he took it in the stateroom it would be stolen, so he put it in his saddlebags and threw the saddlebags on the deck of the War Eagle. He told us children to pay no attention to the saddlebags, but to let him know if anybody started to take them away or open them. We went by stage from St. Paul to Minneapolis. The actual distance is probably not over eight miles, but in those days we followed the river, and on account of poor roads it took us more than half a day to make the 20 miles. I remember very distinctly seeing the falls of St. Anthony on the east side of the river. We stayed that night at the home of William Wales, a Quaker, and next day we crossed the river to Minneapolis where we arrived in September, 1861, and where I lived for the next 40 years.

"Mother went to a yearly meeting of the Friends in Iowa. In crossing the river the ice broke and Mother got wet. She died as a result of this accident. After Father and Mother were dead, my oldest sister kept house for us.

"We had lost practically all our property when we left our home in North Carolina, so it was a case of having to work if we wanted to eat. I got a job piling millwood at ten cents a load. I was paid 15 cents a load for piling slabwood. I had to work hard all day to earn as much as a dollar. Later I got a job wiping joints for a plumber. Still later I went to work for Captain John Horton, a painter. I got lead poisoning and had to quit that work, so I went to Oseo, Minnesota, where I got a job as a farmhand with Isaac Potter, a North Carolina Quaker. On his farm I learned to milk cows, swing a cradle, and do other farm work. Later I came back to Minneapolis and got a job with Nate Roberts, a carpenter and house builder. When I was about 18 I got a job on the geological survey of Pennsylvania.

"I saved my money and went to Cornell University at Ithaca, New York. I took a cold, which turned into pneumonia, so I had to drop out. Later I went to Haverford College, in Pennsylvania, where my father took his degree in 1846. I took my degree there in 1878 and from there went to Amherst and still later to Harvard. I took my A. B. degree at Harvard, and, by the by, when I was there I knew Theodore Roosevelt, whose principal reputation at that time was as a middleweight boxer. I worked during summer vacations while at college. I put in one summer on the geological survey under J. P. Lesley, a noted authority on geology.

"After finishing college, I went back to

Minneapolis and got a job as a clerk in a law office. There were six ahead of me. I had to get the ice, sweep the office and fag for the other law clerks, because I was boy No. 7. In those days all briefs and other legal documents were written in longhand. The firm I was with was Shaw, Levi & Cray. Judge Shaw, seeing some of my work, told me I would be his personal secretary, so that within two months I had graduated form boy No. 7 to boy No. 1.

"One day Charles H. Woods came to our office and said, 'I am going to Europe, and I want one of your law clerks to help my partner, Babcock, while I am gone.' Judge Shaw pointed to me and said, 'Hill can do the work for you.'

"Mr. Woods turned to me and said, 'I will give you $75 a month.'

"I refused the job, as I wanted to stay where I was.

"After Woods had gone I said to Judge Shaw, 'Why did you suggest me? Isn't my work satisfactory here?'

"He said, 'Your work is very satisfactory. That's why I recommended you. I want to see you advance. Babcock is lazy. You will soon be doing all the work. It would be good practice for you. What you ought to do is to be admitted to the bar and take the job.'

"I took his advice. I took the bar examination, was admitted to the bar, and went to Woods & Babcock as a law clerk. Mr. Babcock began putting more and more work on me, and within a month I tried and won my first case. Meanwhile, real estate was moving actively and I had been making some pretty good commissions in selling real estate. Upon the return from Europe of Judge Woods I resigned and went to Harvard Law School.

"I knew that young lawyers had pretty hard sledding, so I decided to be an exception to the general rule, if possible. At that time there were 35 volumes of decisions of the Supreme Court of Minnesota. I committed Volume 35 to memory. I then took Volume 34, and continued till I had got to Volume 1. I annotated all the cases. I decided when I went into a courtrooom I would not have to lug a lot of law books, but would be able to quote, accurately, the book and page of any case I referred to. I made a contract with the owner of the Vanderburgh Block in Minneapolis whereby I would attend to his legal work, draw all leases, collect the rents, etc., in exchange for the use

---

"When you and I are drifting dust, people will realize that I had a vision of the future, when they visit what is to be a beautiful and worthwhile museum at Maryhill."

---

of four rooms on the second floor.

"One of the four rooms I used for a file room. I subscribed for almost every newspaper in Minnesota. I cleaned up $1500 in cash on real estate deals, so I bought a safe and a library.

"I hired a young chap named Charles H. Babcock as a law clerk, and, by the way, he worked for me for the next 48 years. When a client came Babcock would get from him his name and address, which he would bring in to me. Babcock would tell him I would be at leisure in about 15 minutes. I put in this 15 minutes looking over the files of the newspaper from this man's home town, so that when he came in I was thoroughly conversant with the affairs of the town. It certainly made an impression on him, for he took it for granted I was equally familiar with every other small town in Minnesota.

"I worked from 8:00 a.m. to 11:00 p.m., familiarizing myself with the history of Minnesota and the local affairs of the small towns. Saturday night I would get on the train and drop off at some small town and stay over Sunday, getting acquainted with the town and its people. My boast in those days was that if I met a man once I would remember his name, his town, and where we had met. As a matter of fact, I did have an unusually good memory. There is hardly any asset more valuable than a good memory. It will carry you far in law or in politics and in most other relations of life. My visits to the small towns resulted in my being asked to prepare the charters for many of the smaller towns.

"I made it a rule never to take a case that I didn't believe in. I wasn't going to fight on the wrong side. This meant that I often passed up profitable cases, but in the long run it paid, for the juries got to believing that if I appeared in the case, right and justice were on the side of my client. I often heard men in the courtroom whisper, 'No, he doesn't have to carry any books. He's got the law in his head.'

"I took lots of damage cases against the railroad. The railroad attorneys would say to a prospective juror, 'Do you know Sam Hill?' If they did, they would excuse this juror. The railroad attorneys would usually use all of their peremptory challenges. I never used mine. I would look at the jury and say, 'I do not have to challenge any of the jurors, because I know they want to see justice done and I can trust to their sense of honesty and fair play.' The result was I had mighty good luck with my cases.

"I won case after case of personal damages against the Hill railroads. Finally James J. Hill sent for me and said, 'We would rather have you with us than against us. On what terms will you come with me?'

"I said, 'I do not care to be your hired man, Mr. Hill. I doubt if you would care to pay me as much as I am making. The only proposition that would interest me is to be allowed to come here without pay and learn railroading.'

"Mr. Hill finally accepted my proposition, and, as you know, he made me president of the Montana Central and a number of other railroads. James J. Hill was one of the greatest railroad men, one of the shrewdest, most far-seeing, most public spirited men with whom I have ever been associated. I learned more from him than in all the college courses I ever took.

"I don't suppose Henry Ford or John D. Rockefeller will acknowledge the fact that I have had a great deal to do with making them two of the richest men in the United States. Unless we had good roads Henry Ford wouldn't begin to sell as many cars as he has. Unless we had good roads we wouldn't have cars. If we didn't have cars, John D. Rockefeller wouldn't sell as much gasoline as he does.

"Next time you are in New York City, take a few minutes off to go and look at the statue of A. J. Cassatt, one of the men who helped make the Pennsylvania railroad what it is. I first came in contact with A. J. Cassatt when I was 18 years old. He took an interest in young men, and I was one of a group of six young men with whom he discussed road building, railroad problems and other such questions. This was in 1875. I have had an active interest in good roads for 52 years.

"James J. Hill was always with me, heart and soul, in my road building program. He said, "Samuel, we are not in the drayage business.' He believed in having good roads as feeders to the railroads.

"I said to him once, 'Mr. Hill, transportation is the measure of civilization, and our freight rates really begin at the farmhouse door.'

"He said, 'Transportation consists of three branches--waterways, railways, and highways.

"I said, 'Mr. Hill, you have the order wrong. It should be waterways, highways, and railways. You told me once that a railroad without terminals was like a human body without arms and legs. You have been a great builder of terminals, but you forget that you need more than arms and legs for your railroad systems. You must have toes and fingers to reach the men on the farm.'

"The men who are chiefly responsible for the building of the Columbia River Highway are Governor Oswald West, Rufus Holman, John B. Yeon, Amos Benson and Simon Benson. Oh, yes, of course. I come in the list, too. You can put me there, in whatever order you please. I was recently made an honorary member of the Automobile Club of Washington, with dues paid up to 1999.

"Converting the taxpayers of Oregon and Washington to spend money on roads was no small task. I spent my own time and my own money freely for what I knew was the public good, and I had to take lots of abuse and criticism for doing so.

"Charles P. Chamberlain is one of the best politicians I ever met, and on numerous occasions he has saved the day for me. One time we were going to hold a meeting advocating good roads, in the public library in Portland. We got word that a lot of objectors were coming to try to break up the meeting. Chamberlain told me not to worry about it--that the meeting would be held, and there would be no trouble, and there would be an enthusiastic audience. When I and the other speakers arrived the hall was packed, and there wasn't room for another person in it. There were scores of husky-looking men outside the library. We had a very successful meeting and the resolutions for good roads were passed unanimously and the papers played up the enthusiasm of the public for the good roads program. I asked Charlie how he had done it. He said, 'I sent a big bunch of railroad men to go there an hour early and occupy all the seats, so when the objectors came they couldn't even find standing room.

"At an election in Seattle we wanted to put in some officers who were favorable to good roads and to the issuing of bonds. We counted noses pretty carefully, and to my despair I found our opponents had colonized four rooming houses. They

---

"When the Columbia River Highway was being built and I propheside that the time would come when, instead of having five-passenger or seven-passenger cars we would have regular stages and buses, carrying ten to twelve people to Seaside and to other points in the state, people jeered at me and called me a dreamer and a visionary, and yet they have lived to see the stages and buses travel not only between Portland and Seaside but to remote villages all over the state. They have seen buses that carry not 12 people but 40 and 50."

---

were going to vote all these men, which meant we would lose out by a small margin. The city officials and police force were against us, but the sheriff was with us. Charlie told me not to worry--that it would come out all right. The day before the election Charlie slipped a man with varioloid into one of these rooming houses, notified the sheriff that there was smallpox there and next day all four of these rooming houses were guarded by deputy sheriffs, who wouldn't allow any of the men to break the quarantine for smallpox. We won the election, got in the officials we wanted, passed the bonds and got our good roads.

"Frank Terrace is another man who has been a loyal helper. C. S. Jackson stood by me through thick and thin. So did John Carroll. So did Julius Meier. There have been hundreds of far-seeing men who saw that better highways meant a bigger and better Oregon--that they meant not only a greater happiness to the farmer's wife, but greater prosperity to the farmer and the merchant. When the Columbia River Highway was being built and I prophesied that the time would come when, instead of having five-passenger or seven-passenger cars we would have regular stages and buses, carrying 10 to 12 people to Seaside and to other points in the state, people jeered at me and called me a dreamer and a visionary, and yet they have lived to see the stages and buses travel not only between Portland and Seaside, but to remote villages all over the state. They have seen buses that carry not 12 people only, but 40 and 50.

"I have seen wonderful progress in the past 71 years. I wonder what is in store for us during the next 71. I am a Quaker, and I hope to see, during the next 71 years, an era of peace and good will that will make war impossible.

"Oregon has not yet come into its own in the matter of good roads. Tourists want three things--a good road to drive on, something worthwhile to see and something worthwhile to eat. The day will come when Oregon and Washington will be the summer playground of America. We will cash in, year after year, on our crop of scenic beauty, without depleting it in any way.

A week or two ago Sam Hill and myself were eating dinner together on the Princess Alice en route from Victoria to Seattle. Mr. Hill had been discussing the proposed road that goes north to Dawson and connects with the highways already built in Alaska.

"About 36 years ago," said Mr. Hill, "my father-in-law, James J. Hill, and myself drove by team from Brownsville, at that time a five-house town opposite New Westminster, B. C., to Blaine, Washington. There was no bridge across the Fraser River. We crossed it on the ferryboat. The distance from Brownsville to Blaine was 34 miles and much of the road was corduroy. It was a hard all-day drive over this waffle-board road, and I was sore inside and outside when we reached Blaine. I protested so vigorously that Mr. Hill said, 'Sammy, what do you propose to do about it?'

"I said, 'If I live long enough I am going to see a highway built down through British Columbia, down our own coast line, clear to Mexico, and it's going to be a hard-surfaced road.'

"He smiled and said, 'Well, if you say you are going to do it, you will, all right.

"That old waffle-board road is now but a memory. Last year 302,100 autos crossed the border line at Blaine and they carried over 1,000,000 passengers. Do you realize that the gateway between Canada and the United States at Blaine is the most used entrance west of Detroit—in fact, in point of size, it is the fourth most used along the border? Most people think the only road leading north to the gateway at Blaine, Washington, is the Pacific Highway. As a matter of fact, there are three paved roads between Seattle and Blaine.

"The building of the first paved highway to Blaine emphasizes the fact, elemental in transportation, that where traffic forms, there it stays. To care for the ever-increasing traffic Governor Hartley and his very competent director of highways, Samuel J. Humes, recommended the construction of a four-track highway from Olympia to Blaine, and this highway is now under construction.

"How different is the public attitude now to what it was when I first began agitating the building of the Columbia River Highway! The county commissioners and other authorities protested vigorously against the construction of a highway more than 12 feet in width.

"I have built at my place on Maryhill an exact replica of Stonehenge, the famous Druid ruins in England, which are over 4000 years old. It is thought the stones at Stonehenge came from Egypt. The Stonehenge that I have built at Maryhill is a memorial to the soldiers and sailors of Klickitat County who lost their lives in the World War. The diameter of the memorial is 108 feet, the outside stones 29 feet high and the others 215 feet high. Twelve young men from Klickitat County lost their lives in the World War.

"Why did I build a memorial that is a replica of Stonehenge? Because I wanted to remind my fellow men of the incredible folly of sacrificing human life to the god of war. As you know, in the old days at Stonehenge they sacrificed human victims. At the same time I wanted to pay a tribute to the heroic dead of Klickitat County. The inscription on the memorial at Maryhill reads: 'In memory of the soldiers and sailors of Klickitat County who gave their lives in defense of their country.' This monument was erected in the hope that others, inspired by the example of their valor and heroism, might share in their love of liberty and burn with that fire of patriotism that death alone can quench.

"I have built on the bluff overlooking the Columbia River at Maryhill a replica of the gateway of the oldest temple in Japan. It is made of concrete and will be there long after you and I are forgotten. Frank Terrace, who helped so greatly in the agitation for the building of the Columbia River Highway has provided $5000 in his will to be buried there. We should call the loops crossing the coast mountains between Portland and Astoria, Terrace Heights. It is really due to Frank Terrace for the work he did.

"The next time you go to Maryhill I want you to look at the replica I have made of the gateway of the oldest temple in Japan, that I have had built there as a memorial to my old-time friend and long-time associate, Eben F. Wells. The inscription over his grave reads as follows: "In loving remembrance of our associate, Eben F. Wells, who never caused us sorrow save when he left us.'"

"Where are you going to be buried?" I inquired.

Mr. Hill said, "Standing on the bluff in front of my place at Maryhill and looking down the canyon of the Columbia River, you will see a mass of jagged rock. Here, on the bluff, overlooking the Columbia, in time to come there will be a bronze tablet, over my ashes, which will bear these words: 'Sam Hill, amid nature's great unrest, he sought rest.'"

Oregon Journal
February 14, 15, 16, 17, 1928
July 1, 1928
January 19, 1930

SIMON BENSON

Lumberman and Philanthropist

While eating my lunch today at the Hotel
Virginia at Long Beach, I happened to glance over
at a nearby table and discovered Simon Benson,
Oregon's ex-lumberman, hotel builder, capitalist,
and good roads advocate. After lunch we sat in
the hotel lobby for an hour or so and talked
about good roads, politics, prohibition, education and industrial unrest, its cause and cure.
When we had threshed out those questions, I asked:

"Where were you born, Mr. Benson? How did
you make your money. What are you going to do
with it? What do you think of education? How can
Oregon secure some of the overflow of the tourists who are migrating in such countless flocks
to southern California?"

Mr. Benson smiled and said: "Now I see why
the people you write about tell you so many facts
about themselves and their work. You know how to
ask questions.

"I was born in Julbarns-dalen. To put that
into English, I was born in Gilbert's Valley, in
the central part of Norway. My father had a farm,
on which I was born, October 7, 1852. The farms
in Gilbert's Valley were small, ranging in size
from half an acre to as large as five or ten acres. Most of them, though, were from one to three

334

acres. Our farm consisted of an acre and a half.
There were nine in our family--my father and
mother and seven children.

"I decided that some day I would be a land
owner myself, and have a farm even larger than my
father's. I made good on that resolution, for in

"I decided to become one of the leading
loggers and lumbermen of the West...I knew
it would take years and require hard work,
courage and sticktoitiveness, but I knew I
could and would succeed. If you have a
legitimate business, if you will be square
and work hard and plan your work for the
future, if you have faith in yourself, you
can make good. If you have no goal, if you
don't know where you are heading for, you
will never reach the port of success."

---

time I owned in Oregon and Washington over 50,000
acres. No, I never told my boyhood friends in
Norway, for they would have tapped their heads
and smiled and said, 'Still building air cast-
les.' I was always considered a dreamer, a visionary. I looked at the stars in place of the
ground. All the rest of our family were intensely
practical.

"Our land was valued at $60 an acre, so that
my father's farm was worth about $90. When I was
a boy a good man who would work 12 to 15 hours a
day was paid from six to eight dollars a month,
but he had to be strong and willing and know his
work well. There were four boys and three girls
in our family. I was the middle one. On our farm,
in addition to our family, we had two cows, a few
sheep and some pigs, geese, chickens, and ducks,
and we raised all the vegetables we needed to

eat, besides a surplus for sale. Mother and we children did the work on the farm, while Father got work about the neighborhood at carpentering.

"As soon as we children could make our own way we went to work. I was nine when it was decided I was old enough to support myself. I got work with a neighbor, herding his sheep. When I was a little older I graduated to a job in a dairy, milking cows. I worked for my board and lodging. When John, my eldest brother, was 18--that was in 1863--we saved enough to buy a ticket for him to America. He worked and saved for five years in America, and then he had enough money to send for all the family to join him in the United States. He earned the money working in the pine woods in Wisconsin.

"My father's name was Berger Bergerson, but when we came to this country, we shortened the name to Benson. I think all foreigners who come to America should simplify their names so as to make it easier for their children. I think they should become not only in name, but in fact, Americans by learning to speak, read, and write English, and they should become citizens as soon as possible. If this country isn't good enough to become a citizen of, it is too good for the foreigner to stay in and make his living in.

"We came to this country in a sailing vessel. The tickets cost a little less than $50 apiece. The trip across the Atlantic took five weeks. At New York City we secured emigrant tickets to Black River, Wisconsin. All of us secured work at once. I was 16. I got a job on a farm, to work for three months--June, July, and August--for which I was promised $50. It seemed too good to be true. I worked 15 hours a day and milked the cows by lantern light after supper, so I usually put in a 16 hour day, for which I received a little over 50 cents a day. Today workmen will not work that hard. But I did not know it was hard, so I did not mind it. My employer told me he would give me two dollars a month extra if I spoke English, so before the three months was up I spoke English so as to be understood. I owed my brother John $53 for my fare and expenses coming from Norway. At the end of the three months, when I received my pay, I paid him the $50 I received, which left me only $3 in debt. I paid that during the next month. I could not have saved $50 in Norway in several years.

"That winter, the winter of 1868, I got a job on a farm near a school. I worked all winter, doing the chores for my board, so I could go to school. Next winter found me at work in the pine words as a roustabout in a logging camp. I was 17 and a hard worker, so I was paid $18 a month and board. I worked in the woods each winter and in the sawmill each summer, till 1875. In the fall of 1875, when I was 23, I married Ester Searle and started a store in Lynxville, on the Mississippi River. I ran the store four years and was doing fairly well when the building caught fire and burned down. I lost not only my store with all its contents, but my records were burned up. I had no insurance. I was broke and I had a wife and a baby to look out for. The baby was my son Amos. I decided to come west and get work at my old job as a lumberjack. Someone said there was considerable timber around Portland, so I bought our tickets to Portland. We went to the Overland Hotel, on Third Street, to stay till I could find work. This was in 1879.

"I bought a ticket on the boat for St. Helens. On the boat I met John Beavis, who told me he was a lumberman. I asked him if he knew of anyone needing an experienced logger. He said he was looking for a good man and that he would pay a good man $40 a month, but the man must board himself. He told me his camp was on Tide Creek, just below St. Helens. I said, 'I am a good man. I know the work. I will take the job.' Within two months I was able to bring my wife and baby. My boss liked my work. He knew I could get more wages elsewhere, so he raised me to $60 a month.

"We saved every cent we could and next spring I bought 160 acres. In my spare time I put up a good cabin on it and we moved in. I had made a small payment on the place and got long time credit.

"I went to Sam Miles of St. Helens and said, 'You have a lot of wild, unbroken steers. Let me have six of them on credit. If I can't pay for them I will return them and your payment will be that I will have them well broken to work as oxen. You can get a better price for them, so it will be the same as if I paid you rent for them.' He told me to pick out six steers and he would take a chance on me. I had about 6 million board feet of timber on my quarter section. Within three weeks I had broken the steers to work in good shape. I got credit for my groceries by telling the merchant my plans and showing him just what I had. Next winter I put my sawlogs into the river and sold them to the Northern Pacific Lumber Company. I had employed one man to work with me. I paid him $30 a month and board. My wife did the cooking. When I got the money for my logs I paid my workman, paid my store bills, made a payment on the oxen, and paid in what I had left on my land.

"I worked hard the following year, and the next winter when I put my logs into the river I sold them for enough to complete the payment on my three yoke of oxen and also to make a payment of several hundred dollars on my place. At the end of the third year I finished paying for my place, paid all bills, and had money in the bank.

"In 1883 my wife got sick. I called a doctor, who said she would have to go to a drier climate. I sold my quarter section and my oxen for $6000 and went to Colfax, Washington, where I got work at $75 a month as superintendent of the sawmill there. My wife never recovered her health. When we had been in Colfax five years she died. When I had paid the doctors' bills, the bills for drugs and the funeral expenses I had only enough left to get back to St. Helens.

"I was broke, but I didn't mind that. I was used to it, and I knew that with hard work I could get another start. But I had lost my partner, and that was a heavy blow and one hard to recover from. When I landed at St. Helens after my five years' absence I had no money, but my credit was good, so I buckled down to work for all I was worth.

"Losing your money doesn't amount to anything, so long as you don't lose your courage. A wound in the pocketbook is more easily healed than a wound to the spirit. I had made one start toward independence here in Oregon, and after ten years I was back just where I had been when I came to Portland--broke.

"I bought four yoke of oxen on credit from Sam Miles. I contracted to buy some timber near Reuben, just across the river from Kalama, at 50 cents a thousand, stumpage. At the end of the first year I had enough money to pay for the four yoke of oxen and to pay up my bills at the store. At the end of the second year I had $3000 in the bank after all expenses were paid.

"I decided to become one of the leading loggers and lumbermen of the West. I decided to build large and modern sawmills to cut up my logs. I knew it would take years and require hard work, courage and sticktoitiveness, but I knew I could and would succeed. If you have a legitimate business, if you will be square and work hard and plan your work for the future, if you have faith in yourself, you can make good. If you have no goal, if you don't know where you are heading for, you will never reach the port of success.

Ordway & Weidler bought my logs. They had about 4000 acres of timber down the river near Cathlamet. They wanted me to buy it. Like myself,

they had but little money. My credit was good,
for I had always paid my bills on or before the
time I promised payment. I suggested that we go
into partnership. We decided to build a railroad
into their timber. We had no money. We got hold
of some second-hand rails and logging cars. I put
in a mile of track at a cost of $4000. We bought
a small locomotive for $6000. Within four years
we cleared up all notes and outstanding bills and
had $20,000 in the bank.

"We contracted to buy the stumpage of a
large body of fine timber at Oak Point on the
Columbia River, at 50 cents a thousand. Times got
hard. The price of logs went down. Ordway offered
to sell his one third interest for $10,000.
Weidler and I bought him out. A year or so later
Weidler wanted to sell, so I gave him $33,000. I
paid him cash. I had to borrow. I got $18,000
from Everding & Farrel, paying 8 percent interest.

"I was running one camp and employing about
90 men. We were using oxen in our logging operations. Several logging camps had put in donkey
engines, but they had proved unsuccessful and had
been given up. I studied them carefully and found
why they did not succeed. I knew I could remedy
the fault, so I sold all my oxen and bought donkey engines. They were a success from the start.
You may remember how the papers at the time had
articles about my camp being the first in the Pacific Northwest to conduct all operations with
donkey engines. We didn't have an ox or a horse
in the camp. The donkey engines cut the cost of
production from $4.50 to about $2.10 to $2.15 per
thousand, so I made good money. I cleared over
$75,000 the first year.

"I at once put the money into more logging
railroad, to go farther back into the timber,
which, of course, kept the cost of logging down.

340

Every time a settler who had a homestead with from four to seven million feet of timber offered me his place I bought it. Other loggers thought I was crazy to pay from $1500 to $2500 for a homestead, but I looked a few years into the future. I had lots of homesteads offered me, as I was paying what in those days were considered high prices for them. Whenever they fitted into the district so that I could work them profitably I bought them.

"What is the best investment I ever made? I think the Benson fountains, for they helped knock the profit out of the saloon business and were a factor in making Oregon dry, and that means a better Oregon..."

"I soon built up an export demand for special lengths and sizes. For this I received from $10 to $12 per thousand. Soon I was able to borrow all the money I needed, and I borrowed freely to buy land or build mills or logging railroads. I always insisted on knowing each evening how much I had made that day, how much I owed, and all about my financial condition. Soon I was netting a profit of $2800 a day. When I began to make a clear profit of $300,000 a year I saw that I could make my dreams come true.

"I constantly studied how to produce lumber more cheaply, for the more cheaply I could produce it, the more lumber would be used, and the more that was used the more money I would make. Freight on lumber to California was one problem I studied a long time about. I studied the problem of why the rafts of piling broke up while at sea. I found the rafts were not properly made. They had not 'broken bonds' properly, nor used the right system of chaining the rafts. I built a cigar-shaped raft of sawlogs containing 6 million board feet of lumber and shipped it to San Diego. It got there without the least bit of trouble. So I built a big sawmill at San Diego and shipped 12 rafts, or about 75 million board feet of lumber in the form of logs. As I saved two dollars a thousand on freight, this made me an extra profit of $150,000, besides enabling me to fill orders for timbers any length. When we had rough weather, the steamer stood by and let the raft wallow in the trough of the sea; consequently we never lost a raft.

"A man named Frank Lynch, from North Dakota, wanted to buy an interest in my mill at San Diego. It was worth $400,000. That was just what it had cost me. He asked me what the annual profit was. I showed him that I had made about $400,000 in three years. He had only $50,000 and that would buy only an eighth interest. I told him to take the whole mill at $400,000, paying me the $50,000 he had and the mill would soon earn the other $350,000 for him. He accepted the proposition and made good on it within two or three years. Then he wanted to buy one of my logging outfits and the land surrounding it. This amounted to $1,000,000. He was able to finance the deal, so I sold it to him. Then some bankers from Duluth bought 25,000 acres of my timber lands for a price approximating $3,000,000.

"I then built the Benson Hotel and began losing money so rapidly that I had to take it over and run it myself. Just as I studied the mistakes made operating donkey engines and in constructing seagoing rafts, I studied the hotel till I saw where I could cut out waste and, by improving service, increase trade. I soon had it paying, and for the past three years it has paid me a profit of over $100,000 a year. I built it to help Portland, so when I recently sold it for around $1,000,000 I did not worry because I was getting $350,000 less than it cost me. I sold it because I liked the type of people who wanted to buy it. I could have undoubtedly sold it for more money, but I would not sell it to the wrong kind of people. It bears my name and I want its reputation maintained so that I need not be ashamed that it is named for me. A man owes a debt to the state and community which gave him his opportunity of making money, and no man has a right to sell a hotel, a streetcar line, a newspaper, or any other public enterprise that vitally affects the public interest, to a corporation or an interest that will be detrimental to the city or which will be betray the public interest.

"What is the best investment I ever made? I think the Benson fountains, for they helped knock the profit out of the saloon business and were a factor in making Oregon dry, and that means a better Oregon--better for wives and mothers and children. In other words, it means better citizenship. Material things, after all, amount to but little. It is the quality of our citizenship that makes Oregon a great and worthy state."

"You have told me how you made your money, now tell me how you are going to spend it," I said as we ate dinner.

"I'll tell you how I have already spent some of it," said Mr. Benson. "There were seven children in our family. All of them were wage earners, but none of them except myself made any more than just enough to get along on. As soon as I was able to do so I made all of my brothers and sisters independent, so they would have no financial worries. I have five children. Amos was my first child. Besides, there are Alice, now Mrs. Alice Benson Beach; Caroline, now Mrs. Undar; Gilbert, who is 21, and Chester, my youngest, 17. I have given each of my five children half a million apiece, making Amos the trustee, and arranging to have them receive the interest on the amount of their inheritance.

"I have spent about $200,000 on building

roads or buying parks for the good of all people. I gave $100,000 toward the building of the Benson Polytechnic school. The Benson fountains in Portland cost me $10,000. Recently I created a loan fund of $10,000 to help students at the Benson school who need temporary help.

"As to what I am going to do with a good portion of the remainder of my money, I do not wish to announce yet. I will tell you of one good-sized amount which I am going to devote to the public good."

When he had told me, Mr. Benson said, "I would prefer that you do not say anything about it. Just say that I plan, as opportunity offers, to invest my money in education, good roads, public parks, and other enterprises which will, in my judgment, be of benefit to the public.

"Whenever I spend my money I have a definite object in view. Take, for example, the money I spent for the 20 fountains in Portland eight or nine years ago. I used to watch workmen going into saloons with their buckets to buy beer. It seemed strange that in a city whose water was famous for its purity and excellence, workmen had no opportunity to quench their thirst except in a saloon. I had been noticing for years how much liquor cost me in decreased efficiency of the men in my logging camps and sawmills. It also was the cause of numerous accidents, all of which were expensive. It also meant poverty and distress to the families of my workmen, which I felt I should alleviate. For a long time I had been getting more and more disgusted with helping support the saloons, which, producing nothing of value, were parasites on legitimate industry. I decided that if the workmen on the street could get a drink of cold, pure water on the street corner without cost he wouldn't go into a saloon to buy beer.

"When the fountains had been installed I sent a trusted agent around to find out if it cut into the saloon trade. In many saloons sales had decreased from 25 to 40 percent. Better yet, scores of other cities followed Portland's example and installed public drinking fountains.

"The reason I gave $100,000 toward establishing the Benson Polytechnic School was to give our boys and girls a chance to learn trades and thus become self supporting, self respecting ci-

"The reason I gave $100,000 toward establishing the Benson Polytechnic School was to give our boys and girls a chance to learn trades and thus become self supporting, self respecting citizens."

tizens. If a man has a trade he can earn money. This means he can get married and own a home. The IWW can make no converts among workmen who own homes and have family ties. It is the restless, ignorant drifter who, having no home ties or real interests, takes up the doctrines of the Reds or the discontented 'intellectual'.

"I feel very strongly on this subject. Take a young man and keep him in the atmosphere of a strictly cultural college till he is 22, and what is the result? He wants to start at the top. He wants a white collar job. He doesn't want to sweat. I have had lots of them come to me for jobs. I want them to put on overalls and learn the business, but they, with their half-baked theories, want to show me how to run my business. They want easy jobs, where they won't get callouses on their hands. Lots of these chaps succeed in spite of, not through, the help of being educated as they were. What we need is producers--men who are willing to work. This will bring down the high cost of living. Teach more of our boys a trade; teach more of our girls to cook, to raise babies and to be home makers, and there will be less industrial unrest.

"The test of an educational institution should be: Is it turning out good citizens; will its graduates become producers, or parasites; will they be assets or liabilities to a community; has it a real part in the upbuilding of the community and the state?

"The cure for industrial unrest is for all of us, employers and employees, to deal justly with our fellow men. You can't give the public a raw deal nor be crooked in your relations with the public and expect your employees to be straight. If you are a grafter they will follow what you do, not what you say.

"We have got to take action against the millionaire IWW and the parlor Bolshevist as well as round up the red card workers in the woods. Right is right and wrong is wrong, irrespective of the size of your bank balance or the kind of clothes you wear. We must get back to the doctrine of the square deal, and practice it as well as preach it."

While we ate, I noticed that Mr. Benson had ordered a very simple meal for himself. When I spoke of it, he said:

"When you are logging, unless you are using a donkey engine, you don't keep it full of fuel nor stoke it till the steam is escaping at the safety valve. Look around you in any large hotel and you will see people stoking away, shortening their breath and shortening their lives, adding to their girth and weight and spoiling their shape, by stuffing themselves. They seem afraid they won't get their two dollars' worth if they don't eat everything on the bill of fare. They work hard and earnestly three times a day at digging their graves with their teeth. They lose most of the joy of life and look like overfed lap dogs. They have no self-restraint. They are not masters of, but are mastered by, their appetites.

"I believe in temperance in all things, and

that includes eating. I am not working hard, so I eat lightly. In the morning I play golf and get just as much exercise in the fresh air as though I were a good player. In the afternoon I go out in my automobile for a few hours. In the evening I play dominoes. I spend not more than two hours a day on my correspondence, on business matters and in reading.

"I am 67 years old. The longer I live the more I believe in temperance, even in work. You can't direct your work from the grave, nor can you take your money with you; so you should plan to do the utmost good to society with it while you are here.

"Too many men try to cling to power to the last. The result is that their sons have had no practice in handling large affairs and come to grief when they take the helm. Let me show you what I mean."

Taking one man after another whom we both knew, he pointed out fatal flaws in their character.

"The line between success and failure is usually marked and you can trace it clearly if you wish to do so. Usually men fail to succeed because they won't pay the price in effort, in sticking to it long enough, or they haven't the courage. They can't stand the gaff."

Again we went over a group of men we both knew. "No, he never gets where he starts for," said Mr. Benson of one of them," for he can't give and take. Things must be done his way, or he won't go into the plan. He doesn't understand teamwork, and he suffers from a delusion of greatness. His money has spoiled his viewpoint and he is no longer a man among men, but in his fancy he is a demigod."

"How about So-and-So?" I asked.

"He lacks integrity of character. He doesn't ring true. People can read it in his face. He is only plated, and the plating is wearing off.

Character is bound to write its story in your face. Your thoughts chisel your countenance. If you are a counterfeit you won't pass as genuine for very long. If you know you are right, go ahead. You will come out all right. Time justifies many of the things that are derided when they are first proposed. I can remember, seven or eight years ago, when I was working for good roads, people said, 'He's a bore,' or 'Where does he get off? What is there in it for him?' or 'He's one of these good road cranks. Let him alone. He will tire of it and take up something else.'

"Do you know why I kept up such an agitation for better roads? It was because we kept talking about getting back to the land, and what it really meant was 'getting back to the mud'. How could we expect to get more producers upon the land and imprison men each winter on their farms with impassable roads? No wonder children didn't want to stay on the farms.

"I had the means, the time and the inclination, so I traveled to see what good roads were doing in the upbuilding of other states. I saw what good roads meant to California, so I determined to help the good roads movement in my state. Since 1912 I have spent about $200,000 on good roads and playgrounds. Do you remember how the little group of us who advocated the Columbia River Highway were attacked as visionaries and spendthrifts, wasters of the public money? Do you remember how many honest men, and well meaning, called our plan the 'Portland paving graft'? I have worked hard in my day but the hardest work I ever did was to talk and campaign for the $6,000,000 bonds for good roads.

"Let me say now that one of the reasons why we won was because C. S. Jackson of The Journal conducted an intelligent and aggressive campaign that helped win the votes. The bonds carried by over 15,000 in Portland.

"Do you know we are building just as good
roads as California and at less cost? To my mind
roads to a community are like life blood. Without
blood your hand or foot would wither and die.
Impaired circulation means disease and death.
Without roads your village dies of dry rot. With
good roads it becomes prosperous and grows. If
Oregon will connect up with California's roads we
shall get the tourists. They will come one way
and go back the other, so we shall either get
them through Oregon on their way to California or
on their way home again. It will mean investment
in and settlement of our state. Take one instance. The strawberry grower of the Willamette
Valley or of Hood River cannot haul his crops
five miles in a wagon over bad roads. The berries
are crushed and the juice is lost. With good
paved roads and a truck he can haul his berries
25 miles without damage. See how much additional
strawberry land that affects. See how the values
of farm land are increased. Good roads spell
prosperity to a state, and the greatest cost of
all is to spend nothing in improving your roads."

Oregon Journal
December 3-6, 1919

SAM JACKSON

of the

East Oregonian and the Oregon Journal

The first acquaintance C. S. Jackson made
in Oregon was Judge C. B. Watson, now a resident
of Ashland. In 1870, when Judge Watson was 21
years of age, he left his native state, Illinois,
settling in California. After chopping wood all
winter he decided to see if he could not better
his fortune, so he came to Oregon and did chores
for his board while attending school at Ashland
Academy. In 1877 he became editor of the Oregon
Sentinel. In 1878 he went to Lake County and,
with his brother, established the State Line
Herald. In 1880 they made the paper a Republican
paper, and that spring he was the Republican
candidate for presidential elector. In the spring
of that year he was a delegate to the Republican
state convention at Portland. To get to Portland
from his home at Lakeview he had to go by team to
Camp Bidwell, thence to Reno, Nevada, and then
and from there by rail to San Francisco, where he
caught the steamer George W. Elder for Portland.

When Judge Watson boarded the George W. Elder he noticed a tall, slender, dark-skinned
young man who was watching the receding skyline
of San Francisco as the steamer passed out to sea
through the Golden Gate. Judge Watson and his
fellow passenger soon struck up a conversation,
and the young man, in answer to Judge Watson's

question, said his name was Sam Jackson and he was from Virginia and had come West to try his fortune. He said he was 19 years old and was going to Oregon where he hoped to get a job on a newspaper and eventually own a paper. When he learned that Judge Watson owned and edited a

---

"Keep the East Oregonian free and fair, accurate and alert, for an honest, up-to-date newspaper is the noblest work of man."

---

newspaper at Lakeview, he showed insatiable curiosity as to the prospects of securing a paper in Oregon. He also asked innumerable questions about the Oregon Country, particularly the Willamette Valley and the country east of the mountains. He had never seen the ocean before, had never ridden on a large ship, and everything was invested with the glamor of romance. He had no doubt whatever as to his ultimate success, but he was anxious to learn where he could get a start.

He told his newly made acquaintance all about his home and his people in Virginia and about having invested his money in a small hand press on which he had printed cards and announcements. He was anxious to write a piece in a paper and send it back to his folks, so he asked Judge Watson if he would publish a piece in his paper, the State Line Herald, if he sent it to him. Judge Watson took a liking to him and, admiring his earnestness, promised to publish it.

Judge Watson advised him to go to Pendleton or The Dalles and apply for work on the local paper and after he had gained some newspaper experience he might eventually secure an interest in the paper and some day own a paper of his own. When they reached Portland, Judge Watson suggested that he stop at the St. Charles Hotel where he always stopped, so Sam Jackson registered at the St. Charles Hotel and Judge Watson introduced him to R. Alexander, N. A. Connoyer, A. T. Wright, and other delegates from east of the mountains who had come down to attend the Republican convention.

Several weeks later Judge Watson received a letter from Pendleton from Sam Jackson, enclosing a letter for publication. It was crudely written, and W. W. Watson, Judge Watson's brother, wanted to consign it to the waste basket, but Judge Watson told his brother to rewrite it and run it, as he had promised to use it. This was the first newspaper experience C. S. Jackson had in Oregon, or anywhere else, for that matter. He wrote letters for publication in the State Line Herald every week or so and eventually he wrote that he was furnishing news items to the paper at Pendleton.

Of his early experiences in Pendleton many tales are told by the old timers.

Arriving at Pendleton, Sam Jackson began looking for a job. He heard that John Hailey, a proprietor of the Utah, Idaho and Oregon Stage Company, needed a man, so he applied for the job. John Hailey sized him up and said, "You look so much like Abraham Lincoln I'll try you out and see if you can make good." The wage was $40 a month.

John Hailey was a typical pioneer--resourceful, kindly and square. He was born in Tennessee in 1835, and when he was 13 he went to Dade County, Missouri, with his parents. When he was 18 he was hired as a driver and drove a five-yoke ox team across the plains to Salem, Oregon. Reaching Salem in the fall of 1853, he tried his luck mining in Coos County. He served in the Rogue River War, after which he ran a ferry for a while on the Rogue River. He ran a pack train and in 1862 went to Idaho. Moving the next year to

Boise, he lived there to the time of his death, a few years ago.

When Mr. Jackson landed a job with John Hailey, in April, 1880, he shared a room with John Hailey, Jr. Mr. Jackson had not been working for the stage company long before he met L. B. Cox, owner of the East Oregonian, who suggested to him that he keep track of the passengers who came to Pendleton or who were leaving town and write brief personal notices of them for the East Oregonian. Mr. Jackson eagerly accepted this opportunity of doing the work he had a leaning for.

The first paper published in Pendleton, the Pendletonian, was started in 1871, and was printed on a job press. It did not long survive. In 1873 H. M. Abbott came to Pendleton and started the Eastern Oregon Tribune. Two years later he moved his plant to The Dalles and ran the paper under the same name.

On October 16, 1875, the first number of the East Oregonian was published by M. P. Bull. It was Democratic, so much so that the Republicans not only refused to patronize it but did their best to secure control of it. In the fall of 1877, Mr. Bull not being able to meet his obligations, the paper was about to be taken over by the Republicans when G. W. Webb, J. M. Bentley, J. H. Turner, S. Rothschild, J. W. Bowman, A. Jacobsen and Henry Bowman, all staunch Democrats, formed the East Oregonian Publishing Company and took it over. They assumed control on October 9, 1877.

About a year later--on November 25, 1878, to be exact--J. H. Turner, and G. M. Bull, whose father had founded the paper, took it over. G. M. Bull soon disposed of his half interest to B. B. Bishop, who on August 6, 1880, sold out to L.B. Cox. Just a year later, on August 3, 1881, J. H. Turner sold his half interest to John Hailey and C. S. Jackson. Two months later, L. B. Cox, wanting to have entire control of the paper, bought out Mr. Hailey and Mr. Jackson. On January 13, 1882, Mr. Cox sold the paper to Mr. Jackson and J. A. Guyer, a native of Maryland and an attorney, and not long thereafter the new owners hired J. P. Wager, a native of New York state, an able attorney and a brilliant writer, to take editorial charge of the paper.

Three weeks after assuming charge of the paper, Mr. Jackson changed it from a weekly to a semi-weekly and, going to San Francisco, hypnotized a printers' supply house there into selling him steam printing equipment on credit. Mr. Jackson traveled all over Umatilla County, afoot or by team, securing subscribers for the semi-weekly East Oregonian, for the East Oregonian had at that time stiff opposition in the Pendleton Tribune.

On January 3, 1878, Lot Livermore had issued the first number of the Pendleton Independent, hiring I. Disoway as editor. Within the next 12 months it had various owners, and in December, 1879, it was purchased by Sharon & Burroughs, who changed its name to the Pendleton Tribune.

Still another aspirant for business in the county was the Weston Weekly Leader, which was started on December 23, 1879, by W. L. Black. A year later Dr. W. T. Williamson, a druggist of Weston, and G. P. McColl purchased it. Dr. Williamson came from Canada in 1872, and in 1877 graduated from the University of California and immediately thereafter came to Weston. His partner, a native of Scotland and also a physician, graduated in the same class as Dr. Williamson. For many years past Dr. Williamson has been one of Portland's leading physicians.

Before long Mr. Jackson bought out his partner and was the sole owner of the East Oregonian. From the first he made it a power in Pendleton and Umatilla County and before long its influence was felt all over the Inland Empire and it was widely quoted by the press of the state.

Sam Jackson had found his life work.

When G. P. McColl, who with Dr. W. T. Williamson started the Weston Leader, came to Portland he became publisher of the East Portland Packet. Another paper, the East Portland Vindicator, was published in East Portland at that time. Mr. McColl brought Felix Mitchell, who had managed the Weston Leader, to Portland to take charge of the East Portland Packet.

In the spring of 1887, C. S. Jackson met Mitchell on the street in Portland. Both being newspaper men and Mitchell having served as the Weston correspondent for the East Oregonian, they had plenty to say to each other. The result of the talk was that C. S. Jackson offered Mitchell a position as manager of the East Oregonian at satisfactory terms. Mitchell went to Pendleton and became one of the material factors in the success of the East Oregonian. He worked early and late for its interests.

During the 40 years of the association of C. S. Jackson and Felix Mitchell they had only one serious falling out, which resulted in Mitchell resigning and then going back to Mr. Jackson with an increased respect for his employer and friend. The falling out between these two men came about in a curious way. In those days the legal rate for the printing of briefs was $1.25 a page. Mitchell had the interests of the East Oregonian just as much at heart as had its proprietor and was anxious to show good earnings on the part of the East Oregonian. He not only solicited job work but he supervised its printing and relieved Mr. Jackson of all responsibility along that line.

One year the court docket in eastern Oregon was particularly heavy, and Mitchell secured almost all the briefs. One day Mr. Jackson, in looking over the books, commented on the large number of briefs being printed, and said, "I notice you charge $1.25 a page. What is the actual cost of printing them?"

Mr. Mitchell said, "By putting in overtime without charge and working very hard I figure I am getting those briefs out at a cost of 60 cents a page."

Mr. Jackson dipped his pen in the ink and scratched out the charge of $1.25 and made it 60 cents. Mitchell protested, "That is the exact cost. We shouldn't have to work for nothing."

Mr. Jackson responded, "God pity the poor people who get into the hands of lawyers. I am not going to make their lot any harder. The lawyers will get most of what they have. I am not going to try to get the rest. When a man has a lawsuit on his hands he has trouble enough. Let us make it as easy for him as we can."

Mitchell threw up his hands and quit, saying, "What's the use of my working 15 hours a day, to have you come in and cut the rates to cost?" After Mitchell had turned in his resignation, he said, "I will finish what work I have on hand and you can look around for my successor."

Mr. Jackson said to him, "Felix, you know I like you, and you know I need you. You should not throw me down. You ought to be willing to indulge me in this matter. This doesn't cost you any money. I am the only one that suffers."

So they smoked the pipe of peace, and Mitchell went back to work.

Mr. Jackson at that time became very much interested in the books that were being got out by a red-headed printer at San Francisco named Henry George. Mr. Jackson not only preached single tax in the columns of the East Oregonian, but he bought numerous copies of "Progress and Poverty", and other works by Henry George and sent them to his friends.

So strongly did he feel on the subject of the injustices being done to those who could least afford added expenses that he would not charge the legal rate set by law on foreclosure notices and others of that kind. "The poor devil is having grief enough without having to pay additional exactions countenanced by law," he said, so he charged the commercial rate, which at that time was very low, not over one fourth of the

---

"God pity the poor people who get into the hands of lawyers. I am not going to make their lot any harder. The lawyers will get most of what they have. I am not going to try and get the rest."

---

rate charged for legal notices.

One day the Democratic candidate for sheriff came to the East Oregonian office with a number of notices of sheriff's sales and, seeing Mr. Jackson there, he said, "I hope, Jack, you are aware of the fact that I am throwing you the bulk of all my legal notices. You are not supporting me as vigorously as you should."

Mr. Jackson looked up from his writing and said, "Who in hell are you to come in and tell me how to run the East Oregonian, and whom I should or should not support?"

The Democratic sheriff was a man of rather short temper and without any beating about the bush he said, angrily, "I'll tell you one thing, Sam Jackson. If you don't come out and support my candidacy for sheriff vigorously you won't get any more printing or advertising as long as I am sheriff of Umatilla County."

Mr. Jackson looked at him as if he were some curious bug or obnoxious insect, and said, "Whose money do you think you are spending when you give out legal notices? Don't you know it is the people's money, not yours, that you are spending, and that it is your duty to place the business where you can get best results for the least money? You can't buy me with your legal notices, and you can't bluff me. You can get to hell out of here and take your legal notices with you. I don't care to do business with bribe-givers, crooks, and corruptionists."

Mr. Jackson had an almost uncanny sense of what would prove to be popular and successful. On the other hand he could detect a "nigger in the woodpile" more quickly than most men. When a man came to him with some measure in behalf of the people he sized it up quickly and, frequently, put his finger on the fatal flaw in it at once, saying, "I can see where you get off. You fix this bill or measure so it won't bring a personal profit to you, and I will work with you, but you can't use me or my paper to plunder the public for your personal profit."

Whether it was a baseball team, a woolen mill, a proposed road, a Fourth of July celebration or a banquet to visiting notables, the East Oregonian always took the lead, and its publisher not only gave publicity to the movement but headed the list of subscriptions and allowed no one else in town to give any money more than the East Oregonian would for the town's advancement. This attitude of the East Oregonian soon put it in an impregnable position, and though money without stint was spent on the opposition paper to put the East Oregonian out of business, the East Oregonian only grew stronger in public favor as the years went on.

When Mr. Jackson came to Portland to take over the Journal he retained a quarter interest in the East Oregonian, selling a quarter each to the three following newspaper men: Fred Lambkin, Bert Huffman, and myself. To the time of his death he retained an interest in the East Oregonian, for, as much as he loved the Journal, the East Oregonian was his first love and there he had spent his early manhood and developed the ability that made him able to make the Journal a forceful, progressive and influential metropolitan publication.

During the past few days I have been re-reading scores of letters written by C. S. Jackson to me during the past 20 years. When Mr. Jackson came down to Portland, 22 years ago, Scott Bozarth was one of his right-hand men. Mr. Jackson asked Scott if he knew of any reliable man who would serve as outside man for the Journal, traveling over the state and sending in correspondence from the highways and byways, particularly the latter, for in those days there were more byways than highways. Bozarth and I had worked together at Salem, several years before, so he suggested that I might be available. I had already pretty well covered the state on horseback, by rig or by bicycle writing up the various sections of the state for the Salem Capital Journal, the Salem Statesman, and the Pacific Homestead, so I was more or less familiar with the field. In answer to a note from Mr. Jackson asking me to come down and see him, I took the boat at Salem and came down to Portland. I dropped in at the office of the Journal, at that time in the Goodnough Building, and had a talk with Mr. Jackson. In the course of our talk he said:

"What I want of you is to act as eyes for the Journal. I want you to travel over the state and do anything and everything that will promote The Journal's interests. I want you to write up the various sections of the state, also the industries of the state, such as wheat raising, sheep raising, irrigation, fruit raising, dairying and, in fact, anything that you think will interest the readers of the Journal. Naturally, I will not object if you see a chance to pick up any advertising or subscriptions. I am particularly anxious, however, to get hold of a man who can see where the Journal can be made useful in promoting the interests of the various communities and the different sections of Oregon.

"The Journal is not a large paper now, and it can't stand much expense, but it is going to be a large paper, though that doesn't mean that it will ever be wasteful of its money. Some of these days the Journal is going to be the leading paper of the Oregon Country, and I intend to stay by those who stay by me. I can't pay you much of a salary to start with, but I will give you $25 a week and pay your expenses. Traveling on horseback, in a cart, or on your bicycle, your expenses should not be over $12 or $15 a week. I am willing to invest $40 a week in you in the hope that you can interpret to the people you meet throughout the state the puroses and plans for the future of the Journal."

I sat tight, sized Mr. Jackson up carefully, and listened closely to what he had to say. I had never met him before, and he struck me as a very unusual, forceful and original character. I could not quite make him out, so I accepted his proposition so as to study him at my leisure as I became better acquainted with him.

A few days later, according to arrangement, I met Mr. Jackson at Pendleton, so he could explain the work he wanted me to do. Since talking with me he had decided that I could also write articles for the Northwest Livestock Journal, which was published at Pendleton, and which he owned. The Oregon Journal and the Livestock Journal were to share the expense of keeping me in the field and, in addition to writing for the Oregon Journal, taking any subscriptions that I could run across, I was also to write articles for the Livestock Journal and secure advertising for it. This meeting at Pendleton was in the latter part of July, 1902.

To keep down the sum of my traveling expenses I decided to travel over the Inland Empire on a chainless Columbia bicycle. After outlining to me very thoroughly his plans for the Oregon Journal, and also his plans for the Northwest Livestock Journal, about whose future he was quite doubtful, Mr. Jackson said:

"What the Livestock Journal needs more than anything else is advertising. J. E. Smith, head of J. E. Smith Livestock Company at Barnhart, is one of the principal livestock men of eastern Oregon. If you can line up J. E. Smith, Charley Cunningham, Doug Belts, and a few more men of that kind we can make the Livestock Journal a paying proposition. I suggest you go and see J. E. Smith, at Barnhart, and get him to put an ad in for his Rambouillet bucks. I don't suppose he will put in a very large advertisement, but if you can get him to put in an inch or two it will be a start and you can get him for a larger space later."

"I think it will be a mistake," I said, "to get one of the leading sheepmen of eastern Oregon to put in such a small ad. All the other livestock advertisers would be guided by his example. I think I will get him to put in a half page."

I saw a most peculiar look come into Mr. Jackson's eyes, a look I learned to know very well in later years. His lips twitched, and he said, "Yours is much the better plan. Go ahead and line him up for the half page."

It was a hot day, and the road from Pendleton to Barnhart was sandy and in places hilly. When I arrived at Barnhart, I was bathed in perspiration and was determined to take nothing less than half a page, to pay me for making the trip. I introduced myself to Mr. Smith. We shook hands and I said, "I have come to get a half-page ad from you, advertising your Rambouillet bucks in the Northwest Livestock Journal, Mr. Smith."

He was a very kindly man and a man whom I learned later to know intimately, and the longer I knew him, the better I liked him. He looked at me in a surprised and in what seemed to me a most curious manner, as he said, "Who sent you here, Mr. Lockley?"

I said, "C. S. Jackson, owner of the Livestock Journal and also of the East Oregonian and of the Oregon Journal, suggested that I come and see you."

He flushed up, and said, in a low, controlled voice, "Evidently, Mr. Lockley, you are new to this country. If you know anything at all about local conditions you know that I have absolutely no use for Mr. Jackson. I would not spend a nickel with him if you would give me a written guarantee that I could make $1000 by doing so. He and I are bitter enemies. For the sake of Pendleton and eastern Oregon, I am glad he has gone to Portland. I do not wish Portland any bad luck, but I hope he stays there."

I had to readjust my line of argument in a hurry. What he had said had wiped the smile off my face and had roused my fighting spirit. I said, "I am wondering how big a man you are. I am wondering if you are going to let your dislike for C. S. Jackson interfere with the good of the livestock industry of the Inland Empire."

"I don't know what you are driving at," said Mr. Smith.

"You are recognized as one of the leaders of the sheep industry of eastern Oregon," I responded. "You are not in this business entirely for what money there is in it. If you are the type of man I think you are you want to eliminate the scrub sheep from the ranges and see that Oregon becomes known as the home of high-grade sheep. If you advertise your bucks in the Livestock Journal scores of sheepmen, seeing your ad, will order bucks from you and thus improve their herds. I am not even going to dwell on the fact that the sale of these bucks will make money for you, but what I believe you will be interested in is that not only will the sale of your bucks to the sheepmen of the Inland Empire put money in the pockets of the sheepmen and bring prosperity to this whole section, but it will add prestige to Oregon and you will be remembered as a public-spirited man for having brought the livestock industry in Oregon to a higher standard."

Mr. Smith looked at me searchingly and then

"Alertness, observation, promptness and intelligence are the requisites to the success of a newspaper. Little things, the small details, are important and if looked after with thoroughness, a newspaper will become as substantial as the hills."

---

said, in a rather slow, deliberate manner, "I guess the good of the livestock industry is a bigger thing than my dislike for C. S. Jackson. Come on into my office and I will sign a contract for your half-page ad, and I will tell you about what I want you to say in the ad."

When Mr. Smith had signed the contract and I had fixed up copy for his ad and put a cut of one of his Rambouillet bucks into my pocket, he shook hands with me and said, "Don't forget, Mr. Lockley, that at any time I can do anything to help you in your work of advancing the interests of the stockmen of eastern Oregon, feel free to call upon me. I will be glad to give you letters of introduction, furnish you information or give you a list of the leading sheepmen of the Inland Empire."

When I returned to Pendleton Mr. Jackson met me with a twinkle in his eye and said, "Well, what luck did you have? I wanted to see if you could stand the gaff. I knew, in advance, you would be turned down, and I know about what Mr. Smith told you about me. We differ radically on many subjects and he has no use for me. Did he throw you off the place?"

I shook my head and said, "What Mr. Smith said about you was plenty, but I think you are as much at fault as he is because you are not friends." As I said so I handed Mr. Jackson the contract for the half-page ad.

He looked at me and once more looked at the signature, and, pointing to it, he said, "Who signed this contract?"

I said, "J. E. Smith signed it. Don't you know his handwriting? He not only signed that contract but he volunteered to help me all he could and he is going to furnish me a list of the leading sheepmen of eastern Oregon."

Mr. Jackson shook his head in a puzzled way and said, "But what did you say to him? How did he come to give you the contract? What did he say about me?"

"He said he had no use for you and that he was glad you had gone to Portland and he hoped you would stay there," I responded.

"Well, I must say that you and your friend, J. E. Smith, are both brutally frank," said Mr. Jackson. "When you see Mr. Smith thank him, for me, for his good wishes, and tell him I have gone to Portland with the intention of staying there."

The Oregon Journal celebrated its 25th anniversary by a special issue on Sunday, July 24, and by a banquet Monday evening. C. S. Jackson, its founder, has a better monument than the Journal Building, worthy as that is. His monument, the Oregon Journal, is a living, growing institution, whose influence is ever widening and increasing.

I started to work with Mr. Jackson in 1902, when the Journal had less than 1000 circulation. Today the daily Journal has a circulation of over 103,000, the Sunday Journal in excess of 132,000. There are 94 Journal workers who have been with the Journal more than ten years--37 of them more than 20 years.

With figures and graphs you can show the growth of the Journal in equipment, physical assets, circulation, advertising and number of employees, but there is an intangible quality which cannot be so recorded--the influence the Journal has had on the upbuilding of Oregon. Nor can one show by graphs and figures the affection and confidence of Journal readers.

Only through honesty of purpose, sincerity, fearlessness, and devotion to the public good can such confidence be built up and maintained. A paper cannot rise above the level of those who guide its destinies and make it what it is. If a paper's employees are devoted to it, are loyal to it, men of character, integrity, zeal and ability, trying to further its interests, you will have a worthwhile paper. Any paper, to be influential for good, must appeal to the intelligent and thoughtful, for in the long run, the readers' confidence is its greatest asset. No temporary gain can outweigh civic betterment and the paper's responsibility to its public. Not only must editorial columns be sincere, and news given without distortion, but advertising must be clean and honest, and there must be, all along the line, unswerving devotion to principle and a maintenance of high ideals and standards.

Just as Oregon is not made but is in the making, so the Journal will continue to march steadily forward and while the Journal workers pause for a moment with pride over the achievements of the past, they must look forward and have a vision of the future, with its untold possibilities for service.

I have hundreds of letters written to me by Mr. Jackson, from the day the paper was founded up to and including the time I was overseas. Mr. Jackson took control of the Journal on July 23, 1903. In a letter written to me eight days later, he says:

"My dear Lockley: I am glad to hear how successful your efforts have been. We will send the papers by express so that they will arrive in Pendleton at 5:30 in the morning. Prompt delivery is everything. Have the carriers at the depot to receive the Journal. Tell the people you meet that the paper will be improved right along. We are going to enlarge it about September 1. New machinery has been ordered for the purpose. See that Pendleton and Umatilla County news is sent in. Those who stand by me in this hour of trial will be remembered in the hour of success."

On October 19 he wrote me at Canyon City, as follows:

"I am printing your articles on Grant County and am sending marked papers as you suggest. In time, I am going to make the Journal a strong, forceful paper. Tell those you meet it will be a much better and more worthwhile paper as soon as we can buy and install a modern press, capable of printing 16 pages at a time."

Today the Journal has a battery of presses, including a quadruple, a sextuple, and two oc-tuples and right now a new four-unit, super-high speed Scott press is being installed that will print 32 pages at a time, 48,000 an hour.

On July 3, 1903, Mr. Jackson wrote:

"My dear Lockley: I am glad to know every-thing is going so well. Alertness, observation, promptness and intelligence are the requisites to the success of a newspaper. Little things, the small details, are important and if looked after with thoroughness, a newspaper will become as substantial as the hills."

On February 6, 1904, at which time I was a partner of Mr. Jackson in the publication of the East Oregonian at Pendleton, he wrote me:

"It is well to show the county commissioners that the intention of the East Oregonian is to serve the county, not to work it. Let them know that you always want to do the square thing. It is this spirit, sincerely expressed and practiced as well as preached, that will win in the long run. A paper that is fair will secure the confidence of the public and earn its support, but the paper must be fair to its enemies as well as to its friends."

On February 24, 1904, he wrote:

"Your idea is a good one. It is equitable and just. It shows you are resourceful. Keep the East Oregonian free and fair, accurate and alert, for an honest, sincere, up-to-date, forceful newspaper is the noblest work of man. It is the greatest influence for good under our form of civilization, but to make it honest, to keep it honest, and to make the people realize the fact--there's where the rub comes in. Vice pays quicker dividends than virtue. Here you have the reason why unthinking men and many newspapers are out for the stuff, regardless."

On August 30, 1904, Mr. Jackson wrote:

"Subscription receipts for the Journal now exceed $5000 a month--advertising is running over $10,000 a month. We are just beginning to learn how to make a newspaper."

On May 6, 1905, he wrote:

"I enjoyed your letter greatly. Keep up the good work. Keep the paper for law enforcement. Show up every official who does not respect his oath of office. You have gone into the war for better living conditions and for law enforcement. Your decks are cleared for action. Keep up the fight. People like a fighting paper, a paper with

a conscience, just as they like an individual who
will fight for better conditions."

Oregon Journal
January 13, 16, &
17, 1925
July 26, 1927

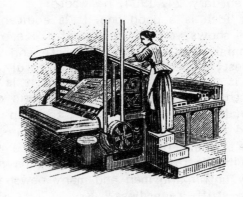

FRED LOCKLEY

The Journal Man

When I was a boy, in the late '80s, I lived for a while on the Ponca Indian Reservation, 35 miles south of Arkansas City, Kansas. My brother-in-law, J. H. Sherburne, was post trader to the Poncas. On the reservation nearby, the Nez Perce prisoners of war were located. This was Chief Joseph's band, which had made the historic fight at and flight from their home near Wallowa Lake in eastern Oregon. The Nez Perces had no trader, so I frequently saw Chief Joseph and his people in my brother-in-law's store.

Many years later, in the spring of 1915, while visiting Miss Kate McBeth and her niece, Miss Crawford, at Lapwai, I attended a service at the Nez Perce Presbyterian Church. On the wall was a motto that has stuck in my memory all these years. It said: "Train up a child in the way he should go and go that way yourself." The church was filled to overflowing with grave-faced Indians whose perfect decorum would put to shame an ordinary assemblage of white churchgoers. After the service, which consisted of a sermon by an Indian preacher in his native Nez Perce, and singing by the Indian congregation in their native language, I was introduced to many of the older Indians. One of the older matrons had known my brother-in-law well and we talked of the old days when she was with her people in the Indian Territory.

Chief Joseph died broken-hearted, September 21, 1904, at the Colville Indian Reservation. He had been promised that he and his people should be returned to the home of their fathers on the shores of Wallowa Lake, but the promise, like most promises of the government and of the white men to the Indians, was not kept.

"Backward, turn backward, O Time, in your flight. Make me a child again, just for tonight." But, alas, we can't turn time's clock back. How many mistakes we would correct if we could but do so.

I am writing this article from Walla Walla, where I used to go to school 40 years ago. We went to Walla Walla in 1880 by wagon, for this was before the era of railroad trains in that part of Washington Territory. I spent today at Whitman College, attending classes and securing interviews. I spent this evening at the home of Mr. and Mrs. Earl McLoughlin...

Sometimes I wonder if the present generation of children realize the advantages they enjoy, compared to their fathers and mothers. My school days are still vivid in my memory. We moved from Walla Walla to Butte, Montana, in the winter of 1881. We went by stage from Walla Walla to Umatilla, where we caught a boat for Portland, where we took passage on the steamer State of California for San Francisco, to take the train for Salt Lake, at which point we transferred to the Montana Central for Silver Bow, Montana, where we caught a bobsled stage for Butte. In those days connections were very roundabout, hence the long trip.

My first teacher at Butte was a woman who had a violent temper and a limber rawhide whip, both of which were in constant evidence.

In those days teachers stressed discipline more than learning. One of her rules was that when we were not reciting we should keep our eyes on our books and not look around. One of my chums was unusually bright and was able to get his

---

"For the past 25 years or so I have been interviewing interesting people—bullwhackers, muleskinners, pioneers, prospectors, '49ers, Indian fighters, trappers, ex-barkeepers, authors, preachers, poets, and near-poets, and all sorts and conditions of men and women..."

---

lessons quicker than most of the rest of us, so he would look around the room to see what he could see. This made the teacher furious. She would say, "Jack, come to my desk." I well remember the first whipping she gave him. He refused to cry. She said, "I'll make you cry if it's the last thing I ever do," and she wielded the rawhide till she was tired and Jack was as white as a ghost.

By this time all the girls in the room were crying. While she was resting to whip him some more, she said, "I'll stop if you'll cry."

Jack said, "You can kill me, but you can't make me cry."

She grabbed him by the collar, shook him till his teeth rattled, and, picking up the rawhide again, said, "I'll break your spirit or know the reason why." But she never did.

She watched him as a cat watches a mouse. The other boys could do things without question that Jack would be whipped for. During the year she had more than 200 cases of corporal punishment, and Jack received 105 beatings, or more than half of them. When we went swimming in the pond near the base of Big Butte, Jack always had new welts and black and blue marks to show from her constant beatings.

Chewing gum was about as serious a crime as murder, and eating an apple behind your geography was equivalent to a life sentence. One day, while out on Timbered Butte, I got a pocketful of tamarack gum from an old tree. I found some of this gum in my pocket during school hours and was tempted and fell. The teacher's eagle eye discovered I was chewing gum. She said, "Fred Lockley, march up to my desk." I marched up to the desk. She held out her hand for my gum, and stuck it on a big ball of gum the size of a walnut, which she had collected from the other students.

She said to the other students, "I am going to make an example of Fred," and, turning to me, she said, "Open your mouth wide." I did so, and she forced that gob of gum into my mouth and told me to chew it till recess. As this gum represented the contributions of anywhere from a dozen to 20 different pupils, I nearly gagged. It was so large I could hardly close my jaws. I would have rebelled, but I knew how expert she was at forcing your fingers down and the palm up when she gave you 20 licks with a ruler. Your hand was sore for a week.

My next teacher said to us at the beginning of the term, "Children, we want to make a record during the entire term of no tardy marks. If you find you are going to be tardy, stay out of school for a half day, for I would rather have you absent than tardy."

One day our cow wandered away, so my father told me to go and find it. I told him I was afraid I would be tardy. He said, "Go and get that cow without any further talk and I'll write you an excuse to the teacher."

It was nearly nine o'clock when I got back with the cow. She had wandered a mile or more away and it took me quite a while to locate her. My father had gone to his work but left an excuse for me to take to the teacher. Without waiting for breakfast I ran all the way to school, but was five minutes late. The teacher said, "Children, Fred has put a black mark on our white record. He has brought us all into disgrace. What shall we do to him?"

Susie Jacobs suggested that she bring her

"After all is said and done, people are just folks, and if you feel a real and sincere interest in them, and if you are a good asker and a good listener, you will be rewarded by getting good human stories."

---

sunbonnet and make me wear it. Another child said, "Make him hold the dictionary at arm's length for 15 minutes." Another said, "Make him sit down on the floor with his legs spread out and hold a nail down with his thumb." Almost every child had a different suggestion. It took three days to use up all the punishments they had suggested.

(Fred Lockley, who has been entertaining Journal readers for many years with his accounts of interesting people and events, tells the story of a most interesting life--his own. The thousands who have followed Mr. Lockley's career know him to be a writer who goes right into the lair after his subject and drags it out by the mane.

No one is his superior at direct and succinct attack. This is one of a series of autobiographies being compiled for Mr. John T. Hotchkiss of the J. K. Gill Company.)

To write about other people is a snap compared to writing about one's self. For the past 25 years or more I have been interviewing interesting people--bullwhackers, muleskinners, pioneers, prospectors, '49ers, Indian fighters, trappers, ex-barkeepers, authors, preachers, poets, and near-poets, and all sorts and conditions of men and women, and I have never refused an assignment, but this particular assignment-- writing an interview with myself--has me stumped. I have shed my coat and rolled up my sleeves and made half a dozen starts, but somehow I don't seem to be a self-starter. Well, there is no use of shivering on the bank or dipping in one toe to see how cold the water is, so here goes:

My father, after reading some of my stories, said: "As a writer you are a fine typesetter or pressman."

C. S. Jackson said: "You are too good a business man to ever make a writer."

All of which made me decide that I would write or bust. I haven't busted yet, though I have sometimes been broke and I have often been pretty badly bent.

Why do I write? Because I like to write. Either learn to like your work or get some job that you will enjoy. My writing is not only my vocation, but it is my recreation. Loafing tires me more than writing. I know of no work that will bring you into contact with more interesting people than reporting.

I have interviewed such people as Woodrow Wilson, Sir Douglas Haig, Tom Lawson, Thomas A. Edison, Jack London, Walt Mason, Booker Washington, Emma Goldman, Eamon DeValera and scores of others of their type, and the more people of their kind I meet the more I realize that the biggest men are the simplest and most friendly, and that it is only the insignificant and unimportant who are unapproachable and difficult.

After all is said and done, people are just folks, and if you feel a real and sincere interest in them, and if you are a good asker and a good listener, you will be rewarded by getting good human stories.

I have published in book form the stories of some of the interesting pioneers I have interviewed, under such titles as "Across the Plains by Prairie Schooner", "To Oregon by Oxteam in '49", "Vigilante Days in Virginia City", and other such titles, which give an indication of the type of writing I enjoy--chronicling the annals of the Oregon pioneers.

Wherever I have been I have run across men--men and action--men who are too busy doing things to stop and write about them. This has been in Alaska, Mexico, Canada, on the British front in Picardy and all over our own country, and my great ambition is to take some of these vital types and make a real book some of these days.

I got into the newspaper game early. I carried papers on the Butte Inter-Mountain when Butte was one of the toughest mining camps in Montana. This was in 1881. Later I worked as printer's devil in Kansas and elsewhere. In 1888 I landed a job as compositor on the Capital Journal at Salem, and during the next few years I worked as typesetter, pressman, reporter, circulation manager, advertising man and manager. Later I served as field editor of the Pacific Homestead, riding on a lineback buckskin pony all over Oregon. Still later I owned a quarter interest in the East Oregonian at Pendleton. After that I worked on the Pacific Monthly here in

Portland and became general manager. From the
Pacific Monthly I came to the Oregon Journal as a
roustabout, and have served in that capacity ever
since.

Oregon Journal
December 1, 1921
February 21, 1928
January 4, year
illegible

Index

382